The Missy Box

By

Anne Emerson

This book is a work of fiction, although the overall framework is based in real historic events. Maria Bourdoux did come alone to St. Thomas with her nanny, and the names of her progeny are real. Her granddaughter did marry Governor Suhm and her great granddaughter did study in Copenhagen, living with her uncle, Thomas de Malleville, and his role in this story is historically accurate. Other names, characters, and events are imagined. Thomas de Malleville is buried in the small cemetery at the Moravian Church on St. Croix, and I scrubbed his gravestone clean.

Anne Emerson

You can contact the author at the below address.

annedemerson@gmail.com

THE EUROPEANS

(Based on the actual family of Thomas Bourdoux)

THE EUROPEANS

1st generation THOMAS BOURDOUX of Soubise, France, b. 1640?, executed in the aftermath of the Revocation of the Edict of Nantes in October, 1687

2nd generation MARIA BOURDOUX, b. 1675, comes to St. Thomas in 1686, marries PIERRE LA SALLE, b. 1670, in 1690

3rd generation MARIA (MORIAH) LA SALLE, b. 1706, marries JEAN DE MALLEVILLE

4th generation THOMAS MALLEVILLE, b.1742, marries JOHANNE MARIE MEYER; MARIA MALLEVILLE, b. 1736, marries 1) CHRISTIAN SUHM, 2) General LUCAS VON BEVERHOUDT

5th generation MARIA MALLEVILLE SUHM, b. January 20, 1758, marries JOHN WHEELOCK in 1786

6th generation MARIA MALLEVILLE WHEELOCK marries Rev. WILLIAM ALLEN

7th generation CHARLOTTE FREYLINGHAUSEN ALLEN HOPKINS

8th generation ANNETTE HOPKINS EMERSON

9th generation KENDALL EMERSON Sr

10th generation KENDALL EMERSON Jr

11th generation ANNE EMERSON (author)

THE AFRICANS

(A fictional family, except for the 6th generation)

THE AFRICANS

1st generation AKILA, b. 1675 in AFRICA, marries SAMUEL in 1692

2nd generation MOHAMMED (MO MO) b. 1696; AMALIE b. 1700, marries HENRY in 1712

3rd generation FREDERICK b. 1713 (MO MO's son), marries ANGELINA in 1733

4th generation CATERINA b. 1738, marries ADAM

5th generation PHEBE b. 1758, marries ANTOINE in 1772; ANGELINA b. 1760

6th generation PHEBE ANN JACOBS, given to Maria Wheelock Allen at birth, buried in the cemetery in Brunswick, Maine, next to Maria Allen. PHEBE ANN JACOBS is reputed to have been model for the pure Christian characters of Uncle Tom in Uncle Tom's Cabin.

Contents

Anne Emerson

Prologue

President's House, Dartmouth College, 1799

I will write it now, the story of great grandmother as I pieced it together, and the story of what happened in Denmark in those two years. Two separate stories, but they are all of a piece, and their legacy is carrying on in this present moment at Dartmouth College, where we are all in a dither about whether our slaves should be freed. The legislature passed a law here ten years ago saying we should go about emancipation gradually. How can one do such a thing gradually? One is either free or not. Our slaves legally belong to my husband, though Angelina and her daughter, Phebe Ann, were gifts from my parents to me and to my daughter at her birth. The thought of losing them is terribly painful. Perhaps they would not leave us, but I cannot bring myself to talk about it with Angelina. All this weighs on my heart, like the terrible sin that it is.

It was the arrival of the trunk some months after we had received the news of Uncle Thomas' death that stirred it all up for me. I recognized the trunk immediately as the one I had brought to Copenhagen all those years before. Inside, with various family relics and papers, was the Missy Box. The valuable jewels had been sold or dispersed with the estate. But the old gris-gris was still inside, and the pearl buttons. And the diary, hidden just as I had left it. Oh, the stories Thomas had told us as he took those treasures out. I think that old Missy Box and all it contained catapulted me out of childhood. How strange that we think our ancestors lived faultless, boring lives.

Those two years were such a peculiar time in Danish history, the time of the mad King Christian. I was twelve—old enough then to be scouted for marriage—but I was innocent, and oblivious to the import of what I was witnessing, until it all came crashing down on us. I will write the story now, in a sequence that will make sense— not always the sequence in which I learned the facts.

Maria Malleville Suhm Wheelock, wife of John Wheelock, second President of Dartmouth College, 1799

Chapter One: Arrival

Hirscholm Castle, Denmark, August 1770

As I step down from the carriage and look up at Uncle Thomas standing on the steps of Hirscholm Castle, a rogue wave of homesickness washes over me. For a moment I cannot speak. He is so like my mother, with his curly black hair and slightly crooked smile. I inhale the smell of roses and push the feeling away. Nothing will be allowed to mar this moment of arrival in Denmark, away from the boredom, the heat, the dust, the smell of rot…and the stifling conventions of St. Croix. My late father,

Christian Suhm, was the island's governor, and I suppose my life was as good as can be in that place, but I am relieved in this moment to be done with it. In Denmark I will further my education, and perhaps find a husband. This is the beginning of my adult life.

It is past midnight, and the strange northern light is otherworldly, casting a soft blue aura over the castle, fuzzing the edges of the formal gardens. The gates remind me of the welcoming arms of the staircases of our best houses in St. Croix. Phebe takes my hand and squeezes hard, then digs out a handkerchief from her bag. She is my slave, given to me at birth, and my dearest friend. Her mother was my uncle Thomas' best friend when they were children, before she had been sent up to the Big House to work. Later he told me that the sight of Phebe had made him homesick too, and that the feeling never quite left him all the time we were there.

"However do they keep their gardens so perfect?" I ask Uncle Thomas.

"Things grow slowly here," he replies. "Not like the wild vegetation of St. Croix that can engulf you if you stand still too long. No, here everything is much more subtle. And the people are a little like those hedges, slow to change, cautious."

Thomas de Malleville is a sainted legend in our family, though he was only thirteen when he left St. Croix and came here twenty years ago. He had come to be educated in the King's court, just as I am doing now. He had stayed on, and three years ago had been appointed Captain of the King's Guards. Anyone in St. Croix aspiring to have a life beyond the Islands went abroad to be educated if they could. My parents wanted that for me, and Uncle Thomas had persuaded them to let me come to Denmark.

That first night we are settled in quickly by my Aunt Johanne in two adjacent rooms. I immediately like her, and as she stands beside Uncle Thomas I think they make a nice couple. Her dark hair is piled high on her head in a bun and her blue eyes have an intelligent, mischievous glint. She has a buoyant enthusiasm that is a delicious contrast to my uncle's sober steadiness. She is not exactly what you would call pretty, but she is handsome…and warm to me. But I don't think she quite knows what to make of Phebe.

Our rooms are on the second floor of the Guardhouse and look down on a courtyard with laundry lines right below our window. Phebe's room is smaller, but the bed, like mine, is lovely and soft. We fall into those beds that first night exhausted, and I wake to a clear blue sky and the sound of birds and the stomping of the changing guard somewhere out in the courtyard. A vigorous wisteria vine grows up the wall and is trying to press its way into my room.

Phebe comes into my room in her nightdress and stands over my bed. "It's a beautiful day, and we don't have to travel anywhere! I so want to unpack. And then let's explore!"

I prop myself up against the pillows and watch her as she flips a dress out of my trunk and holds it up to her chin, looking in the long mirror. She turns and does a little dance for me, and looks back at the mirror, sighing loudly.

"This blue doesn't suit me at all," she pronounces in a high nasal tone.

Matching her snooty tone, I retort, "That old thing? Mama had it made from some old rags she had lying around."

Phebe takes out my hairbrushes and combs and lays them neatly on the dressing table. From the bottom of the trunk she lifts out the petticoats and lace caps. Dressing is an architectural undertaking each morning, what with bum rolls and panniers. At the bottom is the jewelry box my mother has sent with me. Phebe places it carefully on top of the tall dresser.

In truth there is nothing very fine in my trunk. Party dresses I will have to have made here in Denmark, because the fashions change faster than ships can travel. When we are finished in my room we go into hers. Mama had had several warm and serviceable outfits made for her, one in black and one in dark green, with several colorful woolen shawls to wear with them. She pulls one from her trunk that her sister Angelina had made for her in a lovely shade of raspberry and drapes it around her shoulders. I hold up a glass for her to look in.

"It's just for wearing in the house," she whispers.

When we put our proposal to explore to Johanne, she says, "I don't think anyone will mind if you just explore this beautiful place on your own, though don't go opening any doors to private chambers! If anyone asks who you are, just tell them you're Captain de Malleville's niece and companion from St. Croix and it's your first day at Hirschholm. You will be a curiosity to anyone who meets you, I am sure."

Hirscholm Castle is an enchanted place, quite beyond anything I had ever imagined: delicate architecture, yet grand; the air softened by sea breezes, and permeated by the sweet smell of late summer roses that peek above the hedges in succulent shades of peach and raspberry. An allee beneath arching trees leads to the castle, while mossy paths wander through well-tended woods. The whole is constructed carefully to seem both casual and wild. We spend much of that first day creeping around the corridors of the Castle, stunned by its grandeur and elegance. My uncle's guardsmen are posted at all the doors, at rigid attention. We pass a couple of bewigged gentlemen so lost in conversation that we are quite invisible to them. Nothing in our experience has prepared us for these seemingly endless cool, dark corridors.

"Look Sum." Phebe points through a window to the expansive inner courtyard. A very short African is scurrying by. "I wonder who that is? Do you suppose he's another slave? How curious to find him here."

Several times we get lost, but each time we eventually find a guard who aids our escape into the gardens where ladies with parasols stroll and stare unabashedly at Phebe. I clutch her arm, wishing to distract her from curious eyes, and point us down an allee of trees with grand vistas and trellised arches with cascading flowers marking divergent paths. Every flower is perfection, as though a troop of garden gnomes had come to life and tended to them overnight.

That night, Uncle Thomas taps tentatively on my door.

"Maria?" His voice is reedy, a loud whisper. For a moment I wonder who he is addressing.

I open it. "Uncle, hello! Remember, call me Summy. All my friends call me Summy. Please?" I plead.

"It doesn't seem a very dignified use of your late father's name, and you know it is a distinguished name here in Denmark. But if you insist I will use Summy in private." He looks like some hallowed being standing in the doorframe with the soft evening twilight lighting his face.

"Have you settled in all right? Shall we say prayers?" he asks.

"Oh yes. Do come in." I make an elaborate bow and gesture him into the room. "Isn't my chamber lovely?"

I watch his eyes go instantly to the only unusual thing in the room, the jewelry box on the dresser. He moves into the room, staring unblinkingly at the box.

"Is that the Missy Box?" His voice is barely audible.

"Missy Box? Mother never called it that."

"That's what Grandmother called it. She would imitate the voice of the Chinese hawker: 'You want box for Missy?'" He clips his words, and his high nasal imitation makes me smile.

"Mother pulled it out from somewhere and declared that it would serve me better in Copenhagen than ever it had her in Christiansted. She locked it up and put it in my trunk and told me to wear the key around my neck." I slip off the key on its ribbon and hold it out to him. "I don't think there is much jewelry in the box, but perhaps a few nice pieces and I think some things that have sentimental value in the family."

Thomas takes the box reverently in both hands and places it on the bed between us, fitting the key into its lock. He pulls out a necklace of tiny emeralds and diamonds and holds it to the light. "Grandfather gave her the box, you know. And over time, most of the jewels in it. I don't think Grandmother ever wore many of these, but she certainly loved them. She would look at some piece of sparkling stone and it would take her mind off into the past. She would weave the most fascinating tales for me. Now I wonder if they were true." He is suddenly silent, contemplating the fierce spirit of his grandmother.

"Why do you suppose Grandfather gave her the jewelry if she never wore it?" I ask him.

"As a way of storing their wealth, I should think," he replies. "Jewels hold their value in uncertain times. And since women can't own real property, jewels have long been a way to have something you can hide and carry away if need be. A vivid lesson that Grandmother absorbed when she fled France as a ten-year-old in 1685, all her wealth sewn into her dresses and coats, little gold pieces, and a few of these diamonds I am sure. If she hadn't had that wealth concealed, we would probably be the descendants of a seamstress or a baker, poor and uneducated laborers ourselves."

He pauses, watching me while I try to imagine such a twist of fate. "Her husband added to the collection, and probably paid very little for some of these. In wartime, especially at the turn of the last century, St. Thomas was neutral, and almost the only place a seller could get any price at all for such things."

I peer down into the box, looking for the thing that had most mystified me. "I found an odd thing at the bottom. It looks like it was once a rag doll, but now it's just a rag on a bit of carved wood. It seems very peculiar in among all the jewelry. As though it is in there to tell a different kind of story." I take the candle from the night table and slide the bottom drawer of the box open. We both peer down on the faded rag doll.

"It's Akila's gris-gris," Thomas says softly after a long pause.

I wait for him to go on. Of course I know what a gris-gris is. I am an island girl and have grown up seeing these spirit dolls. Most White people poo-poo the idea of gris-gris. But the Blacks attribute extraordinary powers to certain gris-gris. I am always on the side of believing.

"I think I was about ten when she took this gris-gris out of the box," Thomas goes on. "It was just a rag even then, about sixty years old, I guess."

"Oh, let me get Phebe," I cry. "She should pray with us, and I would like to show this to her. It was her grandmother's after all."

I bound from the room in my bare feet and soon reappear pulling Phebe behind me, reluctantly, in her nightdress. She is almost a head taller than I am, and strikingly handsome, with a wide forehead and high cheekbones. In the foggy evening light her figure casts a long, commanding shadow into the room. Her large eyes glisten so, I can see my face reflected in them. Uncle and I realize at the same moment that she has been crying. She quickly looks down, as if caught, and avoids Thomas' gaze.

"Welcome, Phebe." Thomas' voice is gentle and for a moment takes on the lilt of the islands. "Denmark must seem very strange to you, and you must be missing your family greatly. For this time I hope you will consider me to be your uncle too. Your mother and I were very close as children. Seeing you here makes me ever so homesick for her and for that happy time we shared."

I feel a great surge of joy as he speaks these words, for I love Phebe and I want so much for her to feel comfortable here. I can see that the words flow over her like warm honey and for the first time I see some of the tension of her body melt away. She smiles shyly at Uncle Thomas and with a graceful nod of her head says, "Thank you, Sir. I will tell her so next time I write home."

"Uncle says that this was your grandmother Akila's gris-gris," I burst out, holding the rag doll out to her in both my hands.

Picking up the thread, Uncle Thomas says "Yes, I believe it was given to her by Bamadille when she was a small child. For comfort, perhaps to make her feel powerful in a world where comfort and power were very elusive for a small Black child. Her life had some parallels to our great grandmother Maria's. They were two little girls, younger than you are by just two years, who were uprooted abruptly from their contented, rather privileged lives and flung out from their countries. Grandmother from France and Akila from Africa. And, can you imagine, it must have happened to both of them almost at the same time, as though they had been born under the same unlucky star." He gestured to us to kneel at the bedside. "But now let us say our prayers, as God would have us do."

Chapter Two: Africa 1685

Akila, ten years old, was leaning against a woman in the darkness with her eyes closed. Penned like an animal, she was wedged tightly in among some hundred standing bodies. She has travelled for three moons through jungle and desert to this place, harnessed to her fellow captives by leather straps around necks and ankles. New captives have been forcibly dragged or brought at gunpoint each evening to a stopping point on their route. Like a serpent, they have snaked through the jungle, the line growing longer with each passing day. Akila, one of the smallest, has strained to keep up.

She was captured one evening back returning with her mother from the fields to her village, grabbed and tied like an animal by a gang of armed men. Her mother fought back, trying to keep the men from her daughter, and in the struggle she had been hit hard in the head with the butt of a rifle. Akila had watched her fall, and seen her eyes open wide with a look of terror and rage. That vision of her mother's face gripped her like the fangs of a lion for her entire lifetime.

With the smallest thing—a smell or a sound—she would suddenly be in the gaping black hole of those jaws, devoured by gut-wrenching pain, taken to the depths of despair and darkness. Over the years she learned to tame the pain, to feel the lion about to pounce, so that she could turn away before it took her entirely into the darkness.

Akila had been the child of the village head, the beloved daughter of a much respected family. Her language was Soninke, a Mande language, but she had been raised a Muslim and spoke moderately good Arabic as well. Because of the status of her family she had also learned some of the related West African tribal languages. Her father had a Qu'ran and could read it. He had promised he would teach her to read one day. In the tradition of her people she had scars at her temples to indicate her tribal group, marks made soon after her birth. She followed her mother by day to the well where she would play games with the other children while her mother passed an hour in conversation with the village women. She helped her mother prepare the food and she worked with her in the fields, where they planted and harvested beans and melons and maize. She loved the butterflies, and the birds, whose calls she could imitate.

The gecko that lived on the wall of her mud dwelling was her friend. Her mother taught her which plants could be useful for poultices, and she went with her to tend the sick of their village, and sometimes helped her catch a baby.

Slave hunters and the wild beasts of the jungle were the ever-present dangers in West African village life. You could hear the drums beating from far away when disasters like this had struck a village in the area. But there had been no drums this time.

Akila had travelled in a state of numbness, beyond fear and beyond feeling. She knew only one other person in the coffle, a man from her village who had made her laugh with his antics for the children. In her village he had been a slave, but he was not treated badly. There were three ranks of slaves and he was a house slave, the highest rank. His name was Bamadille, which meant 'follow me home'. His name gave her hope, even though she knew in her heart that it was a childish hope. He had talked to her softly along the path, but she could not reply. It was as if her throat were frozen. No breath came to her to push the words out. Bamadille was one of the few in the group who spoke her language, but sometimes his words were like wisps of smoke that vanished as he spoke. Instead, a buzzing like insects thrummed in her head.

"Oh child, will you ever be able to speak to me again? What will it take to heal this terrible time." Bamadille reached his hand out and touched her cheek.

Awake early one morning she lay on her back, her foot roped to a tree. A butterfly, orange and black and iridescent blue, flickered by and alighted on her hand. For a moment time stopped and she and the butterfly and the dappled sunlight were all there was in the world. This at least could not be taken from her. Sometimes she thought she was the butterfly, flying high overhead to look back at her village, and forward to the jungle ahead. The butterfly became the image that held her heart steady in her silent world.

As they passed villages their captors would demand food from the villagers to feed the captives. They were fed in the evenings and the mornings. And then they walked. And walked. They all stank. They had running diarrhea, and sores everywhere from insect bites.

Occasionally they would have to go around the decomposing corpses of those who had fallen and died walking before them, fly ridden and stinking. They filled Akila with horror and her throat with vomit.

They had finally come to a hilltop from which they could see a vast expanse of blue. Akila had never seen anything like it. An endless sky. And she imagined being swallowed alive in its expanse. She stood on the hill and wept with terror. They were above the town of Christianborg, the Danish fort on the west coast of Africa.

As they were herded through the town to the pens around the fort, Akila became suddenly alert. Men in strange, complicated drab clothing, with hair on their faces of all different colors, stared at the women. Some of these people were pink and some were light brown, and they wore odd things on their heads, like gourds with lips. They shouted commands at Akila's captors, who in turn used their rifle butts to prod the group along more quickly. Akila looked down at her bleeding feet and naked body covered in bites. She could see her ribs like the ribs of an animal carcass. She wished desperately to cover herself. The black despair began to envelop her. She closed her eyes and grew her butterfly wings.

They stayed in the pen for several weeks and were fed each day boiled vegetables and a heavy gruel. Sometimes there was even meat. Akila ate silently. Her ribs began to hide again. At night a woman lay curled beside her for warmth. Akila still could not speak, but she was glad for this woman's body in the night. Each day more people were brought to the pen, until there was no room to lie down. On the last night she slept standing up. In the morning they were taken in dugout canoes, still chained, to a sailing ship that sat strangely upon the water.

Chapter Three: Dr. Struensee

Hirscholm, August 1770

I dream that night of St. Croix, that a great wave washed over the island and tossed all the inhabitants into the sea, and when they washed ashore there was nothing left on land, and they were neither White nor Negro, but all alike with nothing to their name, not even clothing. It was a dramatic and frightening dream at first, but finally peaceful, as if we had all been washed clean. In the end there was just beautiful sunlight, with beings shining like crystals, and beautiful shells. In the morning I lie in bed awhile, thinking of that strange dream, waiting for Phebe to come in and dress me. But she doesn't come, so I ring the little bell, just as I would at home. She still doesn't come so I get up and dress myself. The hair I cannot manage as she does though, so finally go and knock on her door.

"Come in." Her voice is raspy. She is sitting in her nightdress on the side of the bed. "Oh Sum, what a night. I dreamt that I was crawling with voracious, nattering insects. I must have cried out, because I woke myself up. My skin was still crawling, so I stood at the window for a long time. Such an eerie light. It must have been the middle of the night, but it was like looking out into midday fog. It took me a long time to go back to sleep. This morning I leapt out of bed thinking I was late for you, but then I was just sick for home. I heard a rooster crow and someone laughing in the courtyard below…and for a moment I thought it was my sister Angelina… And then I burst into tears…" She looks at me in a way that nearly breaks my heart.

I sit on the bed beside her, stricken with the strange contrast of our dreams. It must have been the gris gris. And then the homesickness hits me with a walloping suddenness, as if the bottom had just dropped out of my heart. I put my arms around her and we cry and cry.

We are a silent, red-eyed pair when we emerge. Uncle Thomas is off in the Guardhouse. The sun is warming the sitting room and there are three plates covered with napkins on the table.

I lift one of the napkins. Dark bread and ham.

"Ah, you're awake!" Aunt Johanne bounces into the room, emanating good cheer and I smile tentatively. She is wearing a cheerful red and white dress with a bum roll and buttons up the front. "Eat now, Dr. Struensee will be here any moment."

"And who is Dr. Struensee?" I ask.

"He is the King's special physician and a most clever man." Johanne's ebullient smile makes it clear that this last phrase is loaded with meaning.

"A clever curer, you mean?" I ask.

"It looks to me like he's decided to cure the whole country," Johanne replies.

"Of what? Smallpox?" Phebe asks.

"Among other things. Mostly of its backwardness. I hear he has all kinds of new ideas. But as he is the King's physician you should feel very honored to be in his care."

"Is it true what I have heard about the King? That he has a sickness in his mind?" I murmur.

"Yes sadly, it is true. Sometimes Dr. Struensee is the only one who can control him. The King trusts him completely and seems truly to love him."

"It must be terrible for the Queen to have such a husband." I sigh.

"Yes. It is quite terrible, but not the first time such things have happened in royal families. They do not spend much time together. Mostly on official occasions. But still it is an unhappy situation. It will not affect you, though, dear Summy." Johanne puts her hand on my shoulder in a reassuring way. But my curiosity has been aroused.

A knock at the door prompts Phebe to rise from the table and stack the blue and white plates to clear them. She has been sitting all this time listening to us intently, and I suddenly feel her discomfort. Her eyes are still red. I catch her glance and smile at her, hoping she feels the sympathy I'm trying to send to her.

"Have I the honor of Captain Malleville's wife and niece?" Dr. Struensee speaks to us in German, a language I know from my schooling in St. Croix. He stands smiling in the doorframe, and then with a flip of the tails of his beige waistcoat, he bows, blond curls freely flowing. Quite a contrast to the bewigged gentlemen we had encountered on our walk.

"And who is this beautiful young woman?" he says, indicating Phebe.

"I am Phebe." A quick curtsy and she steps back, warily. Is he making fun of her?

I suddenly feel a twinge of jealousy at the way he is looking at Phebe. And the need to make myself an interesting specimen to him.

He scans the two of us rapidly with his dark blue eyes and says, "You both look splendidly healthy to me."

"You are so kind to pay us a visit, Dr. Struensee," Johanne's eyes are wide with pleasure. He nods, smiling, to her and turns to me.

"Miss Suhm, am I right? A distinguished name here in Copenhagen."

I look down at my hands and smile. "Maria Malleville Suhm, but please call me Summy. My Aunt says I'm too brown and skinny, but I have assured her that it is just the way God made me." I draw myself up straight for his examination, imagining the string from heaven that suspends me on earth that my mother is always talking about.

"Nothing wrong with brown and skinny," Dr. Struensee mutters, looking at me closely. "But it's always a good idea to check people who have arrived from the Islands after a long sea voyage. Sometimes there are parasites, sometimes a touch of scurvy. Curable things that can be a misery if unattended."

He presses my tongue down with a little paddle and peers down my throat. "Your uncle tells me that your grandmother was a famous healer on the island, a woman ahead of her time."

I gurgle and he takes the paddle away. "My great grandmother, actually." I reply, clearing my throat. "Yes, it is true, along with Phebe's great-great grandmother Akila. I never knew my great grandmother, but they must have known some amazing cures, because people still talk about them. Not always positively, because she must have been very different from the usual plantation women. There's not much for women to do in the Islands but rock and sew and be waited upon. To stay upstairs where the breezes are healthier." I blush suddenly with the realization that there was plenty for Black women to do. "The White women, I mean."

I pause, looking at Phebe. "But they say she never did any of those things, but rode horseback all over the island seeing to people with Akila. They were much gossiped about by the other women, and not very kindly for the most part."

Struensee finishes with me and moves on to Phebe, still talking. He takes her chin and looks carefully into her eyes. "I would love to know what medicines and treatments they used." He peers into Phebe's ear. "The Virgin Islands were the center of the world in her time, and ships from all over the globe would have stopped there. They may have encountered some ancient and exotic cures. Extraordinary for a woman to do that in her time, and with her slave by her side." He looks at us strangely for a moment, as if assessing whether we might have any of these qualities of bravery and defiance.

"We took a lot of fruit on the *Christianborg* with us, as our great grandmothers would have had us do, and made it last the voyage. We had some seasickness at the beginning, but never any other problems. Unless you count homesickness. Phebe had a mighty case of that."

The doctor's face is stern but kind, and I blurt out, "I hope I have done right in bringing Phebe with me to Copenhagen. I had not thought how different she would seem here and how lonely she might be."

"A terrible institution, slavery." Struensee is suddenly grave, and I feel as though he had slapped me. As though it were my fault. Tears well up in my eyes. "You will find that there are some other Africans here in Copenhagen. They are quite a symbol of wealth, so people show them off."

I am mortified. All I can think to say is, "I think you will find us both in good health."

The examination over, Struensee settles in an armchair and looks intently at Johanne.

"I wish half the population of Copenhagen were as healthy as these two are." He leans back and crosses his legs. "One of the reasons we're here in the country castle of Hirscholm is to avoid the smallpox raging in Copenhagen. But we will have to return to the city for the winter and when we do I am going to begin a vaccination program. It is a simple enough thing. You infect a person with a tiny amount of the disease, just a little pin-prick. They get a little sick, but the dose is controlled, and it prevents them from ever contracting the illness again." He smiles broadly. "I hope you all will agree to be vaccinated. I am sure Thomas' grandmother would have approved. It's not terribly pleasant, but not awful either, and far better than having the pox."

Johanne looks at him directly. "You are full of amazing ideas, Doctor. I am sure we will follow the Queen in this."

"Prince Fredrick will have the vaccine in a week's time. So I will put you on the schedule too." He pauses as if waiting for her refusal. Then he looks appraisingly at Johanne.

"I have also suggested to the Queen that she widen her circle of social acquaintances and invite more of the general population to her table. I don't think she's ever met anyone below the rank of Count and Countess, unless they were serving her. Being from England, Queen Caroline Mathilda hasn't had the easiest time. I think you and Summy would be good company for her. She needs some friends and a little fun. So don't be surprised if you find yourself dining at the Royal table sometime soon."

He rises from the chair and runs his hand through his hair. "I must take my leave." With a quick bow, he is out the door. Johanne bursts into laughter.

"What an extraordinary man," I mutter.

"You have no idea. He has become our shadow king. The King signs anything that Struensee puts before him, and as you can see, he is not lacking in ideas to improve things," Johanne says with a grin.

Uncle Thomas appears at my door again that night. I sense that our arrival has unleashed something in him, a longing for the Islands, and perhaps for his grandmother, Maria, who lived with him all his growing-up years. His own mother had died giving birth to him, so his grandmother must have been like a mother to him. She lived to an astonishing seventy-five.

The evening light casts long shadows into the corners of the room and a bright orange reflection in the mirror makes the gris-gris that I have propped on the dresser look as if it had been shipwrecked beside a campfire.

"You two look cozy," he says softly.

Phebe cocks her head and blinks. Then she smiles. His tone is warm, as though he were talking to two daughters.

"I hear you met Dr. Struensee today. What did you think of him?" Thomas asks genially.

"He is a most extraordinary man," I cry. "I think he could get one to do almost anything. Very charming, and full of new ideas…like the one about vaccinations."

I see Uncle Thomas stiffen slightly. I have just dampened his pleasure. Could he be jealous that I like the man so much?

"Do you know what he did today?" He presses his fingers into his cheeks and cocks his head. "He signed a proclamation giving the press freedom to say whatever they like. The whole court is outraged about it, except for the King and Queen. I didn't even know we had any press here in Denmark! But we're bound to get some now. He is very bold and he is treading in very dangerous territory. Whether he is an instrument of God or the Devil I have not yet decided. Go cautiously with him, my dear."

I have no need to think on that caution. I have already decided that Struensee is very much a creature of God, if not God himself.

Uncle Thomas goes to the Missy Box and delicately lifts a chain between his thumb and forefinger from which dangles a simple silver medallion. He lets it slide from his palm back into the box and says, "Let's say a special prayer for our ancestors and acknowledge all the suffering they endured in their lives."

Chapter Four: Departure from France

La Rochelle, France, October 1685

Shafts of early morning sunlight filter through the forest trees onto the hidden beach and play upon two groups of Huguenots, French Protestants who are being hunted by the King's men. The Protestants of France are being hunted; those who will not convert to Catholicism are being murdered, sent into convents, stripped of their possessions, in a frenzy of hatred and greed. The Edict of Nantes that held them in relative safety for a hundred years has just been revoked by King Louis.

Thomas Bourdoux has chosen to send his ten year old daughter, Maria, away from France to save her from being put in a Catholic convent. He will follow as soon as he can sell his business. She will be accompanied into exile by her nanny Celine, a simple woman of the village of Soubise who has cared for Maria since the death of her natural mother in childbirth.

Thomas kneels beside Maria and wraps her in his arms, warming her against his body. She puts her small arms around his neck and nuzzles his stubbly cheek, tears flowing. "Papa, oh papa, don't make me leave you."

"You must go Maria, you are not safe now in France. But I will join you soon enough. He pulls a thin, silver chain from his pocket, revealing a small medallion. "This is to be yours now. Take care of it. It will keep you safe and bring you luck. It has been our our family for many generations."

She fingers the medallion and struggles to calm her hiccuping sobs. "I will treasure it, Papa," she whispers.

They watch the dory approach, listening anxiously for the sound of approaching horses. The King's men are watching all the ports.

Nearby, Jacques La Salle, with his manservant Lucien, watches his fifteen-year-old son, Pierre, flick stones into the waves, trying to making them skip.

"You and Lucien must watch out for little Maria, and of course Celine, will you?

She'll be homesick for her father, until he's able to come…And beyond all things, stay close to the Lord, my son, and you will have nothing to fear."

"We will. Do not worry. And I will write to you often."

From the dory Maria never takes her eyes off her father, a dark triangle in the shadows on the edge of the forest. She blinks into the white diamonds of light cast upon the waters by the rising sun. *Just a tiny speck now,* she thinks, and she waves her bonnet, until she sees him turn and slip silently into the woods. She looks up at Pierre and tries to smile, but her lip trembles and she looks away, not wanting him to see her cry. She has grown up with Pierre and is pleased that he is to take care of them and to help secure them passage from the intermediate port of Funchal in the Madeira Islands to somewhere in the Americas. She has great confidence that her father will follow and make a new life with them as soon as he can secure his business affairs.

Maria and Celine settle into their snug cabin on the barque. In other circumstances Maria might have found it enchanting. There are two berths, upper and lower, made up neatly with heavy quilts. Everything in the cabin is mahogany, varnished to a high gloss. Resting in the corner is a washstand with a blue and white porcelain basin. "Hot water every morning at sunrise" declares the cabin boy. "But don't drink it. Ever. Two portholes let in bright streams of morning light. "Portholes closed at all times," intones the boy, as the ship heels over and their trunks slide across the floorboards. "No candles, or fire of any kind."

"Oh my, how dark it will be." says Celine, lurching against the washstand. Maria and Celine lie for days on their berths.

"I wish I could die," Celine moans.

"No, no, Celine. This will pass. We will be in Funchal soon Pierre says."

With the help of Pierre and Lucien, Maria tends to Celine, lugging buckets up and down. When they arrive in Funchal Pierre scours the harbor for a suitable vessel to take them west. The next departure is on the *Fortuna,* a Danish ship of the Royal Navy, carrying a new governor to the Virgin Islands. It is a much grander ship than what they have just been on, and Pierre arranges passage for all four of them to St. Thomas in the Danish Virgin Islands.

Being gentry, they eat at the Captain's table. His cozy dining quarters are a wonder to Maria, who at her first meal sits quietly as she has been taught and speaks only when spoken to. She observes and listens. Next to her is Dr. Pundit, an exotic young Indian man in a strange white garment. To Maria's pleasure, he speaks to her in French. He is a very young man to be so learned, but he eats with his fingers and Maria is appalled at his manners. But she likes his deep brown eyes and wild mop of black hair.

He turns to the ship's surgeon beside him.

"Have you heard of the new fever treatment? Made from the bark of the Chinchona tree. From Peru!" Maria strains to hear what he is saying as she thinks this a very interesting topic.

"Is it a stimulant or a purgative?" the surgeon asks. Back and forth they go, and Maria tries to follow. But the men are in disagreement about whether fevers should be treated with stimulants such as wine, distilled bark water and cold plunges, or by depleting remedies like purges with calomel, and copious bleeding with lancets or leeches. There is much discussion of leeches, at which point Maria loses her interest, and nearly her breakfast, and leaves off listening to the doctors.

Pierre sits at the other end of the table with Lucien, whom Maria has always found comical because he is so tall and odd. Practically coiled in his chair, he reminds her of a garter snake with a floppy mustache and flaming red hair. Pierre himself is talking very seriously to a man named Mikkelsohn, the incoming Governor of St. Thomas. What Mikkelsohn sees before him in that moment is a young man of unusual education, languages and demeanor, qualities that are practically nonexistent in the rough world of the Danish

Virgin Islands. He will take Pierre on as his assistant the moment they land.

Maria feels so like she is at a tea party that she is greatly surprised by the food, which is quite disgusting. The bread is hard as a rock and there is no jam or honey. The conversation turns to the passengers on the ship, and the Captain, addressing them all, says, "You will soon be aware, if you are not already, that we are carrying a number of convicts. Petty criminals for the most part, nothing to be afraid of, but not an element to socialize with. They have signed themselves up to be indentured for seven years of labor in the plantations, after which time they will be given a bit of land and some tobacco. Most of them were lifers in Bremerholm Prison, so they found this an attractive alternative. They are confined to the forward area of the gun deck, though we will give them air topside for a portion of each day to keep their health. Be alert with this element. There are some strange ones among them. You, of course, are all free to be on deck anytime, unless I specifically command otherwise. But please stay clear of the crew and their work."

Their days gradually take on a rhythm. The November cold of France has given way to the balmy breezes of the southern seas. An albatross has taken to following the ship, and Maria names him Albert and feeds him table scraps each day at the stern of the ship. At night Maria and Pierre stand on the deck together and watch the bow waves, like rolling mountains of fire glowing with tiny sea creatures. Maria is up with the sun each day and creeps silently out on the deck to say her prayers in the wind and spray, watching the peachy golden light come up over the horizon. Her bonnet is soon carried away and her wildly curly brown hair whips in the wind. She is becoming a shade of mahogany and she knows her father would not approve, but she thinks it is a most beautiful color, the color of a sailor's skin.

The sailors are a wild and rough bunch of men, quite terrifying to Maria at first with their jumble of dialects and sweaty male smells. But they are charmed to have this little girl in their midst and in small ways compete for her attention. They teach her dirty songs in languages she doesn't understand and laugh heartily to hear her singing them. They sleep in four-hour shifts, as there are only forty hammocks for eighty men, so there are always forty sleeping and forty working. She has a little box on deck where she sits when the sailors are busy and want her out of the way. When the captain shouts an order, she runs to her box, and the sailors rush about making a great clatter adjusting the sails. Pierre has taken to helping them and they have instructed him in many things of the sea.

Sometimes Pierre will sit beside her box, his long legs tucked beneath him to avoid tripping the sailors, and teach her how to tie a knot, or whisper to her a little gossip about one of the sailors. "See that man up in the rigging with the mermaid tattoo? He just came off a pirate ship. You wouldn't believe the things they did. And I can't tell you." Maria longs to be a boy, to share the secrets of men. Her eyes follow his pointing finger and she sees the man, who seems almost a monkey, so muscular and agile is he in the rigging, and so hairy. Pierre is not hairy. He is smooth and brown. But he has an extraordinary head of curls, a mix of blond and chestnut from the salt and sun. It has grown into a great mop on the voyage, and she can see that a bit of beard and mustache is fuzzing up around his mouth.

When the convicts come on deck Maria watches them curiously. A woman called Mette stands out, being astonishingly dirty and loud, with a harsh Danish very different from the Captain and Mr. Mikkelsohn's speech. She keeps staring at the medallion around Maria's neck until Maria starts wearing a wide ribbon to hide it. The sailors try to teach Mette to milk the cows, but she is no good at it at all, and once spits in the pail of fresh milk, so they make her drink the whole pail.

At the beginning of December they are rocked by a fierce gale from the northeast.Piglets get loose from their crates and go flying through the air like pink bowling balls. The gaff on the mizzen splinters to matchsticks, and one of the sailors is knocked off the rigging into the hold, suffering a broken arm.

Two sailors come lurching to their cabin and tie them with rope into their bunks, tucking them in tightly under their quilts. Over and over the ship leaps into the air on enormous waves and slams downward at a terrifying angle. Maria closes her eyes and pictures her father, Thomas, with his comforting big mustache, and she hears him say: "Put your little heart there now, right in His outstretched palm," and a steadying calm comes over her in the pitching ship.

Celine does not fare so well. She retches into the bucket by her berth for the long duration of the storm. Maria, desperate for something to do to comfort her, sings hymns from the top berth. Dr. Pundit pays them several visits, clutching the rails of the cabin to stay upright and promising to take the buckets topside when the sea calms.

After three days the rain becomes mist. The waves calm a bit. Gradually ashen faces appear on deck and meals in the Captain's quarters resume. One day as the sun is setting a great column of water rises to the clouds. Maria stands transfixed at the wonderous waterspout, thinking that the Lord must surely be giving them some kind of sign. This is just like a story from the Bible. For the rest of her life she will long to see such a miracle again.

Several days later, while Maria watches the sun sink on the horizon, she suddenly feels the medallion chain around her neck tighten. Just as she reaches for the chain, the air splits with an ungodly shriek from Albert, the albatross. He swoops over Maria to land his great bulk on the lice-infested head of Mette Petersen, who falls to the deck screaming obscenities in her guttural Danish. A collection of sailors comes out of the dusk and gathers around the prone figure of Mette, who sits up screaming and points a long, dirty fingernail at Maria. The girl looks at her dumbfounded, but the hairs on the back of her neck rise as she realizes the woman is cursing her in Danish. The sailors laugh and look at Maria with new admiration. They drag Mette to her feet and escort her below, while Albert preens himself on the stern of the ship.

"Oh Albert, you are a very smart bird," Maria whispers. "I think the Lord has sent you to protect me." A great flood of love for the bird washes over her. She goes down to her cabin to report the incident to Celine who, though better, is far from spry. That night they pray together for protection from Mette's curse, whatever it might have been.

As they get nearer to the Caribbean, weeks into the voyage, more ships appear on the horizon, flying Dutch, English, Spanish, French and Portuguese flags. Captain Meyer puts it this way to his dinner guests one evening after several glasses of Madeira. "Right now, the West Indies," he waves his glass in an westerly direction, "is the center of the world. Who knows how long it will last, but here on these islands is where the wealth of the world is about to be made. You will either get rich or you will die in the effort. Denmark has done well to remain neutral in these endless squabbles among the kings of Europe. No one will disturb our Danish ship but pirates, and they are not likely to approach a forty-gun warship."

The weather has warmed as they enter the tropics, and now it becomes unbearably hot. The passengers strip off as many of their garments as is decently acceptable. Maria has never experienced this kind of heat and the new odors that come with it. The smell of sweat, rot and the occasional whiff of excrement. She has shed her heavy woolen undergarments and stands at the rail each evening, her cotton skirts fluttering as she strains to see a speck of land. Dr. Pundit often comes and stands beside her, hand to his brow to share in her scrutiny of the horizon. He smells of some spice that makes her think of the cook at home making a lovely confection with cinnamon and nutmeg.

"And what do you expect this place you are going to be like?" he asks one evening.

"A paradise. Don't you think so?" Dr. Pundit does not respond right away, so she goes on. "With beautiful beaches and swaying trees, and simple people who will be kind to us."

"What a lovely image. I would like to think that is what we shall find, but I've been to many places and not one of them turned out to be a paradise, though I do think we'll find beautiful beaches and some lovely vegetation. I am afraid you will not find the simple people… they were the Ciboney, the Caribs and the Arawak tribes. But there are few of them left—they had no immunity to the diseases of the Europeans and had no match for their weapons. I am afraid almost all of them have died."

"Oh, that's dreadful."

Dr. Pundit looks down on her shocked face and decides to change the subject. "Some of these Caribbean islands might still be active volcanos! You can see on any map they are an archipelago, just like the mountains that divide our borders in Europe, but here, just the tops are showing."

"Oh, I hope we'll not be living on a volcano! My father would not be at all happy with that," she says softly. Remembering that she is not to talk too much about herself she smiles up at him. "Where are you going exactly, and why?"

"I am headed for Curaçao. Interesting plants there I am told, and I am a collector. For medicines."

"How did you come to leave India?"

"Ah, that is a long story, and perhaps not one suited to a young girl's ears."

After that Maria begins to imagine Dr. Pundit's family dying of dreadful diseases, or savage warriors killing them all, but nothing in her world experience would enable her to imagine the truth.

Not long after that conversation Maria, in the stern of the ship, is just about to beat Pierre in a game of quoits, when from high in the rigging comes a sailor's cry: "Land Ho."

Chapter Five: Vaccinations

Hirscholm, Denmark, 1770

We have permission to wander as we wish, though Uncle Thomas has cautioned me to keep our distance from the King should I encounter him. But if by chance I should come face to face with him, to curtsy nicely, smile and scamper off like a deer. "Likely, he will think you are one," he mutters.

In the end it is not the King that we encounter, but the Queen, walking with Struensee in the rose garden one midmorning. Phebe is trailing a little behind me and I am startled from my examination of a rose bush by her sharp intake of breath.

"Why it is Miss Maria Suhm and her companion, Miss Phebe," says the doctor amiably. He bows to each of us as he had when we first met. Since I have never seen anyone bow to a slave I am disconcerted, but in a pleasing way, as if a new vista had suddenly opened before me. "Let me introduce you, Caroline. Miss Suhm is the niece of Captain Thomas de Malleville, come from the islands to get a bit of Danish polishing. It is the De Mallevilles and Summy whom I have proposed you invite to dinner."

Queen Caroline Mathilda smiles at me with a distracted air. In a quick glance, for I know it is impolite to stare, I take in that the Queen is lovely in the foggy soft way of Denmark, all pastel colors and no hard edges. Blond and blue eyed. I know that she is nineteen, not so very much older than I am, though we are opposites in coloring. I curtsy, slowly and formally, and bow my head. Phebe, standing tall beside me, makes a fair imitation of the same.

The Queen smiles. "Welcome! I hope you do not suffer from homesickness as I did!

Please come to the nursery sometime and play with Prince Frederick. He would be delighted. He's only three, but such fun, and there must be very little of that for girls your age." Chin up and cleared-eyed, she looks directly at Struensee and continues. "Frederick has just been returned here to me thanks to our Dr. Struensee, who finally persuaded the Dowager Queen Juliana that a boy belongs with his mother."

"We would enjoy that very much, Your Majesty." And wondering at the emotion behind her little speech, I curtsy again, just a bob this time.

"Frederick is going to be vaccinated tomorrow," Struensee says. "Why don't you come along at the same time, both of you, and do the same. Bring your aunt and uncle. Nine o'clock in the morning. Be prepared to feel a little unwell for a few days, but it will be nothing much. It will be a distraction for Frederick to have you there, and if you are brave at the prick, maybe he will be too."

"You always have the best ideas, Herr Doctor." The Queen smiles as she says this and moves past us. "Good day then. We shall see you anon," she calls back over her shoulder. We return to the guardhouse for our midday meal and I describe the encounter to Johanne.

"Vaccination? Terrifying! But I suppose…it is better to do it before we go back to the city. And how delightful it would be to be invited to dinner," Johanne's face lights up. "You can't imagine how hard it is to be inside the palace but excluded from its grand activities. I would rather be back in my old country life where at least I had my sisters and my animals for company."

"An invitation to dinner is a nice reward," I reply. "And I'm sure it will come. It does give some urgency to the question of my wardrobe."

"And my wardrobe too! I have nothing I could wear to the King's table. If we live through the vaccination, and if the invitation is forthcoming, we will call in a seamstress." I can see by her dreamy look that she has already been transported to a glittering royal dinner in her head.

The center of attention in the nursery is little Frederick, a blur of dark curls, rocking wildly on a wooden horse, through tiny dust motes that dance in the morning sunlight. Struensee and the Queen stand together nearby, and after being announced, we parade before them to bow and curtsy. Two of Frederick's nursemaids attend the galloping horse.

"The procedure is simple enough," Struensee begins. "I will start with Thomas. I have done this on myself, and several others. Since then, I have been in the company of the afflicted many times since with no ill effects, as have many others. I will prick each of you with a tiny dose of the disease in a fatty place, perhaps your leg or your arm. You can come with me behind that curtain for privacy but let's have Frederick watch…if we can get him off his horse… so that he will see it's harmless."

Each of us in turn gets a prick behind the curtain, with Frederick watching intently. But when it is his turn, he begins to howl anyway, until Phebe brilliantly produces a lump of sugar. He closes his mouth around it and the Queen smiles gratefully at Phebe.

By evening we are all feeling unwell to varying degrees. But Phebe claims to feel fine and prepares us a little supper in the apartment. After a few days of mild fever, life returns to normal.

Normal has its own tedium. In the mornings I go to the schoolroom to have my lessons with a series of tutors: Latin, French and English, mathematics and music. In the afternoons I am free to wander the beautiful grounds of Hirscholm, but this is boring without Phebe who has been put to work by Johanne polishing everything from floors to silverware.

The afternoon is the lowest part of the day and in my boredom I retreat to my room and play with the Missy Box and its contents, hoping to find a secret compartment. I have noticed that the bottom is larger than the drawer that seems to be the last. I dump all the jewelry on the bed and turn the box upside down. How to get it open? I spend a few moments running my fingers around all the corners, pressing this and that. I look at the key that opens the main lock. It is an unusual thing, a key at one end and at the other a lovely spherical silver knob with four sharp points, as though it were meant to spin on its end. I take the pointy end and begin to press on all the indentations in the box I can find.

Suddenly the bottom drops off. I had pressed a little indentation that was hardly visible.

There, tied in a soft blue ribbon, fresh and bright as the day the loops were made by my great grandmother's fingers, is a sheaf of papers two inches thick. For I am convinced that this must be what these papers contain, all those private things that Uncle Thomas never knew himself, though he may have suspected.

The rainy afternoons are suddenly a treasure, a private time to read the innermost thoughts of the Maria of Uncle Thomas' stories.

I untie the ribbon with trembling fingers and look down on the first page. My excitement dampens to gloom. The diary seems to be in some kind of code. The pages are just crammed, indecipherable. First there is the problem of the handwriting, tiny, crabbed. And everything seems to be abbreviated. Did great grandmother not have enough paper? Or did she want to make sure no one could read this but herself?

I look out the window at the drizzling rain and take a deep breath. "I'll just have to begin at the beginning and try to figure it out. If she made it that hard to read, there's probably something interesting here." I take the diary over to the window where the light is better and get to work. After forty minutes I have worked out these sentences. *Oh, my heart. I cannot make it still. It pounds as if it will fly apart inside me. I grow hot thinking of what I have witnessed, but I am also suddenly calmed, as if the Lord has just taken me into his confidence and revealed why my marriage has been such a struggle.*

Definitely worthwhile. I struggle on, barely breathing. Not quite knowing what it is I am reading about. The diary is so personal to me I don't want another living soul to know about it.

These were great grandmother's most private thoughts and secrets. That is very plain. But it is going to take months to decipher. She wouldn't have written this down if she never wanted anyone to know the contents, but she didn't want just anyone to know. She wanted someone who really cares to know. At this moment I feel a deep loving connection to this woman, as though she is speaking to me alone. We have entered an intimate space together, just the two of us. I have taken my own paper and ink and am carefully making a new version of what I think my great grandmother has written.

In the evening Uncle Thomas details the plans for church in the morning. He will ride ahead of the carriage with the King and Queen and Dr. Struensee.

"Of course it is a not a Moravian Church as you and I are accustomed to, but a Lutheran Church."

"Oh I hope it will not be as dull as the Lutherans at home," I mutter. Uncle Thomas looks at me gravely, but I can see the corners of his mouth twitch.

"The Lutherans used our islands as a land of exile for their worst behaved ministers," he says quietly. "When I was eight years old Phebe's mother led me to the Moravians. Their missionaries were holding secret services in the hills for the slaves of the Island. It was thrilling, I can tell you, the power of those meetings. And what a contrast to the Lutherans."

"Your parents must have been horrified!"

"My mother was dead by then and no one was paying much attention to me. God entered my soul at that moment and I brought your mother along on my next visit. We both ended up as converts and I'm hoping one day that Johanne will be one too when we return to the Islands. There are very few Moravians here in Denmark but I know some, and we worship together occasionally."

The church at Hirscholm is by the lake. It is an impressive structure, stolid, white and without ornamentation. I walk to it with Johanne and Phebe. Thomas is riding at the head of the Guards, making way for the King's carriage. Dr. Struensee smiles at us and raises a hand in greeting as they roll by. The breath goes right out of me and I think what a silly fool I am.

My heart is still racing as the service begins, but the austere liturgy sobers me quickly. I reflect upon my sins: my longing for Dr. Struensee's attention, my concealment of the diary. I think of God's judgment, and then Johanne begins to snore, and I nudge her, trying to keep a straight face.

Chapter Six: Voyage of the Hope

Akila lies in the hold of the slave galley *Hope* for many weeks, like a sapling tossed by the wind among tall trees. All she can see is a bit of sky above her through the grid of the hatch cover. Blue sky, grey sky, starry sky and sky that turns into torrents of water for days at a time. But for those little squares of bouncing sky she is in a dark box, as if she had been buried alive with just enough air to breathe. The air is vile. She is conscious of each breath through her mouth, as though she were inhaling the excrement and sweat of all the bodies around her. They are crying out in a cacophony of unintelligible languages, but the keening and sighing is like the sounds of the forest in a storm. She closes her eyes and summons her butterfly. For an instant she can feel the breath of its wings on her cheek.

For some period of every day when the weather is fine they are taken to the deck. It seems to her that there are hundreds of them, and she cannot imagine how so many could fit below decks. The men are chained, but Akila and some of the women are allowed to sit unchained. They are in the tropics. The sun is hot. The air stinks. On some days the sea spray washes over them and they try to cleanse themselves from the filth of the hold. The sailors eye them warily, especially the men, despite their chains. Akila stays close to Bamadille when they are on deck, but below he is chained with the men, and she with the women. He speaks to her softly.

"You are not chained, child. If you chance to get anything that might be a tool, or a weapon, seize that chance. Something to saw through these chains. Take it. Hide it. We must watch for every chance." She turns her face towards him silently, wanting him to see in her eyes her eagerness to please him. But they are put back in the hold and Akila does not see any chance. She can't imagine where she could hide anything on her naked body. She looks out over the vast and empty sea. She too is empty, and she no longer cares.

The *Hope* is rocked by a series of tremendous gales each lasting three days, with a few days of sunshine between. The bodies in the hold are tossed like sticks into the air by the slamming of the boat against mountainous waves. Akila's head pounds against the floorboards over and over until she thinks she will lose her teeth and her skull will crack. Torrents of water flow in through the scuppers. A great chanting begins among the chained bodies. With all their different languages they find a common chant of pain and outrage, drumming against the storm. The chants drown out the moaning and the retching. At the end of each storm the sailors come down to the hold. Akila sees one of them gag into the kerchief he has tied over his nose and mouth. They unchain the dead and carry them to the deck. Moments later she hears a series of splashes as the bodies are tossed over the rail into the sea.

The weather turns fine and hot. The captives are unchained and taken on deck. The sailors make a kind of music, beating on pots, one of them sawing on a little stringed instrument with a stick. They prod the captives to dance, and some of them dance with pleasure. A chanting begins as they move. It feels good to move. For a moment Akila thinks of moving right over the rail of the ship, into the water. To be free. But she is afraid of the beasts in the water. She raises her arms and moves them, chanting to Allah. Begging him to take her home.

On a morning when the sea is calm and Akila can see blue through the grate, a sailor comes and unchains her and takes her above, alone. She blinks in the bright light and follows him, with another sailor coming behind her. Her heart pounds. Her mouth is dry. They take her and wash her, heaving buckets of cold seawater over her. She begins sobbing at the shock of it.

They take her to a cabin door, and after a knock, the captain opens it and beckons her in, shutting the sailors out. The size of him, and the shiny blackness of his hair and whiskery cheek takes her breath away. She stops crying and turns away from him, looking warily around the cabin. A monkey with a little bowl of peanuts is chirping in the corner. The captain puts his hands on her shoulders and steers her toward the bed and presses her down to a sitting posture.

She recoils with terror at his touch. Her eyes dart around the cabin and rest on the monkey. He is so like the monkeys in her village. She feels a shaft of the deepest pain in her heart as she looks at him, and tears well up in her eyes.

The captain says something in his strange language, a language that makes him sound like he is swallowing a whole banana. He holds out a basket of dried fruit and Akila just looks at it, weeping. He offers her a basket of bread still warm from the oven. The monkey leaps suddenly onto the bed, jumping up and down beside her, grabbing a piece of the bread. He squeals and chirps and touches her cheek, as if to wipe away her tears. Akila cannot help but smile. The Captain's face softens and lifts and he offers the fruit again. She puts out her hand and he puts a dried apple into it. He holds out a tankard of small beer. She gulps it thirstily.

For three days they repeat this ritual. On the third day the captain is called away, and he locks Akila into his cabin, saying something to her in his banana talk. She sits on the bed and looks around the cabin, examining each thing. There is the monkey's crate with a nest of straw in it. She has no name for most of the objects she sees, but she sees that everything is snug, tidy, fastened down. There is a little desk with a writing quill and a bound notebook, much like her father has. A small painting in a frame shows three girls that look a little like the captain. "His daughters?" and she wonders if that is why she has been chosen by him for this treatment. On the desk she sees a small metal thing, pointed at the end. A tool of some kind, like a dull knife. She remembers Bamadille's words. She grabs the file. She has been thinking about hiding places. She spreads the place between her legs and with the round end first, pushes the file into her skinny body. It fits neatly. She sits back down on the bed and waits.

The Captain returns. He sits facing her, silently. She can see that something about her has touched him. Does it have something to do with the young women in the picture frame? Or perhaps it is her silence among all the others? She almost wishes she could ask him, but she is too weary.

Akila is returned to the hold, wedging herself between the bodies of two women, making herself as tiny as she can. She raises her knees and slips the file out from between her legs.

In her mind she calls out, "Bamadille, I have something for you." She tries to make the sounds but no words come. Silently she passes the file to the woman next to her, who looks at it, and then at Akila, her bloodshot eyes wide with admiration. She passes it on in the direction of the men. Akila doesn't know where it ends up, but in the quiet of the night she hears a rasping sound, timed with the slapping of the waves.

Some days later Akila is on deck in the hot sun. She watches the rhythmic cresting waves and weighs the idea of throwing herself into the sea, as she does each time she comes on deck. But the terror of the sea is greater than the terror of whatever unknown fate lies ahead. She is no longer starving or thirsty. The captain's ministrations have taken care of that. But a bottomless well of grief seems to have displaced all that ever was inside her.

She stares into the waves. Suddenly a tremendous noise erupts behind her and she turns to see four of the male slaves unshackled, each lunging for a sailor. She watches one as he wraps himself around the sailor like a giant serpent, his forearm against the man's Adam's apple. He takes his sword with one hand and his pistol with the other, and shoots into the massing crowd of sailors. Firing begins all around her and instinctively she flattens herself on the deck in the bow of the boat and listens to the sounds of clashing steel and gunfire. The air is filled with the acrid smoke of it, and the screams and shouts of the mutinous slaves and the furious sailors.

Lying face down on the deck she prays to Allah that her people will throw the white men overboard, that they will turn the ship around and take her home. But even before her prayer is finished she can hear the roaring anguish of defeat, the rising rage and vengeance of the sailors. She lifts her head and sees Bamadille, alive but bleeding. Then she sees that they have tied one of the rebel slaves to the mast, his mouth stuffed with canvas, his manhood severed, an empty slick red gaping chasm. She looks away, her heart swallowed up, and vomits into the vast and empty horizon.

Chapter Seven: Anker Suhm

Copenhagen, 1770

In early October we leave Hirscholm Castle and go to Christianborg Castle in Copenhagen. Thomas has gone on with the King, and Phebe and I travel by carriage with Johanne. We plan to stay the night at the home of my uncle, the judge Anker Suhm. I am sad to leave Hirscholm, but the long daylight has shriveled to an early twilight and the cold has set in. I have made little progress with the diary but I know I will have many dreary winter hours in Copenhagen to work on it.

I feel slightly sick from the jostling of the carriage and I ask Johanne if I may get out and walk a bit.

"Not suitable, I'm afraid," is her reply, as she scratches behind her ear. "The city is ridden with vermin, both human and animal. Your uncle would be sure to point out that they are the Lord's creatures just as we are, but I say 'tis safer to be in a carriage. And besides, your boots would never recover."

Bumping along on slimy cobbles we peer out and are stunned into silence. There is a packed-down sense of filth, as though the ground had been tramped upon for a thousand years and had layers upon layers to release to the passing nose. The smell of horse dung is the freshest aroma to be had. People watch our passing carriage warily, unsmiling, their faces a greyish brown, creased with little riverbeds of streaky sweat and grime from their labors. But the buildings are a swirl of color, the kind of color I love in St. Croix. Yellows and oranges and blues, but here they have green copper roofs, not the tin of home.

The market squares are shrill, and our movement through them slow: coopers and carters, fishmongers and farmers are each in their personal dramas. Around them a swirl of errand boys scurry with overflowing canvas sacks. Occasional flashes of island colors, pink conchs and bright baskets that conjure in my mind the flying fingers of women weaving and chatting under softly moving palm trees.

"Look Sum, there's a cart of hogsheads," Phebe murmurs, pointing to the cartload of barrels passing us.

"I wonder if it's sugar from home." I look off at the forest of masts on the waterfront. "Maybe a ship has just arrived from St. Croix." My heart clutches with homesickness but it passes with the distraction of our arrival.

Anker Suhm's house is at a corner, with a gable angled over the street as if the bottom of the house had been cut off for a passing wide carriage. We are admitted by a tidy woman in a white apron, and my father's younger brother is soon holding me by the shoulders, scrutinizing me carefully. Gazing back, I wonder if this is what my father would have looked like had he lived. He had been the Governor of St. Croix and had died when I was two. I find myself staring at my uncle, but he is looking at me just as intently, so I am unembarrassed. I take in a tall, elegant man, simply dressed, with startling grey eyes and a shock of white hair. His long nose is a larger version of my own. He wears simple brown breeches and waistcoat over a white shirt, and he looks at me thoughtfully.

"You have a handsome, intelligent face, quite like my mother's, though she was fair where you are dark. That must be your French side. Do you speak French, by the way?" He looks up as he says this, taking in Johanne and Phebe with a smile.

"I will have a tutor soon at the Castle. I speak German and Dutch along with my Danish, such as it is. A little too much of the islands in it, Uncle Thomas tells me. And I have been learning English.

He turns and bows lightly. "I am being rude. Johanne, it is good to see you."

I grab Phebe's hand and pull her forward. "Uncle, this is Phebe, whose family has been part of ours for four generations now."

Gazing down at Phebe, he pauses somewhat uncomfortably. He is a man of his time and it is a time in which large fortunes, including his, have been made in the slave trade. But I suspect that he himself, once beyond childhood, has had little to do with Africans or their descendants. Perhaps he is somewhat afraid of them, thinking, on the fringe of his consciousness, that they have every reason to hate him.

So I am not entirely surprised when he says to Phebe, "Perhaps you would like to go to the kitchen and see what's about there."

Phebe looks down at the parquet floor and then at me. We lock eyes for a moment and then I turn to my uncle soberly.

"Let me go with her to the kitchen, Uncle, and make introductions to your cook."

Later as we walk in the garden, I listen distractedly to my uncle on the subject of language.

"We all felt the standard of our Danish rather low when we first arrived here. Personally, I love the creole of the islands…the fluid way it is created out of any language at hand. A while at court will bring your Danish higher, but it is quite acceptable now. Comprehensible, and charming if you ask me." I wince at this description. "The Danish of the capital is stiff and unmelodious in comparison."

The leaves drift down from the pollarded trees in the garden, and I think to myself that it is strange to see death so present in nature.

"Can we go in, Uncle. I am cold." At least, I think, Phebe is in the warm kitchen.

In the parlor my uncle continues his soliloquy.

"I was born in Africa, you know. In the truly frightening Christianborg Castle, not a bit like the one here of the same name. Though it did look like a castle to a small boy. White and elegant with its flying flags, but inside it was a prison where the slaves, captured from all of western Africa, were kept before being shipped to the Danish West Indies. It is still in operation, but I don't think that trade can last much longer. My father did great service to his king in taking that job. It was a difficult time for all of us."

I press my lips together, holding in the bubble of speech that is welling up, starting with "Difficult for you?" and instead I say, "General Van Beverhoudt, my stepfather, has had his fill of the sugar trade in the West Indies. He has bought property in the colony of New Jersey, though they have not moved there yet. For my part, I will not be sad if I never see St. Croix again. I think it is a cruel place for too many, and boring for a woman. I have told Mama that I am quite determined to go to the Moravian School in Pennsylvania." I surreptitiously take a deep breath, quite startled at myself for this daring speech, given the muddle of my feelings.

"I would agree," said Uncle Anker. "There is no reason for a young woman like you to go back to the Islands. Find yourself a good intelligent man in the colonies. That's where the future lies. Or stay here in Denmark. I daresay that is what your parents had in mind when they sent you here. You are close enough to marrying age, and I am sure there will be offers for your hand before you leave. And if you leave, I might consider buying that slave of yours. It is quite the thing right now to have an African slave in Denmark."

I am speechless. Horrified. I could not be more appalled if he had proposed locking Phebe up in a closet for the rest of her life. It suddenly strikes me in a way it never quite has before that Phebe's life could indeed be disposed of in this cavalier way. After a couple of minutes, I pull myself together and try to muster some more conversation.

"I don't think so, Uncle. Phebe is an island girl. By the way, have you heard about Dr. Johan Struensee?" My equilibrium restored, I blurt out, "He's like a troop of galloping horses. So many ideas. I think he is quite brilliant." Anker Suhm harrumphs. The silence is awkward. I wonder if I have overstepped. "I don't care," I think defiantly.

"He is certainly the talk of all the Council," my uncle finally responds. "A follower of Voltaire, they say. Perhaps that is not such a bad thing. Except that, if he threatens the privileges of the nobility, they will not take it kindly. But who am I to judge?" and he smiles placatingly at me.

But, of course, he is a judge.

Later Phebe describes to me the steamy scene that had transpired in the kitchen.

"Oh Sum, wasn't the cook something to behold? She looked like a giant pastry, with ruffles of fat at her wrists and neck, and a starched cap that looked like a dollop of whipped cream atop her head. Oh my, she was so large and white. And I felt so black beside her. She grunted while she attacked a mound of dough with her pin. And every once in a while she would look up at me suspiciously. Like I was a bad dog. I felt badly for her you know. She probably had never seen a Black person up close before. But you know, Sum, I just transported myself to the cookhouse at home, with all its wonderful smells, and into Mama's arms. Finally, to put her at her ease, I started describing the cookhouse to her, and Mama's baking. In the end we were actually laughing together."

She sighs softly after she tells me this, and I close my eyes and lean into the softness of a tropical day, and hear her little sisters playing in the courtyard and her mama humming and scraping rhythmically on the pot as she stirs. When I open my eyes I can see Phebe squeezing back her tears.

Christianborg Castle is as different as can be from Hirscholm. The difference between winter and summer, I suppose. An ancient structure, built on the bones of Vikings, it was renovated just twenty-five years ago and is now considered to rival the French palace at Versailles. Our new quarters are larger than at Hirscholm but spare, with the plain wooden furniture of a barracks. We have brought the eiderdown duvets with us, and I sigh with pleasure when I get under mine that first night. We are to begin our new life the very next day: Phebe is to be given a list of tasks she must accomplish each day and I will begin my lessons with a phalanx of tutors.

Three days after our arrival we are visited by a lady-in-waiting to the Queen, who smiles at Johanne as if her face were made of plaster. The corners of Johanne's mouth twitch as she is handed a creamy piece of paper bearing the King's arms, the awaited invitation to dinner. When the door is firmly shut on the messenger, she breaks into a grin, waving the invitation.

"The revolution begins! I guess that woman is not too happy about it." Looking me up and down she declares, "Time for the dressmaker, my sweet!" And she does a little dance around the room, like a bird hopping from a cage.

A dressmaker of indeterminate age, with wide-set blue eyes and a bird's nest of wispy blond hair, appears in our quarters the next day. She takes my chin in her hand and whispers, "I have been sent by the Queen to put you in proper order. Now that I see you, I am sure that Dr. Struensee is behind it all." I feel an uncontrollable urge to giggle. I want to hug this woman. But I rein myself in to a demure smile. The dressmaker assumes a more formal manner. She begins with Johanne, taking her measurements.

"I think blue is the color for you, but let me see what would work for the young lady."

She pulls me to the window, tilts my head back and stares into my face, I assume appraising its color scheme. "A creamy yellow and maybe a mossy green too, my sweet. Not many can wear those colors in Denmark. But with that coal black hair it will suit you. I will return with some fabric for your approval."

She is back in two days with a roll of buttery silk embroidered with a broad vine, and a moss-green brocade for me, and the sweetest sky blue silk for Johanne. She measures and appraises us. Five days later we are both twirling and blushing in our new gowns before Thomas and Phebe. I feel as if I am about to step into a brighter pool of light, and I am full of anticipatory joy. I so wish my mama could see me… I will slip a sample of the fabrics into my next letter. I think Johanne was feeling much the same sense of liberation and delight.

I go to my room to rummage through the Missy Box. The diary is safely hidden in its secret compartment and I turn the key and lift the lid. I will wear the green brocade to the dinner. Should I wear the diamond necklace?

Thomas comes that night to my room for evening prayers, and I pose the question to him.

"Wear something delicate and subtle, Summy. You never want to call too much attention to yourself in your dress. Your face will do that nicely."

He pulls out a necklace of gold bows enameled in green and white and set with tiny diamonds.

"French. Grandmother loved this piece especially, because it is so French. It was one of the few pieces that she was able to hold onto that came over with her sewn into her cloak."

Standing behind me he fastens the necklace and we look together at my image in the mirror. The necklace in the candlelight explodes in a sparkling shower of light.

Chapter Eight: Akila's Arrival

kila and Maria arrive in the harbor of St. Thomas on the very same day of February, 1686—on very different vessels. Akila, naked, half starved, traumatized into speechlessness. Maria, a sober child, an orphan, though she does not yet know it. But she has her protector Celine, and young Pierre. And she has money, though it is mostly at this moment in the form of jewelry sewn into her clothes. But yes, she has some wealth. And that makes all the difference.

The *Fortuna* drops anchor at dawn. With Celine's help Maria packs her trunk and drags it to the deck. They wait impatiently to be assigned to a dory. It is December and the air is cool; the harbor sparkles in the sunlight and it does truly seem like a paradise. But as they approach the dock a grim sight looms up: two corpses hanging on gibbets that have been partially devoured by the birds.

"That's what happens to thieves in Tapphus," says the oarsman seeing the blood drain from Maria's face. Maria and Celine are housed in Fort Christian, a formidable, many-sided, three-level white stone structure with a walkway at the top that is used as a lookout by the soldiers. They are assigned a corner room off the big center courtyard with solid green arched doors. It has a little gun embrasure for a window and two straw mattresses on wooden bed frames. A barracks. Plain and simple.

Not fifty feet away, across the courtyard, is the Governor's office, right beside the chapel where all the island inhabitants—that is the White inhabitants—are summoned to worship every Sunday. A Lutheran service. Those who fail to appear at the sound of the trumpet pay a fine in sugar.

Pierre has been employed from his first moment on land by Mikklesohn, who has been sent on a special mission by the Danish Company to investigate the corruption of Governor Milan. Pierre records the events of the trial and summons the witnesses. Planters file in and out all day, testifying to the venality of Milan. Though the sun shines like a vigilant eye above them, and the aqua sea shimmers like paradise, the human element is raging noisily in Fort Christian.

Steaming, sweat-filled days pass. The bodies of the captive slaves recover slowly from their ordeal on the ship. The bright turquoise sea is visible through the narrow embrasures in each of the dungeon's cells. In the morning, a shaft of sunlight goes like a spear right through the line of bodies where Akila and Bamadille sit in the dirt on the floor. Akila's eyes communicate her terror to Bamadille.

"They will sell us," he says. "We are like cattle to them. Each of us has a price, and they will sell us for as much as they can get. I will do everything I can to keep us together."

The keening and wailing of the captives rises up to Maria and Celine, throbbing endlessly on the air. Their spirits sink. What kind of hell is this, masquerading as a paradise?

The indentured are housed here too, in quarters not unlike the slaves, but they are not locked in. Free to come and go, Mette Petersen wanders within the Fort and watches Maria, resenting her privilege and remembering the failed attempt to get her medallion. She is shrewd and looking for other opportunities for advancement.

Born in a brothel in Copenhagen, Mette was orphaned early. She was trained nonetheless in her dead mother's trade at a very tender age, and continued to live in the brothel. But her features were pinched, her complexion sallow, and her expression wary and sullen. She was not high on the list of the customers' favorites. She fell to petty thievery within the house to satisfy her own needs. By the age of fifteen she was on the streets, living a vagabond life, keeping warm by burning garbage and nestling against whatever warm body could be found at night in lean-tos and abandoned buildings.

Gradually she became part of a pack, and then of a gang of thieves. She has been caught, sentenced, transported. Now, she is to be indentured on St. Thomas, but she is still wily, looking for opportunity. Before she is assigned to one of the planters' families, she has a few days of liberty. She thinks of running away, but there is no running from here.

Mette sees her chance on the third afternoon. She approaches the soldier who is guarding some slaves being exercised in the courtyard. Akila is among them. A coin flashes in the sunlight.

Mette grabs Akila's arm and pulls her along. Akila struggles, wanting to call out for Bamadille, but no sound comes. Dragged along, she stares fixedly at the greasy black bun at the top of the woman's head. She reeks like rotten vegetables. Not the sharp familiar animal smell of Akila's people. No, this is more like something moldering, dead.

The woman's dark eyes sweep across the courtyard as she leads Akila out through the great door on the north side. Emerging onto a pathway, they walk beside the sea. Strange iron barrel-shaped things protrude from the walls of the fort. Akila had seen these things explode, and she crouches before them, scared that they will suddenly erupt. The woman keeps hold of her arm forcefully, her long nails digging into Akila's skin. She drags her along quickly, and after some minutes they arrive at a small wooden lean-to not far from the beach, away from the pier that juts out into the harbor, and away from the enormous building on the other side of the fort.

She sits with the woman in the dirt. The woman babbles at her in the banana talk that the Captain had used on the ship, but her voice rasps like two rocks rubbed together. As dusk comes on a cacaphony of sounds from night creatures closes in around them like an attacking armada. Sitting beside this filthy woman, Akila feels as if her skin were crawling with ants. In the little wooden shack is a straw pallet. Just beyond the wall is a little cooking area, not unlike the place by her own house in the village where her mother cooked. There is an iron pot, and the woman gives her a small bowl of cooked vegetables. She watches as the sun begins to dip over the mountains behind them. Darkness comes quickly and along with it the rushing, clattering sound of the night insects and frogs. For a moment she lets the familiar sounds wrap themselves around her like a comforting black blanket, and she loses herself in the insistence of the sound.

A sailor approaches the hut and speaks with the woman. A big man with a black beard and loose pantaloons. His chest is covered with black fur, like an animal, but he reeks of the same rotten vegetable smell. He gives the woman a coin and a strange smile and she walks off down the street. The sailor pulls Akila to her feet and pushes her into the hut ahead of him and pulls a burlap sheet over the opening. The closed space is sweltering. He drops his pants and she sees his huge member, stiff and red, inflamed, like a hot anvil. She stares. She has never seen anything so ugly. The sailor pulls the skin on it back and the tip glistens in the dim light. Akila's heart leaps and pounds like a trapped animal desperate to get out of a cage.

She pushes herself back against the wall of the shack and the sailor takes her hand and puts it on his member. She pulls her hand back, and he pushes her down and rises over her, straddling her body with his. She tries to scream, but no sound comes. He pushes her shift up and presses her body down on the pallet with his great bulk. With a great thrust he forces his member between her legs and lies on top of her, pounding into her. It feels like a fire is inside of her, as if she is being ripped apart from the great size of the thing. She cannot breathe from his weight on her chest. Akila beats on him with her small fists. And then he stops moving and just lies on top of her, crushing the air from her. Tears stream down her small face, in little rivers around her ears, over the delicate scars of her tribe. She closes her eyes. He gets up and is gone, leaving her with a sticky mess between her legs, her heart pounding, unable to draw breath.

Akila lies for a long time on the pallet trying to calm herself. She feels as if the great weight of the man is still on her, sitting on her chest, and that it will always be thus. The woman returns and looks at her with disgust, throwing a crusty rag in her direction. Akila lies with her face to the wall, her eyes open, staring at a little lizard that flicks its tongue. The woman drags her outside and pushes her down the path by the bright moonlight. Yellow flashes of light dance on the black ocean, beckoning to Akila: "Come sink into this blackness." The soldier who had released her earlier is waiting in the shadows of the Fort. He ties Akila's hands with a rope and leads her back into the dungeon of the Fort and pushes her into the first cell he comes to. Where is Bamadille? Akila throws back her head and tries desperately to call his name. But no sound comes.

The next day Akila is brought again to the courtyard in the morning. She sits on the ground in the dirt. She is waiting for Bamadille. Her legs are smeared with dried blood. Maria sits thirty feet away, working on a piece of embroidery. She looks up and, seeing Akila, makes an involuntary strangled cry. She jumps up and crosses to her, kneeling beside her.

"Are you all right?" she asks. "No, of course you're not," she answers her own question under her breath. She calls to Celine. "Bring water, Celine. And some cloth. This girl has been hurt."

Together they bathe her gently. Tears trickle silently down her cheeks.

While they are with her, Mette walks into the courtyard and looks around. Akila shrinks back at the sight of her. Maria and Celine recognize Mette from the *Fortuna.*

"What have you done to this girl," Celine calls out to her angrily.

"You stupid cow," Mette mutters, and turns on her heel and goes back out the door.

Akila had felt such shame when the big woman sponged between her legs. She felt herself turn phantom, up in a wisp of smoke. She closed her eyes and summoned the beautiful black and orange butterfly. They floated together on the wind.

Chapter Nine: The Dinner

Christianborg Palace, October 1770

Uncle Thomas is pacing at the doorway, chewing his thumbnail. Phebe hovers behind him, her eyes glowing in the shadows. Is it with satisfaction at the way she has triumphed with my hair? Or is it with yearning? I glance at her and smile as I stand at attention awaiting Uncle's inspection.

I am supremely happy in this moment. I have never been dressed in such a grown-up, elegant fashion. My black hair is piled high on my head in the most amazing swirling coils, which Phebe has masterfully arranged, and my face has been handsomely powdered and pinked. She's been practicing all this for days. My green brocade gown flashes subtly in the light as I move, and shows just a tantalizing hint of a bosom. Topped by the French necklace, I am radiating confidence.

Johanne rolls her eyes at Thomas impatiently. His gold braid shimmers in the candlelight, and I think for a moment that he looks more like he is trying to play the part of a military man, than actually succeeding at it. He is much too gentle a soul for the rôle he has been cast into…I think he looks rather more like a dancing master at this moment. But Johanne looks amazing.

Her sky blue gown and her blond hair are like the best part of summer, and she has a delectable lightness emanating from her.

"Thomas, we'll be late." Johanne looks longingly out the second-story window at the covered bridge that arches across to the palace. His return look silences her but there is a flicker of distain in her expression.

"Be sure to divide your attention equally between those on your right and on your left, even if you must make an effort—which you very likely will." This last remark Thomas says under his breath. "Be a good listener and don't prattle on about inane things." He looks directly at me, but I think it is meant more for Johanne, whose impulsiveness I know makes him nervous. "Above all, keep smiling at whatever the King says, no matter how odd. Remember he is not well, and his illness makes him prone to do and say strange things. You don't want to attract his attention."

I can see that his palms are sweaty and his face is flushed, which I know mortifies him. I am sure he is thinking that there is altogether too much that can go awry this evening. What if the King takes a fancy to one of us? We do look sparkling. Johanne taps her delicate foot impatiently. She is glowing with the anticipation of her introduction to Royal society. She must be thinking that this will be the end of boredom. And in that she would be perfectly correct.

We leave our apartment through the great wooden door with its diagonal panels and enter the second-floor corridor that leads over the enclosed bridge into the palace. It is a lovely thing, this bridge. It has an arched span the length of six carriages and is made of white stone, with glass windows that look out toward the canals on both sides of the palace. All along its length candles have been lit. Below, pale faces in the twilight look up at us as we pass. Ahead the towering white palace with candles in all its windows, beckons.

Phebe will stay alone in our quarters. I guess that she will eat a little bread and meat, and knit. She will sing to herself for company. Now when I think back on that night, I am mortified at how self-absorbed I was, how oblivious of her homesickness and misery, when I was so full of joy and anticipation.

We arrive precisely on time. Quivering, with a stomach-churning mixture of terror and delight, I step into a wondrous hall of mirrors, with its brilliant candles flashing from all the sconces, and multiplied into infinity in receding angles and galaxies of light. A fairyland of possibility. Thomas is between the two of us and we are quietly announced, if anyone cares to listen. There are perhaps thirty people in the room, milling before the bell is rung. Dr. Struensee comes up to us directly, affable and smiling. Relaxed. He is attired in a robin's-egg-blue tailored waistcoat. His wig is powdered white. He looks like an entirely different person.

"Captain de Malleville, and his beautiful ladies. What a splendid addition to our party!" He leans over to Johanne and says quietly, "I have seated you across from the Queen. I think you will enjoy her conversation, and she yours. Do not be shy." Then he whispers to me, "You I have seated with the charming young Count

Brockdorff, but to keep you safe I have put myself on your other side."

With no fanfare the King and Queen are announced. Christian shambles into the room and I cannot help but stare for a moment. There is certainly something odd about him, but what is it? His eyes? His awkward tall frame? Perhaps it is the look around his mouth, a cross between a sneer and a grin. I look away. We are soon seated. Introductions are made. I assess the young Count in a swift glance, with a smile that feels pasted on my face. I put his age at perhaps sixteen. He is blond and looks solid and well-tanned, as though he has had some time at sea.

He turns to me with a quick, small bow, and says, "I understand you are from the Islands. Do you like Copenhagen? You must find it very different."

"It is certainly colder," I reply merrily. "But a woman's life is a little dull wherever she finds herself. In the Islands we are kept indoors most of the time for fear of fevers, sunburn, the rowdy elements…whatever crosses Mama's mind. But we have many friends who visit. I miss that here. I know hardly anyone. And in the Islands I do ride with my friends, a tradition started by my great grandmother in our family. She was of a very independent mind and even wore men's clothing when she rode." It suddenly occurs to me that this is what Uncle Thomas meant by prattling on.

"Ah, that is a fashion that our Queen has begun here. Perhaps you would like to go riding one day? That could easily be arranged."

"Oh, I would be delighted."

A man in livery inserts a silver platter of meat between us and the Count's attention is momentarily diverted. Struensee takes the opportunity to ask me what I think of the evening so far.

"Oh, just magical, with all this shimmering light and beautiful people," I reply in a voice that I hope is redolent of teacups and drawing rooms. After a pause, I sally forth in my best German with the question I had prepared in advance for this occasion.

"And what do you think of the likelihood of revolution in the American colonies, Dr. Struensee. The news of the massacre of citizens in Boston is quite shocking. I am sure it has stirred much feeling among the colonists. Do you think they will revolt?"

"It is only a matter of time. Britain cannot keep control of so vast a continent." Struensee speaks quietly to me alone.

"Surely it is the right of the monarchy to keep the populace under control," I offer tentatively.

"It is never the right of one people to impose their will upon another, without consent." I feel a frisson of excitement at this comment, as though I had come upon a hidden treasure in a dessert. I turn to him, chin down, looking up at him coyly.

"You are a revolutionary! I knew it from our first conversation. From your comments about slavery."

"Slavery is the worst of all. But the oldest of all. Ending it will be very complicated.

But it will happen."

"In our lifetime, do you think? My parents will bring their slaves with them to New Jersey, I am sure. They don't know how to do anything for themselves…and of course their slaves are like money to them."

The King flicks a pea off his spoon and hits Struensee squarely in the forehead.

Struensee looks at him directly and holds up his hand, palm forward. But the King just makes a little pouting face and then grins, and rises. He is just a few places down the table across from us. The

Queen looks anxious, but follows his lead, rising. Christian's motions are jerky, awkward. He shoots his hands into the air and harrumphs. "I welcome you, my drunkards of the first estate. Eat up. 'Til you're all sick." He appears ready to go on to more expansive oratory, but Struensee smiles at him broadly, and begins clapping. He gestures for the King to sit, as everyone else begins tentatively to clap.

And the King does sit, abruptly. He smiles back at Struensee as though he has just delivered a fine parliamentary address. The Queen sits down beside him and locks eyes with Struensee across the table. After a moment her glance shifts to Johanne, and she leans forward, smiles, and begins a conversation as if nothing out of the ordinary had happened.

As the room fills again with the clinking of glasses and the murmured rumble of conversation, Count Brockdorff whispers to me, "And what do you think of our King?"

"He is everything I had heard, though perhaps more handsome than I had expected. It is a very good thing that Dr. Struensee is by his side at every moment, is it not?"

Brockdorff replies, "Well someone he trusts surely needs to be. What say you and I go riding soon? I will make the arrangements and let you know the date."

In the two weeks that follow, Thomas is absent, off with the King and Struensee in Schleswig- Holstein. Johanne has been in the company of the Queen quite a bit in this time, having been invited to her private quarters for cards on several occasions. I have had a communication from Count Brockdorff and we have made a rendezvous to ride. For me everything is new, full of interest and promise. I am taking lessons with excellent tutors, along with some of the children of the palace, most of them younger. In free moments I continue to puzzle over the diary. But Phebe has been assigned a grueling list of chores by Johanne and I am seeing less and less of her.

Chapter Ten: The Von Bergens

Tapphus, St. Thomas, January 1687

Standing in the courtyard of the Fort, Maria looks at him so imploringly Pierre cannot say no.

"You have the power to save her. We have the power to save her." She leans into him, punching the words to make her point. "Celine will give you the money. Oh hurry, Pierre. There's no saying what may happen to her. She was bleeding. She's been hurt."

"You will have to come and show me which one she is." His voice has a sinking note of resignation.

Maria's heart leaps with the bounding energy of terror and curiosity as he says this.

She has a terrible dread of going into the slave dungeon where the wailing has been coming from. But she must see the girl again, see where she has been held. She pushes the fear down.

To the ship's captain, Bardewinkel, Pierre says, "You won't regret the time spent… but I don't want to wait for the auction. It seems the child is injured, and my friend has taken a particular interest in her."

Maria and Pierre follow Captain Bardewinkel down the stone steps of the Fort to the cells below. He does not seem to have quite got his land legs, and he holds the wall to steady himself as he descends. Maria's eyes are slow in adjusting to the light, but then she sees that the slaves are so packed in that they cannot sit or lie down. A cry escapes her at the sight and her heart pounds.

Bardewinkel holds a rag to his nose and mutters with undisguised disgust, "The next load I'll sell off the ship. Looks like some of these will die down here before they're sold." He turns to Pierre.

"Which one is it you want?"

Pierre and Maria walk down the line of cells looking for Akila. In the enclosed stone space the sounds reverberate. Maria realizes that it is singing, so mournful that it sounds like wailing, but as she listens, she blinks back tears. The sound is achingly beautiful.

A lightning strike of pain goes through her when she spots the child. She is sheltered against the huge shiny black body of a man, her bony arm wrapped tight around his. She is wearing some kind of burlap sack and the man, a loincloth.

"That's her." Maria's words come out in a whisper and she summons her louder voice. "That must be her father. Oh, we must buy them both. We cannot separate them."

Pierre turns to Bardewinkel and then back to Akila, pointing. "That's her. And I'll take him, too. I'll give you 150 rix-dollars for the pair…and I'll take care of the port taxes."

"Those two?" Bardewinkel says, with a startled catch in his voice. Maria sees surprise and confusion on his face. "The man alone is worth more than that," he mutters.

"The girl doesn't look like she'll survive. I'll make it 160 but that's my last offer," Pierre responds.

"I grew a little fond of this girl on the ship, and I like the idea of selling them as a pair. I'm not really supposed to do this though. There will be an auction soon, can't you wait for that?"

"No, she's been injured, can't you see? She needs care. The Company will have no use for her dead, you know." Maria stomps her foot for emphasis.

"All right then. They're yours. You're getting quite a bargain. I can tell you she'll be a powerful good worker. As long as you treat her well."

Pierre and Bardewinkel go into Pierre's little office to do the paperwork. It seems to Maria to take an eternity, but eventually Pierre returns to Maria later holding the documents.

Back in the dungeon Bardewinkel says to the guard, "You can unlock those two," and shows him the bill of sale.

Up the stone stairs they go, Maria leading the way. They emerge into the hot light of the courtyard. The tall African speaks softly to the girl and then sweeps her up on his shoulders. This is how they arrive at widow Von Bergen's daub and wattle house on

Konge Gade, the establishment Celine had selected as the safest home for Maria at this moment.

Maria had wept miserably when Celine had announced that they would, of necessity, live apart on St. Thomas. Celine had married Lucien unceremoniously in the Lutheran church in the Fort the second day after their arrival. Together they will build a small shelter of their own, close to the plot of land they have been given to establish a bakery by the Danish West India Company. The baking of bread is a skill they have brought from France, and ready money will soon be needed.

But now all Maria's attention has turned to Akila.

As soon as they arrive at Mrs. von Bergen's, Maria takes Akila to the wash tub in the courtyard at the back of the house. Akila keeps her solemn eyes on Bamadille, who sits nearby on a stool with his back turned.

"You'll be next," Mrs. von Bergen wags her finger at him. A smile plays across her face and Bamadille nods at her solemnly in return. She leaves Maria to wash Akila and gestures to him to follow her to a hut in the courtyard, blathering to him in Danish and gesturing to indicate that this will be his abode.

Mimba, her slave woman, follows them, curious about the newcomers. "Can the child speak?" she asks him in Mande. He gives her a slightly puzzled look as he sorts through the words, but they have common roots with his own Soninke.

"She was the chief's daughter and chattered night and day in our village," he replies. "She was more learned than any of the other children. But she has had a very hard time. She has not spoken in a long time." He looks at the ground and kicks the dust. "Maybe she will talk again someday."

In the corner by the wash tub, Maria pulls the rush screen across for privacy, and taking her lavender soap, gently washes Akila. She fetches one of her own chemises, a simple white thing with six pearl buttons down the front. Akila touches the soft fabric and Maria sees a glimmer of pleasure on her face. She raises her arms, letting Maria slip it over her head. Akila touches one of the buttons and begins to worry it with her fingers.

That first night in their tiny room, Maria looks over at Akila as they prepare for bed.

All the pearl buttons on the chemise are missing.

"Where are your buttons?" she exclaims, pointing to the front of her own dress, a blue version of the one Akila is wearing. Akila looks at the floor and reaching into her pocket, holds out six buttons in the palm of her hand. Maria exhales and gives her a half smile, taking the buttons. "You have worried them all right off. Oh, Keela, what terrible things you must have in your head." She lifts the chemise over Akila's head and exchanges it for a soft white cotton nightgown.

Maria takes her hands and looks solemnly into her eyes. Akila does not look away and Maria feels a current of strength flow between them. "Never mind. I'll sew them back on in the morning." She kneels beside the bed to pray and pulls Akila gently down beside her.

"Heavenly Father…" she begins softly. Akila stares at her a moment and then prostrates herself on her sleeping mat, silently attentive to the sound of Maria's strengthening prayer. It is a great surprise to Akila that Maria is praying to Allah, and she feels their room has suddenly become a glowing sanctuary, a refuge of holiness as the two of them kneel humbly before God. The terrible pain and shame are, for a moment, lifted.

"You know who I'm speaking to, don't you," Maria whispers, pointing upward. For the first time, Akila smiles, briefly, hesitantly, but Maria sees it and she feels it as a smile from God. She gestures to her to lie down and she strokes her hair, feeling its strange wooly texture. "Like a spring lamb…The Lord is my shepherd," she murmurs. "Our shepherd." Then she climbs on her bed and sets to work by the flickering candlelight, sewing all the pearl buttons back on the chemise, and trying to imagine all that might have happened to Akila. She does this every night for the next week.

Akila remains watchful, anxious. Mimba, Mrs. von Bergen's slave woman, is kind to her, and hearing the sweet, familiar sounds of her singing as she moves about the house, works wonders on Akila's spirit. Mimba's language is Mande, and Akila understands much of what she is saying. She knows immediately from her muscular build and way of speaking and moving that Mimba was a household slave in Africa, like Bamadille in her own village.

On their third day at the house Mimba comes into their room just as the sun is rising and wakes Akila. Maria sits up and rubs her eyes.

"Where are you taking Akila?" Mimba looks at her and smiles and nods, trying to be reassuring. Maria leaps out of bed and grabs Akila's arm. A modest tug of war ensues and Maria is the winner. Mimba leaves the room and returns ten minutes later with a fistful of corn tassels, and in a bubbling stream of Mande instructs Akila in their use. Akila nods solemnly and for the first time grins at Maria.

Shortly afterward Maria sits on the bucket to do her morning business. The wet rag she is accustomed to use for wiping is at hand, and she looks quizzically at Mimba and Akila, who stand patiently over her.

"What are you doing? Leave me now please."

Mimba shakes her head and smiles. And when she perceives that Maria's business is done, she takes the cornsilk and firmly bends Maria over and begins to wipe, nodding vehemently to Akila.

"ACCCH," Maria bellows. Mimba chuckles but her grip is firm. Maria sees she has no choice but to submit. But she looks over at Akila and, grimacing, she shakes her head in a firm "NO."

Maria watches Mimba's attempts at training Akila with growing anxiety and begins insistently to keep her close by her side, despite Mrs. von Bergen's head wagging.

Outside their bedroom window, the girls can hear the screeching gulls and the tap, tap tap of the shoemaker's hammer. From the wharf and the tavern farther down Konge Gade come the percussive shouts of sailors. The girls sometimes sit at the window, Maria in front looking out at the wharf and the ships in the harbor, longing to be out in the world, and Akila hidden behind her, twisting the buttons that Maria has just sewn on her dress, terrified of the white men and the din.

Maria sees Pierre down the street and leaning out the window calls to him. "Pierre, can we come down to the wharf with you?"

"No Maria, it's no place for a girl. There's a French barquentine that just came into the harbor. It may have news—maybe even a letter—and if it does I will return." Maria turns to Akila and babbles her frustration to her, mollified to have an audience that can at least read her mood.

He does return, but there is no letter.

"Oh Pierre, can't you at least tell us more of this place we're in? How many people are there living here?"

"Oh, fewer than thirty in the town, I should think. But during the year around fifty ships will come into this port, from all sorts of countries, and their crews will pour into the town looking for taverns and women, dwarfing the population that actually lives here. But on the whole island I understand there are around 300 White people and some 420 Africans."

"What are they all doing? Growing things?"

"Well at the moment, as you can smell, they are very busy burning brush to clear the land for the cultivation of sugar, tobacco and indigo. Personally I don't mind the burning smell as much as all the others it masks!" He tells her all this through the window and then heads off to the Fort.

Maria is trying to learn the languages of the island, starting with Mrs. von Bergen's Danish. In the evenings she sits at the table in the parlor by the lamplight while Mrs. von Bergen embroiders. She writes down words in Danish and their French equivalent, and any other equivalents that Mrs. Bergen happens to know. Akila sits beside her and watches and listens, but she still cannot speak. Something hard and black as a stone is lodged somewhere between her throat and her heart. It refuses to be swallowed away.

Listening, Akila begins to distinguish different kinds of banana talk. Maria's tongue has a soft and gentle sound, not unlike the sound of the Mande languages. But Mrs. von Bergen's sounds are harsh, like the low roar of a lion. And they bring something of the same chill to Akila's heart.

"I'll draw you some pictures" Maria says one evening. She makes a map of the town, with the Fort and the wharf, and different kinds of ships and oar boats, and the taverns, the bakery and the Company Warehouse. Then she says each of the words in French, and Mrs. von Bergen says them in Danish. Maria looks at Akila questioningly, hoping to coax a sound from her, but she just nods, indicating that she understands. Day after day, Maria practices her Danish, exaggerating the guttural consonants in the back of her throat until they sound like she is gargling, and drawing a tentative smile from Akila.

Bamadille and Celine's husband, Lucien, have taken a great liking to each other and are inventing their own pidgin out of whatever words come to mind. Bamadille finds helping with the building of the bakery to be a more satisfying occupation than minding little girls. So he often brings them along.

On this day Maria holds tight to Akila's hand and tries not to recoil from the strong smelling men she passes. She wishes she could converse with Akila, for she has many opinions she would like to share. She suspects that most of these people were not particularly welcome or successful in their place of origin. Like those indentured prisoners on the *Fortuna*.

When they are well past a sailor speaking some Germanic language to his companion, Maria imitates him with a series of choking guttural expectorations and Akila laughs.

Maria breaks into smile. "You laughed!" Then she is overtaken by a flash of empathy: how much more foreign all this must be to Akila. She tries to imagine what Akila's life must have been like in Africa, and all she can picture is jungle and wildness. But they must have had huts. Maybe not so different from the daub and wattle structures springing up around the town.

When they arrive at the building site Bamadille leaves them with Celine under the great spreading flame tree that gives shade to a table and chairs. The three women work together to weave sticks and palm fronds into a sheltering roof for the bakery, while the men haul huge rocks to build the ovens. Akila always sits as near as she can to Bamadille.

One day he calls her over to him and he carves a little doll from wood. With a glue he has made from pitch and charcoal, he attaches dried grasses and a piece of red cloth. He touches chicken blood to its head and tells her it has special powers to protect her, and to cast spells. He tells her to use it carefully, for it is a powerful gris-gris. Akila is delighted by the doll and plays with it while Bamadille goes back to work. Unobserved, she builds a little shelter for her doll out of palm leaves and twigs. And then her doll kills all the terrible men who come and try to capture her, turning them into mangled heaps of twigs and grass. Eventually she wanders back to Celine and Maria, her little doll hidden in her pocket.

The sun is a huge orange orb on the horizon as Bamadille walks the girls home.

Mountains of glowing cumulus clouds are stacked behind it, and they stop to watch as the day vanishes below the horizon. For a moment the vision lifts all three of them into a magical place of peace.

Maria holds her hand up to Bamadille in a motion that says "stop," and then she points to the beach just below the road. She clambers down the embankment and pokes around on the beach. A few minutes later she returns with three small smooth stones, one white, one bluish and one black. She closes her hand around the stones and rubs one with her thumb. She rolls them in her hand, making a quiet clicking sound and then shakes them. Taking Akila's hand, she places two of the stones in her palm, wrapping Akila's fingers around them.

"For worrying," she says. "Instead of the buttons." She points to the buttons and shakes her head no, and then to the stones, nodding. She opens the pocket on Akila's chemise and puts the third stone inside. Akila slips the other two stones in her pocket and clicks them together, rocking back and forth, smiling at Maria.

That evening, Maria tells Mrs. von Bergen of their day's adventures, ending with the sunset.

"Just you wait until July," exclaims Mrs. von Bergen. "It'll be like walking through hot steam. And that is the fever season. By then most of those indentured people who came on the boat with you will be dead from fever and field work."

Chapter Eleven: Winter

Christianborg Castle, Copenhagen, November 1770

One frigid November morning I open my eyes and see my breath emerge in a small cloud and disperse. The sight is so interesting I am momentarily distracted from the cold. I must ask someone what this is. I roll over and pull the duvet up to my chin and reach out for the bell. I ring for Phebe.

After a while I grow impatient and throw off the cover and leap from the bed, grabbing a shawl to wrap around me and patter across the hall to Phebe's room. I crack the door open and see Phebe lying there, the same little cloud coming out of her mouth. I stand over her bed. Her lip trembles and tears roll down the sides of her face into her ears. She rolls over to hide her face from me and starts to sob.

My heart opens and my impatience vanishes. I climb in beside her and wrap my arms around her. She is shaking uncontrollably, sobbing. We stay like that for a long time. I try to think what to do. I must get Dr. Struensee.

As I rise off the bed, she turns her face into the pillow to try to muffle her crying. In the hallway I almost crash into Johanne.

"Homesick probably…poor thing," Johanne says.

In fifteen minutes Struensee is with us, wigless now, tufts of blond hair going in all directions, an ink blot on his sleeve. He examines Phebe and then steps out of the room to speak with me. Standing beside him, I feel heat rising in my face. He compresses his lips and then speaks.

"This was entirely predictable. How do you suppose a human creature can bear such loneliness as must occur when she is separated from all her people, and given no proper rôle to play in the world, but minion to a child?"

At this I burst into tears. "But she is my dearest friend."

"But how much time do you actually spend caring for your friend? Do not delude yourself, Maria Suhm. You may love her, yes, but you are not accustomed to treating her as an equal or caring for her and looking out for her needs. Indeed, it would seem very odd to your family if you did, and they would not allow it. The care has always been in the other direction. I do not blame you, you have been raised in a perverted society. How could you know otherwise?"

I have the sick feeling that all he says is true, and that I am quite helpless to change myself, much less the society I have grown up in. "What shall we do to make her better?"

"Her spirits are very low and that is not easy to reverse and can be dangerous. Either send her home, or treat her here as your equal, at least in most things. Let her go with you to be tutored. Get outside with her."

When he is gone, I return to Phebe's bedside. Her face looks very small in the puffs of white down. The tears have dried, but she stares listlessly at the ceiling. I sit on the bed beside her.

"Do you want to go home?" Silence. "You can if you want to. You know it is a much longer voyage returning, and you would be alone. But I do not want you to be this unhappy. For now, let's get you up and we'll take a long walk." I pull Phebe gently from the bed and hug her. She responds with more tears.

I ask Johanne if we may go for a walk. "Perhaps you'd like to come with us?" I suggest.

"I've been invited to the Queen's quarters to play cards, but you go. A walk will do you both good."

"Oh, what fun! Do you play for money?"

"Of course. But don't tell your uncle. He would most certainly disapprove." She giggles as she says this and I feel myself blushing. I am embarrassed. I really don't want to be keeping her secrets.

We bundle into warm layers, topped by capes, mine a carmine red and Phebe's a dark navy. As we walk in the gardens our breath freezes in clouds. We pass through the big iron gates across the canal and into the city. The day is bright, and we look at the store fronts: a clock maker with a funny cuckoo clock in his window, and a hat maker with the most gorgeous broad-brimmed red felt hat with a feather. This is a much nicer part of town than the market area we had driven through coming here. People stare at Phebe, and I tuck her arm in mine and smile defiantly. We walk a long way but finally get hungry and are guided home by the copper roofs of the palace.

Later I make tea for Phebe and we have it in my room. Looking into the Missy Box I find something that has always charmed me: a necklace with just six pearls strung with knots that keep them in inch or two apart. A simple thing, not valuable I suppose, but pretty. I tie it around her neck. "It suits you somehow. It's an odd piece. I wonder why it's in here. But now it's for you. Let's consider it your lucky talisman."

Struensee returns in the evening to see his patient.

"I am feeling better, Sir," Phebe says in a barely audible voice. "I do not want to go home alone."

He takes her hand, feeling her pulse. I notice how gently he holds it and the way he holds her eyes with his as he feels the beat.

"The exercise has done some good. The best remedy for low spirits is activity. Perhaps you would like to assist me in giving vaccinations in the city in a few weeks when the clinic is set up."

His eyebrows go up in a question and Phebe looks in turn at me. "Well, don't look at her. We don't have slavery here in Denmark. Or at least we don't call it that." He pauses. "I am asking you, Phebe. The clinic is just two days a week, and your help would be welcome." Phebe nods her assent.

"Can I come too?" I ask in a barely audible squeak. He smiles at me and nods.

Chapter Twelve: Isaac Benjamin

Tapphus, St. Thomas, April 1687

Mrs. von Bergen summons Maria to the parlor one morning while it is still cool. She opens the shutters a crack, letting ribbons of daylight stream in. Maria comes barefoot into the room and stops in a pool of sunlight. A man stands by the window in a well-worn white shirt and brown pantaloons, his feet in dusty leather slippers. His skin is tanned and his hair is almost white, though whether bleached by sunlight or by time is not clear. He does not look particularly old, just weary. To Maria his watery blue eyes seem to look through her far into the distance, with a kind of deep sadness that reminds her of Akila.

Mrs. von Bergen, licking the last crumbs of her breakfast from her lips, says, "This is Isaac Benjamin, Maria. He was tutor to my little Anastasia before she passed away of fever. He will be your tutor from now on. You will have lessons every morning and you may as well get started right away. Akila, you come with me."

"No, no no." Maria jumps up and down, and says with all the force she can muster. "I want her to stay with me."

"It is forbidden, Maria, for slaves to learn to read."

"Why should you worry about that when she cannot even speak," Maria declares.

Isaac Benjamin's eyelids lower as the corners of his mouth twitch into the hint of a smile. "You cannot argue with that Madame. It can do no harm to let the child stay."

Mrs. von Bergen cocks her head and looks at him. Then she throws up her hands and declares, "You always win Isaac, so I may as well give in right now. But just don't let anyone find out."

He smiles and sighs. "No ma'am. No need for anyone ever to know. Now you shoo and leave us to our lessons."

"Mimba will bring you a drink in a bit," she coos as she leaves the room.

There is a long pause as Isaac stops to study his two new charges. His eyes glisten and twinkle in the flickering light. Then he turns to Akila and says something to her softly in Arabic. A slow smile spreads across her face and she nods slowly. He continues to speak to her softly. Maria watches the two of them, all mundane thoughts suddenly driven from her head.

"Why, she understands you!" Maria's blue eyes sparkle and grow wide. "What language is that you are speaking?"

"It's Arabic. She is clearly an educated person in her homeland to know this language. Let's see if she can write it. It is exceedingly difficult to do so, but perhaps she has some training." He puts a slate in front of Akila and a thin sharp rock in her hand. She begins to write the alphabet. Maria's jaw drops.

"What strange marks. Are they letters? That looks like a very difficult language." "Possibly the most difficult," Isaac says quietly.

Akila is beaming as she writes each letter with care. Isaac leans over and whispers to Maria.

"Why don't we just keep this our secret for now. No good ever comes from people knowing that a slave is smarter than they are."

Their daily lessons take place at a round mahogany table in the parlor, with bleaching bars of sunlight coming through the jalousied windows. Across the way is the cobbler's shop; the smell of leather drifts over to them and their morning lessons are punctuated with the tapping of a hammer.

Very soon the girls are looking forward to seeing what treasure Isaac Benjamin might bring along with him to the house. A teapot from China one day, a scrap of lace from Belgium on the next. He sits in a shaft of sunlight, spinning magical stories around the object and its country in the language they are supposed to be learning, sometimes Dutch, sometimes English. He translates bits into Arabic and French. Akila smiles silently and nods, indicating her comprehension, but she does not speak. He dips the quill into a pot of ink and carefully writes the letters of each word. Akila watches, silent and intent, occasionally clicking the stones together in her pocket.

Celine visits occasionally and watches their lessons. She is delighted to find another person to speak French with, because communicating on the island has been a puzzlement to her. As her bread business has developed, she has learned a kind of pidgin strictly for the purposes of commerce. But along with Lucien, she is gradually learning the Creole of the island, which seems to evolve like a bartering exchange in which the higher status person becomes the linguistic winner.

"Isaac Benjamin," Celine explains to Maria one day, "is a Jew, which means that he has always been persecuted, just as we have been as Protestants in France. You can see from his face that he has suffered."

In addition to his personal treasures, almost every day Isaac Benjamin brings with him a plant from the island. He picks them along the way, or, if they are harder to find, he brings a dried sample. The girls draw pictures of the plant and also of the human form, from pictures he has in a book. Isaac Benjamin explains the medicinal uses of the plant, how to prepare it, and what ailments it cures. Maria takes notes. Akila draws pictures. Most of the ailments are familiar enough to the girls: stomach aches, fevers, burns and wounds. But some are for body parts they have no idea of, though they do understand something of the heart. Over time they accumulate many pages of drawings and notes. They each, in their way, enjoy this exercise and begin to look for the plants as they go on their walks in the afternoons.

One afternoon Isaac Benjamin joins them. Maria has developed a passion for mangos, and she runs ahead, scouting for a mango tree. Isaac and Akila walk side-by-side and he begins to talk quietly to her in Arabic.

"I dearly hope, Akila, that one day you will be able to speak to me, to tell me of your family in Africa. I think it will help you to keep them alive in your heart if you can talk about them. And that is a very important thing. You and Maria help me to keep my family alive in my heart, you know.

"I had two little girls who would be now the ages that you and Maria are, had they lived." He kicks the dust as he walks. "Their mother died with them in the Inquisition in Mallorca, where we lived. A terrible death by fire."

Akila looks up at him, her eyes wide and her mouth open. She puts her hand gently on his arm and the two of them stop in the road. Isaac looks down at her brown bare feet, now ashen with dust.

"I was traveling at the time, staying in the home of a rabbi in Salamanca when the word reached me. I was warned not ever to go back there." He is silent for a time, and then he puts his arm around Akila. "So now you see why the two of you are so important to me."

Akila looks up at him, hoping that her eyes will express what is in her heart, yearning to find a voice of solace.

Walking by the wharf buildings one day with Akila and Bamadille, a whiff of cinnamon wafts over Maria and she pauses, looking around. Just across the way she sees an unmistakable figure wearing his distinctive white outfit of a cool white shirt and saggy diaper.

" Dr. Pundit!"

"Well, halloo there," he greets her with a flashing smile. She looks at him and is flooded with delight at his cheerful wiry young form, the memory of his quick wit and humor. The thought of introducing him to Isaac Benjamin makes her almost dizzy with delight. As though he were an exotic specimen she had herself found.

"Why halloo to you," she replies. "What a lovely, divinely directed encounter this is! Oh, you must come tomorrow morning! You will find a mate in our tutor. He is so knowledgeable about plants and medicines. I know you will like each other and have ever so much to talk about."

"How grand! I have managed to procure a trunkful of Chinchona bark in Curaçao. I am sure it will interest him. And we will put it to good purpose on this feverish island, I am sure."

Dr. Pundit joins their round table the next morning and the two men are quickly deep in conversation. For a brief moment Maria feels almost jealous of the instant connection she senses between them, but then her affection for them both wins out. Dr. Pundit will bring an entire new continent of knowledge with him to their group, and he will ease dear Isaac's loneliness. She nudges Akila's knee under the table and grins at her.

Celine and Lucien have built their bakery in the center of Tapphus, making a delicious, yeasty, slightly sour bread with the strange varieties of flour they can buy from passing ships. They soon draw a devoted early-morning crowd from every walk of life. Slaves from the plantations line up in one line and share their gossip, and the townsfolk and sailors form another line. It is there that the news of the day gets exchanged, Black to Black and White to White, with occasional crossover if the news is sensational enough.

Mimba is walking along this morning to fetch bread for the dinner that Mrs. von Bergen has planned for that day. People across the island vie for an invitation to eat Mimba's fish stew. Young Lucas von Bergen trots along behind her with his best friend, Pierre de Malleville, hoping she will give them an end off the bread she buys. They lounge under a tree in the courtyard waiting for her to finish in line, but she is deep in conversation with a slave from a plantation on the East End.

"People are gossiping, Mimba, about those two girls you've got living at the house. They're saying that Soninkan girl has bewitched that White girl."

"Now don't be telling tales. They're just two girls acting like two girls, is all. Everybody's got a best friend at that age. Did you hear that Jango went maroon yesterday? Hope he'll get clear away. But there's no way off this island but to swim." She shakes her head mournfully, and then spots the boys over in the shade waiting for their treat. Her face brightens and she nods at them. "If I get you all a treat, will you be good to those girls now?"

It is a bribe, plain and simple. They are always underfoot, tormenting Maria about her relationship with Akila. For it is an unusual relationship and everyone has noticed. The two girls are inseparable, as though completely unaware of each other's skin color, and as one holds the voice for both of them, they seem even more like two halves of the same person. Maria can be heard day and night talking to Akila, *sotto voce*, hoping that one day Akila will talk back.

When Dr. Pundit next appears at their morning table, he is carrying a small parcel which he ceremoniously hands to Isaac.

"For your collection, my dear Isaac. A sailor on the wharf begged me to give him ready money for it so that he could go to the tavern. I obliged him because it brought back memories and because I thought it belonged in your collection."

Isaac carefully unties the string and folds back the paper, revealing a blue and white porcelain bowl with a simple pattern of chrysanthemums. "Oh my. A beautiful purity about it."

"There were many things I found beautiful about Japan. Simple and calming, like this bowl." Akila and Maria take turns examining the bowl. Dr. Pundit watches Akila with special interest, and then makes her open her mouth wide so he can look down her throat. He palpates her glands. He peers into her ears.

"I don't think there is anything physically wrong with her," he asserts. "Which means that there is hope that by gentle persuasion and encouragement she will speak again. You know, she's a little like a turtle that's pulled its head in for protection." Dr. Pundit takes Akila's chin in his hand and gently raises her face so that they are looking directly at each other.

"I believe that with some effort we can not only put our turtle heads out and look around, but with practice we can begin to shed our shells altogether. We can become invulnerable, fearless. Try it. Each time a little hurt comes along, just sit and look at it, watch what your body does. You will see that each time it will hurt a little less, as you expand your sense of peace in the world."

"If we're not speaking any language she knows, how is she going to learn?" Maria asks, stroking Akila's arm gently.

"It is not a matter of learning; it is a matter of making a sound. You are learning Dutch and English. She'll learn them with you. And we know she understands Arabic and can write its alphabet. And we are all learning—and inventing— a Creole that draws on any language available to communicate. So she'll learn that too, along with you. The important thing is to get her to try to make a sound."

"What language did you grow up speaking, Dr. Pundit?" Maria asks.

He sighs. "Hindi, my dear. But in India there are so many languages, sometimes people who live in the same large family speak different languages…and cannot always understand each other. Quite like this place!" Smiling, he brushes away the dragonfly that has just landed in her hair. "But the language of love is the very best, and that is the language that you speak with Akila."

That night Maria kneels by her bed, as she always does, with Akila prostrate beside her. She knows now from Isaac that this is Akila's prayer posture. She thinks of Dr. Pundit's turtle and tries to soften a little, to shed a little of the fear that she feels in this place. She opens her heart to God and prays vigorously that he will give Akila her voice back, that he put his power in her and let her speak. She tries saying this in Dutch and English as well as French, in case there is a language problem in heaven.

Mette Pedersen has supplied much of the gossip on the island since their arrival, and now she has been caught stealing some of the Company's sugar. She will be whipped and branded beneath the gallows just under the high wall of the Fort. Isaac hears the news at the bakery and brings it to their morning table, delivering it in both French and Arabic. Akila looks at him, her eyes wide. She sinks suddenly into a chair and shudders violently. Her body goes limp, her eyes almost closing.

Maria sinks to the floor and puts her head in Akila's lap, wrapping her arms around her knees. "Oh, Keela! Mette Pedersen is that terrible woman…the one who hurt you. The one who was trying to get you the morning we found you."

"No need to be afraid of her now," Isaac mutters.

As it happens, Pierre is always the first on the island to see the mail that comes off the ships in the harbor, as letters are deposited in his office in the Fort. On this day in February 1688 there is a black-bordered envelope addressed to Celine. He carries it to the bakery, grabs a buttery roll, and sits with her while she reads it. She is unnaturally still.

"Who is it from? What does it say?"

"It is from François, my master's manservant." She blinks and puts the back of her arm up to her eyes. "Maria's father has died a fearsome death. At the hands of the Catholic zealots. In our own town. I am sick to think of it. And sicker still to think of telling Maria."

They walk slowly to the Von Bergen house, along the beach at the edge of the swirl where the sand is light and dark.

"I do not want her to know how he died, not just yet. She is too young. Perhaps we can say it was fever," Celine says scratching her head, "though fever is what we die of here, not there."

"She will want to see the letter."

She did, of course, want to see the letter.

"When you are older," Celine says to Maria, "I will give it to you, for it is truly yours. He died in the way the Catholics have for heretics. But you may be sure that he is with our Lord. He was a holy man." They are seated in the Von Bergen salon. Akila stands gravely beside Maria, looking down at the Turkey carpet.

"Do you mean that he was *ecartelé*? Drawn and quartered? Surely not. Please not that." Maria's words stutter out like the sounds of a tortured animal.

Celine is silent. Maria lurches forward, curling herself up in a ball, rocking desperately.

Akila sits beside her and puts her arms around her. "Maria, Maria," she whispers. A croaking little breath from a voice so long unused, freighted with love.

Chapter Thirteen: Phebe in Copenhagen

Copenhagen, November 1770

My schoolwork has started in earnest and it has for the moment taken my mind off Dr. Struensee. I had been see-sawing back and forth between the anxiety of knowing his secret and the passion of my childish heart, and I am having trouble focussing on my lessons. Phebe comes with me each morning to my English tutor. I am determined that she will not go back to the Virgin Islands, but somehow stay with me when I go to America. She will need to speak English there. Though I am stumped by what she will do when I am at the Moravian School. I doubt they will allow me to bring my slave.

While I am with my other tutor she is left on her own. She always has a long list of chores from Johanne, but as I discover later with some surprise, she sometimes goes out exploring in the city if she has extra time.

"Surely you don't expect me to just look out the window. I'm an island girl! I know how to take care of myself!" she declares, cocking her head. "I pull my cape around me so my face is nearly invisible. I never know what kind of reaction people will have to my dark skin, though I know that at best it will be curiosity. And at worst it might be quite hateful. But I love seeing the city. It is a beautiful place. Even on grey days the colors of the buildings are so beautiful...all that yellow and orange and azure blue...with those green copper roofs. In the sunlight it just glows...and the sea air makes me feel alive." She looks down at her boots. "But don't tell Johanne. I'm afraid she would forbid it."

So I keep it to myself.

"I saw two ships from home today—one from St. Thomas and one from St. Croix! I watched them for a while as they unloaded. Don't worry, I always find an unobtrusive spot in the shadows."

I picture her stepping gingerly over the entrails of fish and rotting leaves of cabbage, looking for a shadow to lurk in. Watching those ships from home unloading hogsheads of sugar. I know that many of the sailors are Black.

"You don't talk to the sailors, do you?"

"Oh no," she says, a bit too emphatically. "That would be foolish...I'm not an idiot!"

I feel an ember of envy glowing deep in me. There is a freedom in all this that I never get to have. She turns heads, of that I am sure.

She is beautiful and it is a kind of beauty people in Denmark don't often see.

Then one day she comes home with a different kind of story. I think she might not have told even me, but her dress was torn. "What happened to you?" I exclaim.

"A bit of an adventure." She takes a deep breath and smiles. "I was in my usual hiding place under the eaves of a building and a big sailor came up to me. He seemed friendly enough at first, but of course I didn't speak to him. I think he was Norwegian. He stood in front of me for a minute with his huge hands. Then he grabbed me and spun me around and yanked my arm, pinning it behind me. I couldn't move, and it hurt. I couldn't draw a breath. I was utterly unable to speak or cry out."

"But I finally found my voice and screamed… so loud I think I even scared him! And the minute I screamed a man appeared around the corner of the building and grabbed this fellow. He wasn't a sailor. He was a Frenchman I think. He just tackled the man and then there was a great sprawl of legs and arms, and puffing and panting, until the Frenchman was seated upon the belly of the Norwegian with his hands at his throat. The man was screaming and struggling, and then he just went limp. I thought he was dead. I just stood there in stunned silence.

"You've killed him," I said.

"No, just broken his arm I would wager, my rescuer replied. "I think he passed out."

"And I thanked him for his service and he looked up at me and said, 'Well you are a handsome one. I can see why he wanted to abduct you.'"

Phebe is grinning now. "And then he laughed and said, 'Are you safe to get home now? Where is your home, by the way?"

"The Christianborg Palace. I am in service there," I replied.

I can picture their exchange perfectly. Phebe, I am sure, looks him in the eye as she says this, not only because she is curious and he is handsome, but because that is the kind of girl she is.

"Such a nice fellow," she muses. She sounds wistful.

When I think about this later, I am horrified. It had not occurred to me that a slave could actually be kidnapped…stolen…just like any piece of property! I determine to be more attentive to her from now on and I tell her that she must not leave the Palace without me.

Later that week I startle from my reading as Thomas comes thumping into the room in his big black boots. Phebe looks up from her efforts to arrange Chrysanthemums in a blue Japanese bowl painted with the same flower.

"Well now he has established an agrarian commission," Thomas says, drawing a deep breath. Hatless, black hair tumbling untied, his brown eyes bright, he looks quite unsettled. "Struensee I mean, though the King signed the writ. A commission of the most liberal sort…the kind of men who look very critically upon the way the nobility is using their laborers. They will surely be making some new labor laws next. Can you believe it?" He is half smiling, and I can hear that part of him is thrilled at this boldness. But there is also an edge of fear about what has been set in motion.

I feel my cheeks flush as I catch his mood.

"That means he can start making the lives of the poor less miserable, doesn't it." I go up and touch his arm.

"And the lives of the nobility more miserable." He pats my hand. "But you are right to be on the side of the poor. Perhaps we should look on Struensee as God's messenger. But people who think of themselves as God's messenger usually get themselves in a heap of trouble.

I don't quite know what to think. But I fear that somehow it will end in bloodshed." He looks down on me solemnly.

"Well surely the nobles could stand to be a little less grand, so the lives of the serfs could be improved a bit," I posit tentatively.

"Oh child, you are naïve. Imagine saying that in St. Croix about the lives of the slaves."

A weight of sadness drops over me as I realize the truth of his statement. It is easy to be generous with other people's privileges. "Yes, I see your point. Uncle."

Johanne enters the room and sinks into a chair. She seems in a dreamy state of mind and takes a moment to tune into Thomas as he repeats his performance.

"Hmm, well, I think it's all for the good, Thomas. The nobility will never make any changes on their own. There will have to be new laws and now we have the instrument. Change is much needed if we are not to have a revolution. The Queen is very much of the same mind."

"Well of course she is. Struensee tells her what to think."

"She is an intelligent woman with a mind of her own." Johanne knows this firsthand because she has become a favorite of the Queen and is now regularly in her apartments. I have not been included in this circle. Even if I weren't with my tutors, theirs is an intimate friendship between women who are sharing secrets they don't want me privy to.

Chapter Fourteen: Dr. Pundit

St. Thomas, 1688

D r. Pundit, while he delights in Akila's new voice and cheers her regular use of it, is alarmed at the state Maria is in. She sits staring for long periods of time. She is poking at her food. Her answers to his questions are monosyllabic. It is as though she and Akila had traded places in their silence. Pierre, sharing his concern, visits often, trying to cheer her.

"Horseback riding," Pierre says one morning to no one in particular. He is gazing out the window at the rare sight of a passing rider in the street. "I will get you all horses. Then you can have your lessons out-of-doors for a bit."

"Ah, Pierre, you're a treasure. What a brilliant idea!" Dr. Pundit claps him on the back, eyes glittering at the thought.

Horses are scarce on the island and so they must settle for three mules and a mare. Pierre is well positioned to make the impossible happen, and he sees to it that Maria gets, from one of the plantations, a young mare that has been well trained. Dr. Pundit insists that the girls make themselves riding outfits of his own design from cotton that they manage to purchase from one of the ships from India in the harbor. He draws them a simple pattern for loose-fitting pantaloons, closed at the bottoms around the ankle, with a light flowing tunic top much the same as the one he wears himself.

"It will protect you from the sun, from insects, and it will keep you cool." Dr. Pundit is full of strange wisdom, and is extremely focused on cleanliness, insisting that the girls wash their hands many times a day. He is a Brahmin and comes with the somewhat obsessive habits of his class. He explains to them that at home if someone sneezes in the kitchen all the food must be thrown out.

"How wasteful" says Isaac.

"Perhaps, but Brahmins get sick much less than other people."

The four of them ride along the beaches and see turtles swimming under water, and beautiful pink conch shells. They ride into the hills and smell the fires lit by the settlers to clear the nearly impassable tropical forest for planting. They collect plant samples and identify trees. Pundit and Isaac between them have an extraordinary grasp of their strange and magical properties. They see a mongoose and iguanas, huge tarantulas and velvety butterflies.

"Leave them be, they have their own place in the universe and we have ours." On this Isaac and Dr. Pundit agree. Maria has named her horse Cibonie, and she whispers words of comfort and love to her. Sometimes she gallops off, leaving the other three plodding along on their mules. Gradually the magic of the island begins to penetrate Maria's heavy shell of grief.

"Dr. Pundit," she says, with the rising inflection of a question, when the two of them are riding side by side.

"Oh, just call me Pundi, Maria," he responds, turning to look at her with an affectionate smile.

"All right then, Pundi." She pauses and looks at him gravely. "I want to know how you came to leave India and what your life there was like. You told me on the ship I was too young then to hear the story, but I'm older now and you are dear to me. I want to know."

Pundi is silent for a long moment.

"Then I will tell you." They are moving in a slow rhythm, Pundi on his mule and Maria on Cibonie. "I come from Kozhikode, a large city on the western coast of India in a place called Kerala. My family were Brahmins, the caste of priests and teachers. Brahmins have many rules of living, of prayer and cleanliness, and we lived according to strict practices. I grew up in a large family compound with aunts and uncles and five brothers and two sisters and many cousins. And servants. Many servants. My father was a Vedic physician who specialized in herbal preparations and was well known in our district.

"Our home was a lovely place with bowers of colorful vines and flowers, with many rooms around a central courtyard. It was always full of people, so many they didn't all speak the same languages. And we had monkeys climbing about and they were a terrible nuisance! A very well-treated cow lived in our courtyard, because cows hold all spirits and are sacred in India. You would have loved our cow." Pundi flicks his thick black hair back and wags his head from side to side, his eyes glistening.

"Kozhikode is on the sea and we lived not far from the port. My brothers and I loved to go to the docks and watch the ships come in, to see what they were unloading. Spices from Zanzibar, silks from China…sometimes even camels. Oh you would have been enchanted with all there was to see…heavenly for a boy. My father had forbidden us to do it, but it was irresistible and we did it nonetheless. You might be able to imagine it if you can picture the harbor and dock of St. Thomas several times bigger." He makes a grand gesture with arms wide and grins down at her.

"But one day I was peering over a railing and the next thing I knew I was in a scratchy burlap bag. A sailor had come up behind me, stuffed a cloth in my mouth and put the bag over my head. Then with his mate he pushed me over and bound the bag with me in it and took me to their ship. People must have thought there was some wriggling animal like a pig inside.

"My brothers must have looked for me frantically, for this was the very thing we had been warned of. The sailors tied me in a cabin on the ship until we were well out of port. Oh, I cried my eyes out, but then I could see there was no use struggling and I accepted my fate. It was a dreadful moment of my life, but I was still a boy and had no idea at that moment that I would never see my family again. It is strictly forbidden for Brahmins to travel across the sea, and the sin of this weighed heavily on my mind.

"I was put to work, all the work that no one else wanted to do. It was a dreadful time. I will not even describe to you the terrible work they put me to and what they did to me if I resisted. The ship was Portuguese, one of the first to carry opium from India to sell it in China, a trade that is no doubt still flourishing, as it was very lucrative."

"How long were you on that ship?" There was a tremor in her voice that caused Pundi to smile gently at her.

"About a year, but then I jumped ship in Canton. I blended into the crowd there and I remade myself. I found an excellent tailor and outfitted myself in a manner suited to an educated man…and because I was educated, I was able to present myself to the next captain as a surgeon. Compared to the rest of them my medical knowledge was vast!" Pundi chuckles.

"What happened next?" Maria turns a curious face up to him.

"I ended up as the surgeon on a Dutch ship. You know I had a considerable knowledge of Vedic medicine from my father, and our traditions of cleanliness alone kept sailors much more healthy…though they all thought it was womanish to bathe. At that time I was collecting plants wherever I could find them and experimenting with them. There was never any shortage of sick men on the ships, but they didn't have a great variety of ailments. I ended up in Japan with the Dutch."

"Japan! How wonderful!"

"We spent some months on the tiny island of Dejima. A very odd place. It was an artificial island created in the middle of Nagasaki, and the gaijin, the foreigners, were isolated there so we wouldn't taint the great culture of Japan." Pundi chuckles.

"But our sailors caught on to the idea of bathing there… The Japanese have lovely ways of bathing… I was glad when we departed. There was no opportunity to collect plants, and to be locked away with a bunch of sailors on land was worse than being at sea, where at least you know you are going somewhere.

I left that ship in Cape Town and then ended up in the Azores…and that's when I joined you on the Fortuna."

Maria beams at him. "And here you have Isaac! And Akila and I can be your helpers…and I'm sure you'll have a more interesting variety of ailments to study!"

"To encounter Isaac has been a great gift. He has been doing similar work but has different knowledge from another part of the world, so we have had much of interest to share."

They ride on in companionable silence, listening to the calling of the doves.

Maria wanders in her dreams that night through a vast house covered in vines, and wakens suddenly with the feeling that she is being suffocated. She goes to the window and looks out at the moonlit harbor with its tall ships bobbing peacefully. The thought of Pundi as a boy stolen from his family opens her heart as wide as the moon.

In May, just as life is beginning to develop a rhythm and as the humidity and heat of summer begin to sink upon St. Thomas, Maria feels a tickle in her throat. Sitting at the round table with Akila, Isaac Benjamin and Dr. Pundit, she keeps swallowing and shifting in her chair.

"Are you not feeling well, child?" Isaac asks.

"My throat is sore, just a little."

Isaac looks gravely at her for a long moment and then at Pundit. "We must isolate her. Until we see if it develops into something."

Within a day Maria is restlessly turning in her bed with a high fever, drifting in and out of sleep. Mrs. von Bergen sits in the salon twisting a handkerchief and looking out to the sea with tears streaming down her cheeks. "All my babies die," she whispers. "This is such a cruel place."

Maria is relieved to see Celine appear at her bedside the first morning of her fever. Her throat is so sore she doesn't even try to speak.

"Lucien will just have to cope with the customers this morning," Celine whispers. "I've a good strong constitution because I've had the pox, as you can see well enough from my face. But I don't think this is the pox," she says, looking closely at Maria. "There are no pustules. I think you may have had a tiny case when I was sick with it all those years ago. You just sleep now and we'll get you well."

Isaac, seeing that Akila is distraught at the thought that Maria will die, takes her off into the hills to search for a Gamalamee tree. As they walk he points out medicinal plants along the way, putting some aloe and some Billy Web leaves into her basket. They walk along the edge of the Van Beverhoudt plantation, next to a field where thirty slaves are hoeing rows for the planting of sugarcane. Isaac points to a tall, thin Negro some distance off, working in the field shirtless and glistening with sweat in the hot sun.

"That man's name is Samuel." Isaac tells her in Arabic. "I met him a few weeks ago at the Sunday market. He was selling tinctures he had made for various things. He told me his father had been the medicine man in his own village and I was impressed with his knowledge. We will come back tonight and pay him a visit."

They walk on past the plantation and into the woods. Akila feels at home here with the sunlight filtering through the leaves. She closes her eyes and lets herself become a part of the jungle; she can feel her mother's warm body by her side, sense the bright colors of her buba. She cocks her head at the sound of a Jumbee bird and opens her eyes, trying to see where he is hiding. She creeps silently toward the sound and points up to the high branches of a tree. "Jumbee!" she cries.

Isaac follows her and laughs, "You have found us a Gamalamee tree, and a Jumbee bird too." They set to work. The bark peels away easily enough, and Akila fills her basket with the dusty brown strips.

"Boiled up this makes a bitter, pretty nasty tea, but it will bring a fever down quickly. You can use the leaves as a poultice for insect bites or sunburn, or worse diseases of the skin. It's a plant with many uses," Isaac says. Akila is familiar with the idea of boiling leaves and bark into a tea. Her mama did it all the time.

Back in the kitchen, Akila boils the water and pounds the bark into a pulp to make a strong tea. Celine sponges Maria with cool water to keep her temperature down and gets her to sip on the Gamalamee tea.

"Drink," Akila murmurs in every language she can think of. "Drink the tea, Maria."

Celine sits on the edge of her bed hour after hour praying aloud, and Akila goes back and forth to the kitchen for fresh water and tea, murmuring to Allah.

As the sun is setting, Isaac and Akila retrace their steps up the hillside to the street of the slaves of the Van Beverhoudt family. Huts are lined up on either side of a wide path, and behind each is a patch for a vegetable garden. Isaac inquires of an old slave woman which is the hut of Samuel. She looks at Akila.

"Soninke," the woman declares. She points to the scars at Akila's temples, and then to a hut down the path. "Thar be Samuel's hut."

They sit on a rough bench outside of Samuel's hut watching the radiant last beams of the sun disappearing over the horizon. A few torches are lit along the path and exhausted slaves begin to trickle in from the fields. But there is a modest sense of cheer among them.

The workday is over. Some are singing, some head to their vegetable patches to catch the last rays of light.

"The people here raise their own food. Nothing is provided by the Van Beverhouts, but they do get Sunday off to work their own patches, and then they go sell some in the market for a few rix-dollars, or they barter," Isaac explains, looking down at Akila thoughtfully. "What a blessing that you ended up with Maria. We must get her well."

The tall Negro from the field is suddenly standing before them. Akila's heart begins a punching drumbeat. She recognizes him.

"MANDA!" And a great stream of the Soninke language flows from her like a high river whose dam has burst.

He responds with a matching torrent, and the two of them fall into each other's arms.

Isaac watches with amazement. Samuel looks over Akila's shoulder at him. "You be the man from the market, neh? This girl is the first-born girl child of our chief. How she come here?" He pauses and looks to the sky. "Why do I ask? I know how she come"

Akila turns to Isaac with luminous wide eyes, a look of pure joy. In Arabic she says, "It's Manda from my village. The son of our medicine man."

"So you know this Samuel?"

Akila nods and then does a little dance, waving her arms in the air and jumping from left to right, as though every part of her has just been unshackled.

Isaac's blue eyes begin to water, and then he starts laughing. Akila lets loose a stream of Soninke and Samuel turns to Isaac.

"She is very fond of her mistress! I will give you something strong for the fever." In a few moments he is back with a pouch woven from soft grasses.

"Tie this around her neck. Helps the throat, drives out bad spirits. Put these drops on her tongue." He hands Isaac the small pouch on a string, and a bottle with a brown liquid in it.

"Go now, I will come see Akila soon. And visit the mistress."

When they return they find Maria delirious with a high fever, and Celine wailing by her bed. Akila gently lifts Maria's head and Celine ties the pouch around her neck. They open her mouth and puts the drops on her tongue. Isaac sits at the table with his head in his hands. He has grown very fond of this child, who so reminds him of his own daughters.

On the fifth day Akila sits down suddenly and says, "I don't feel well."

Celine wails, "Oh no, not you, too! We must get Isaac. And Samuel. Oh Lord, protect us."

On the eighth day Maria's fever breaks and Celine weeps with relief. Now they watch Akila thrashing on her pallet. "Please put her in the bed beside me, Celine. I'm sure I can't catch it again, and she'll be more comfortable here." Side by side they look like spoon and fork: Maria round and flushed pink, Akila spiky thin, with her high cheekbones, sharp elbows and rosy brown complexion, the color of the Gamalamee tree.

Isaac and Dr. Pundit have set up camp outside by the cookhouse, where they are experimenting with combining various plants to augment their medicinal properties. Akila is gradually getting better, and they realize that Samuel's concoction has been quite effective.

Isaac climbs the hill to the Van Beverhoudt slave encampment and finds Samuel.

"Come down and join my Indian friend and me. We are experimenting with plants and you know many things we don't."

Samuel looks for a long moment at Isaac and then kicks the dirt at his feet. "I must feed myself you know…and that requires that I work on my little garden, or I will have no food."

"You'll have a meal with us, and we'll make sure you go home with something too. And maybe you can let a neighbor cultivate your plot and give you a little in exchange. What you know of plants and medicine is too valuable to waste."

"Oh, it is not wasted. I treat our whole little village you know. They may be suspicious if I start working with White men."

"Well, I can't blame them for that. And I am sure there are quite a few things that only you can treat them for…you know their minds, and much that bedevils the body comes from the mind. But please think about it. We sorely need you."

In a very few days Akila is sitting up and taking food again, and Isaac invites Samuel in to see her. Mrs. von Bergen is rendered speechless to see this stunning specimen of Black manhood in the girls' bedroom.

A few evenings later Samuel comes into the little "pharmacy" beside the cookhouse, bringing with him a sampling of his own favorite plant specimens. The three men sit together in a circle as the moon rises. With their combined knowledge from three continents they begin to plan their experiments, thinking of all the distressing illnesses that they have encountered in their lives, and here on the island. In one of their first discussions, Pundi muses on why Akila has recovered faster than Maria.

"Akila has had fevers like this before I am sure," says Samuel. "Lots of fevers in Africa. If you have lots of them they get milder."

"Well, they've both survived this one and I suspect it will protect them for a long while," Isaac says. "I hope so. Fevers are the scourge of this island, mysterious and deadly."

Chapter Fifteen: The Ride

Copenhagen, November 1770

Count von Brockdorff sends a message that he will pick me up in a carriage midday a week hence. I am instructed to wear my riding clothes. I have none, so again the seamstress is called for.

"The Queen is now wearing men's pantaloons for riding. Dr. Struensee was the instigator of that. I think it is causing quite a stir. Do you wish me to make you a pair?"

"Oh yes. Certainly if Dr. Struensee thinks it a good idea."

So on the appointed day I descend the staircase in a form-fitting rust-colored wool jacket, flaring at the hips over a pair of velvet green pantaloons. Boots, gloves and a manly hat complete the outfit.

"Oh, how very *à la mode* of you," the Count declares admiringly. He stands close, bending over me slightly. I feel the warmth of his breath. He is in a black riding costume, striking beside his fair skin and blond hair. I suddenly feel very self-conscious.

"I never have ridden side saddle. It seems a very precarious thing to do. I hope you do not mind if I do not." We set out through the city streets for the stable in which he keeps his horse.

He has selected a beautiful black palfrey for me. "I think she is a good match for you, both in bold temperament and coloring. But she is a respectful beast, I assure you. Like her master," he says with a little bow. "I call her Cunegonde."

"Not really!" I have just learned about Voltaire from my tutors. "Yes, indeed. She is a very clever beast. And full of surprises."

The sun is bright but strangely without warmth, and I put the collar of my jacket up around my neck. I mount the horse from a box, insisting all the while that the box is entirely unnecessary. A surge of contentment settles over me at being astride this powerful animal, at the familiar pungent smell, the alive sense of connection to another being. Her breath, like my own, forms little clouds of steam in the cold air. I lean forward and whisper my joy in her ear. I still have my little-girl passion for animals but have learned not to show it as I once would have. We start. First walking, then trotting, and finally cantering into the woods. We are quickly out of the city and I can hear the rhythmic surf breaking against the shore in the distance. The familiarity of the sound seems oddly out of place in this world of dead leaves and paillarded trees.

The landscape is flat, a little like St. Croix if St. Croix had trees, and not at all like the mountainous terrain of St. Thomas.

We ride for over an hour and then come to a lookout point on a little hill above the sea, the only high spot for miles around. Dismounting we sit on a fallen log and share some biscuits and cheese the Count has brought along. At his insistence I have started calling him Heinrich.

"Well Heinrich, what do you think of the goings-on at court?" I ask him. "Isn't it amazing what's happening?"

"Simply terrific, I think. But you should hear my father," Heinrich snorts. "I don't mean to be disloyal to him, but I do think the country has been shackled by these old men long enough. There is no excuse for such misery as you may encounter on any random day. I heard that the King was taken ill not long ago at the sight of a man flayed nearly to death while strapped to a wooden saw-horse. That may have been a decisive moment. The power of the nobility has been without reasonable limits and that must end."

"I am surprised that you would say so, being nobility yourself." I look at him with new interest. His face is burnished with the glow of the afternoon sun.

"It is not gallantry speaking, but self-preservation. It makes no sense to keep people in misery. Look around the world and the agitation that is happening. The boiling hatred. In France, in America. You must know it well in the islands. Did you not live in constant fear?"

"Yes, fear of revolt is always with us. And of course, we did have a terrible revolt on St. John in 1733. Very fortunately limited to that one very small island."

Heinrich rises to attend to one of the horses, who has wandered into the woods.

Sitting by myself on our log I see a bright flash in the woods beyond, just at the edge of the beach. A glint of something that moves. I stand up and look again. There is no mistaking. It is the Queen in her own famous riding outfit, and she is encircled in the arms of Dr. Struensee. I almost choke on the biscuit in my mouth, then swallow it without chewing, just barely getting it down.

I continue staring. Their mouths are locked together. For a moment I am completely frozen in place. Then a wave of panic washes over me.

"I think we should be going," I shout loudly at Heinrich, hoping that he will not see what I have seen. And that my shout will alert them. I must distract him. I must protect them. Heinrich reappears and I chatter brightly at him, claiming the beginnings of a headache. I throw myself up on Cunegonde, and Heinrich follows my lead, though I suspect he is quite dumbfounded.

At home Phebe remarks that I am distracted, her eyes a flash of gold and licorice in the ill-lit room. "You are not yourself, Sum. Are you in love with the young man?" She giggles at her own presumed shrewdness.

"Not that I perceive," I say wryly with an answering smile. "But there is much around here that gives pause, do you not think so?"

"Well, it is I who gives pause to most people I meet, and that's not much fun."

"Yes, I can imagine it might." I am resting my elbow on the table and I put my chin in my hand and contemplate my friend, my slave. I think of her sometimes as my wisest self and with that thought I decide to share my secret with her. I describe the embrace I had witnessed that afternoon.

"Oh my." Phebe says after a long pause, her eyes locked with mine. "What to do? That is a very big secret indeed."

"Do you think I should say anything?"

"I think you should confront him. Let him know what you've seen. Perhaps it will put an end to his recklessness, for that is what it is…and it puts the Queen in as much danger as it does him. How careless of him. It makes me so sad because his ideas are very fine."

I encounter Struensee two days later in a corridor of the palace. He is walking towards me, wigless, mind elsewhere, as I can easily see. I have thought about this moment, hoped this opportunity might come.

"Dr. Struensee."

"Oh, Miss Suhm. Where are you off to?"

"To the garden. It beckoned. I was feeling like a chicken in a coop." Here I pause, weighing my approach. "Might you join me?"

He looks at me with an indulgent air, a look that says, "Oh you have no idea, do you?" But what comes from his mouth is simply, "Too much to do I'm afraid. A pity. It would be nice."

"Then I must say what I have to say here. It is important. I hope you will not be offended." The words come out as if from behind a collapsing dam.

There is a short pause. "Of course not. Speak up."

"I was riding the other day, off by the beach. With the kind Count Brockdorff you sat me next to at dinner. I saw you and the Queen together. Down by the beach in the woods. In a somewhat compromising posture. My companion did not see you, I think." Here I rush on. "I want to say that if I can ever be of use to you, to the Queen. It would be my honor."

Struensee is entirely still, staring at me, a glow of pink has risen from his neck into his cheeks. Then a smile like the sun beaming over the horizon lights up his face, and he slowly runs the tip of his tongue over his lips. In a quick and gentle movement he puts his arms around me and tilts my head up and kisses me softly, affectionately. "Is this what you saw?" And his eyes crinkle with humor. "Think nothing of it. I just have a weakness for women. But it passes. The Queen is quite safe." And he tilts my head back again and kisses me again, this time a little longer, his tongue playing softly with my lips.

I feel as if the blood in my veins has all just started to flow backwards. I am hot and cold by turns and cannot speak at all. I have never been kissed before like this, never felt anything quite like what has just gone on in my body.

"Ooh," I say. Then a long pause. "I see."

"Now you know what a kiss is like. Consider it a lesson. You can try it out with Heinrich." Pause. "But let's keep this our secret. No good will come of telling anyone of this, or what you saw with the Queen. Not even Phebe, please."

The avalanche of feelings that comes crashing down upon me as he says this takes my breath away…starting with the powerful desire to feel his lips on mine again. Then comes shame… that I have already told Phebe. Then jealousy and finally, fear. A big enveloping fear that drops like a dark miasmic cloud over me…that he will be discovered…and all that would befall him if that happened.

Chapter Sixteen: Weddings

Tapphus, St. Thomas, 1689

Standing by the narrow gun slit embrasure in the treasury room of Fort Christian, Pierre La Salle looks down into the harbor at the gulls squabbling over the garbage being dumped from a black galleon. The morning sun beats down like an unblinking eye. He fingers the bolt of India cotton he has just procured off a Dutch vessel in the harbor. In his mind's eye he drapes it gracefully around Maria. And perhaps a shirt for himself?

Johan Lorenz grips his shoulder from behind, startling him from his reverie. "Beautiful cloth!" Johan purrs. "For Maria? God's teeth, you are a lucky one. First pick of all the goods…And the women too, I perceive! I trust you not to forget me when you're out in the harbor on your inspections. Hasn't our King put us in a fine position? All Europe with their daggers drawn, save for dear old neutral Denmark…making us the provisioners of the Atlantic… the only port where they can buy anything!"

"And how are you supplied for rum?" Pierre whispers with a conspiratorial grin, clapping his arm around his friend.

Lorenz had been Pierre's first friend on the island. He had spotted Pierre in the courtyard of the Fort on that first day, a gangly youngster with an intelligent face.

"Do you know that Mikklesohn fellow?" he had asked Pierre, pointing to the tall Dane holding forth to a crowd.

"Been at sea with him for four weeks now. He's a good enough fellow. But his mission is to arrest your Governor."

"Gadzooks!" Lorenz had exclaimed. "We've already got one governor, Esmit, and his beautiful wife, Charity, locked up right behind you!" And he pointed to the corner of the Fort, grinning. Within the hour Lorenz had installed Pierre on barstool at a local tavern, handed him a mug of rum, and begun to explain the scandalous and peculiar politics of Tapphus. Pierre had been absurdly relieved to find another educated person his age in this hellhole. The sea of toothless, rank characters that had closed around him on the docks when he had come off the *Fortuna* had convinced him that he had arrived in a nest of vipers.

Lorenz had given him a quick overview of the tensions between the planters here on the island and the governors of the Danish West India Company in Copenhagen. Now, looking out the window, Pierre remembers the vivid image he had conjured: a tight wire strung across the Atlantic. A wire they all must learn to walk with care. And now his dear friend Lorenz had been voted governor of the island by the planters.

His shirt is sodden with sweat moments after he steps out of the cool stone office into the noon sunlight. He nods at the guard, who salutes him as he heads to the Company warehouse. An image of his father rises in his mind's eye. How amazed he would be if he could see how prosperous Pierre is becoming…as a Calvinist, he would surely consider him one of the elect. But he would not approve of the means. Compared to trafficking in slaves, the bit of skimming Pierre does would be a minor offense to his father, who was himself a businessman.

But he would be fierce on the subject of slavery. In truth, his father would have harsh judgments to make on every aspect of this life.

A planter yells across the road at him in Dutch. "Hey La Salle! Any news of a slaver coming to port soon? Hard to grow cane without more labor. Black labor! The Whites just can't do this work. They don't last a month. I heard that the Brandenburgers have a couple of slave ships headed our way."

"Soon, my man. Soon." He puts up a placating palm. In truth the news had just arrived that a Company slaver had gone down off Cuba just a week ago, losing the whole cargo and crew. But he wasn't going to spread that news around. He hated the thought that the Brandenburgers would beat the Company in this slaving business. He thinks of David Bordeaux, who has just arrived as the representative of the Elector of Brandenburg. Maria barely knows him, though he is her father's cousin. The Elector needs a place in the Americas where he can sell the slaves he is acquiring in Africa. The King of Denmark has agreed to this as long as they develop a plantation on the island and contribute to the flow of trade.

As the right hand to the new governor, Pierre has his fingers in everything. Nothing can be sold without his inspection. He determines which planters will get their goods shipped to Europe, and when. He oversees the weighing of cargos, coming and going, and the paying of taxes thereon. He lives in a world of guttural Danish and Dutch, of mijnheers and rix-dollars, of very bendable laws.

Always at the back of Pierre's mind is the shadow: the knowledge that the fundamental trade of this island, the trade in slaves and all that their labor produces, is against God's morality. Pierre can see clearly enough that he is witnessing the beginnings of a truly grinding plantation economy. He can hear his father on the subject, to say nothing of his future wife, who reminds him of its offensiveness every day, not just by what she says, but by her very gentle and compassionate way of being…and her tie to Akila.

The relationship puzzles him. He understood her first impulse to rescue Akila, but the closeness that has developed between them is disquieting. He fears it to be the subject of much gossip. But the one time he tried to broach the subject, Maria had just held up her hand in a gesture that clearly meant Say No More.

Ah well, he thinks, "when we are married, Akila will be mine by law."

He is very fond of Maria, but he feels slightly guilty there too. She is his muse, his touchstone from home, but not his passion.

He inhales the saltiness of the sea and the sweat coming off the passing sailors. His passions are locked deep away inside of him, for the moment out of his own reach and understanding. But they are stirred by those smells. Is it the smell of power? Money?

Pushing all these thoughts from his mind, he signals a dory to take him out to inspect the French ship that has just dropped anchor.

"Hold still," Akila's mouth is full of hairpins and she takes them, one by one, and jabs them into the giant confection she is fashioning out of Maria's thick, curly hair. They have been absorbed in wedding plans for weeks. The ceremony is to take place in the church within the Fort, and invitations have been much sought after.

"Arms up!" Akila slides the grey silk dress, made especially for the occasion, over Maria's head and smooths the skirt out around her crinolines. "Now turn around." And she fastens the familiar pearl buttons all the way down the back of her dress. Next, she carefully hooks the clasp of the diamond necklace. She and Celine had struggled to string these diamonds, once hidden in the hems of Maria's clothing. "Oh, let's have a look." She spins Maria around and steps back to look at her handiwork. "You are too beautiful. He doesn't deserve you." Maria wraps her arms around Akila and hugs her for a long moment.

"For the sake of Allah, do not cry! Your eyes will puff!"

"But I love him so, Keela," Maria hiccups, and then her eyes go wide. "The medallion! Oh, I must put the medallion in my shoe. Papa said that it will bring me luck!"

The marriage takes place in the dark church within the Fort, heavy with the scent of lilies and burning candles. Maria glows in the flickering light, with her blue eyes shining and little tendrils of curls falling to her shoulders. Her heart pounds like a caged bird against the whalebone of the unaccustomed corset, and she wishes that Akila could stand beside her to steady her. She turns and looks longingly at Akila, in the very back row, the only slave in the room. Akila smiles and gives a nod of encouragement.

Pierre has borrowed a costume from Lorentz for the occasion: wide pantaloons that come just to his boot tops, a blue silk waistcoat and a contrasting yellow doublet. An outrageously hot outfit, but he will shed most of it as soon as he is properly married. The

Company's Lutheran minister of the moment officiates. Johan Lorentz stands by Pierre. Celine and Lucien walk the bride down the aisle, Lucien's unmistakable red hair like shimmering gold in the candlelight.

Isaac Benjamin and Dr. Pundit sign the official documents as witnesses. Pundit, glowing in the candlelight, in his dhoti and flowing white shirt, seems to Maria like a being from a magical kingdom, sent to protect her in this strange place.

As a result of Maria's perpetual lament over the mosquitoes of the island, Dr. Pundit has given them a very special present. She had proclaimed in exasperation one day, "Look at this cloud of mosquitoes following me!"

Pundi had tossed his head back as if examining his own personal swarm, and replied with a snort, "The mosquitoes are always bad here! Personally, I always use my domatera at night and don't quite understand why it has never traveled beyond India except in my duffle."

"Oh Pundi, you are always so far ahead of us all. What, pray tell, is a domatera?" Maria was alternately fanning herself and Akila with a palm frond as she said this.

With great satisfaction and abundant use of his hands he had described to her a mosquito net.

"Gads, why don't we have the whole island wrapped up in one? Can you at least get me a few for the house?"

"I will inquire in the harbor. If no one has them aboard I can perhaps command a shipment from India. I suppose the Chinese have them too."

He had succeeded in his search for a domatera and had personally wrapped their marriage bed with the netting.

As the marriage revelry begins in the Fort, Akila slips off to join the other slaves. She finds them in a field around a campfire, fingers flying wildly over drums that have been crafted of wood and animal hide, bodies swirling in hypnotic dancing that serves as liquor does to the planters. At the Fort the party is hardly sedate. Rum is flowing freely and the sounds of the crumhorn and the bagpipe drift over the island as the revelers spin one other around the courtyard.

The married couple go that night to their own house, newly built of wattle and daub, with a fine thatched roof. Just two large rooms so that the breezes can pass through, it is close to the Fort, set just a little above it on the hill overlooking the harbor. Slave huts and a cookhouse encircle a courtyard in the back. All is pristine and yet to be occupied, save by a few geckos.

Pierre and Maria are escorted to the door and serenaded by a now bawdy assortment of revelers who are quite prepared to follow them to the bedroom. At the threshold Pierre tumbles into the house, and Maria blocks the door with her small authoritative self, putting up both hands and bowing in a small salaam. She bids them goodnight and lights a candle.

By the time she enters the bedroom Pierre has managed to find a way in through the domatera and is snoring softly in the bed. She looks down on him with loving exasperation.

"Oh, my dear Pierre. My husband!"

She turns to the window and opens the shutters, inhaling the night perfume with a deep sigh. The moon is full, owlish, casting undulations of yellow light on the sea. Suddenly an avalanche of feelings tumbles down upon her. Most of all she is missing Akila, who has slept by her bed on a pallet for the past four years. She tries to picture her in her little hut by the courtyard. Her tears gather and flow. Gradually the rhythmic sound of the water lapping against the wharves below calms her. She turns back into the room and unfastens the sparkling necklace and places it in a drawer, hidden beneath her undergarments. Then she struggles with the intricate buttons on the back of her gown and realizes she can't get out of the dress. She goes to the back window and whispers loudly, "Akila." And again, "Akila."

Akila appears at the door.

"Oh Keela, I'm so sorry to wake you, but I can't get the button undone."

"I thought Pierre would help with that!"

"He's asleep. I think he had a bit too much rum." Akila unbuttons her dress and Maria lets it drop to the floor around her. The medallion, on a soft blue ribbon, she takes from her shoe.

"I must not wait for it to bring me luck, I must make it for myself, with the help of God."

Standing in the pool of moonlight and dress, she looks longingly at the outstretched form of Pierre, and reaches for Akila's hand. "Go back to bed, dear Akila. I'm sorry to have disturbed you."

"Let's say our prayers, first."

"Urrgh…" Pierre groans upon waking on their wedding morning. The house has filled magically overnight with their small troop of slaves returning from their own revels. The sounds of their morning ablutions, the clanking of pots, the cry of a child all have combined to jar him from his slumber.

He props himself up on one elbow and looks at the tangled mass of brown curls on the pillow beside him. "Oh Lord," he mutters, "I am disgraced." He leans over and kisses the sleeping form gently. "Forgive me, my sweet." She rolls over, opens her eyes and looks up at him. Smiles. He is relieved. He swings his feet to the floor and pulls the bell cord for his manservant. "It's nice, this room," he comments, stepping over the puddle of her dress.

The sun is slatting through the shutters. The day is already hot. Marcus, his manservant, a houseslave of delicate proportions and ebony skin, sticks his shorn head into the room after a knock. He carries a pitcher of water. He is all propriety. "Send Akila to me, Marcus," Maria says softly.

Pierre goes behind a curtain to the washstand and Akila comes and sweeps the dress up off the floor. Dropping it at the foot of the bed, she sits down beside Maria and gives her a hug. "Bonjour" she says with a meaningful smile. Looking around at the mess, she bursts into a patter of sounds, clicking her tongue and smiling. Maria smiles. She loves the sibilant sounds of Akila's language. They have their own patois. All over the island a new kind of language is developing, a combination of infinitely simple and complex, a mishmash of African dialects, Dutch, English, Danish, French and German that will gradually develop into several varieties of creole depending on who is speaking to whom. It will be a language of the sibilant sounds of the sea and the percussive crashing of wave on rock, marrying them to the ancient whispers and cries of Europe and Africa. And it will be a language of gesture.

Akila settles into a hut in the courtyard by the cookhouse. She is not unhappy, because it is her very own place, something she has never had. She savors solitude like a new-grown fruit, and when it ripens precipitously into loneliness, she has but to step out into the courtyard and into the company of Anna and Sophia and occasionally Samuel, whom she finds sitting quietly some mornings by her door. She has become shy with Samuel. But his presence makes her feel at home and secure.

Her days begin with the cacaphonous chatter of birds rising in volume with the sun's first rays. She tosses her chemise over her head and pulls back the drapery that serves as a door to her hut, unfurling her prayer mat in the direction of the rising sun. She is the only one in the courtyard to do this. The others steal glances at her and go about their own ablutions.

She is soon off to the bakery, stirring up the red dust with her bare feet as the doves light on the branches above her and weave through the air. She fairly dances down the road, a distinct series of geometric shapes, her oval head upon the beautiful line of her long neck, her back curving into the rounds of her buttocks, and her long legs reaching for the path. Along the way, she greets friends, other house slaves streaming in from all the plantations within walking distance. They come here for the news of the day, and their bread, though sometimes it seems that the bread is an afterthought. Not a native thing, this French bread, more something for status. The masters send their brightest because they want their news fresh and true, she thinks.

Conversations from the bakery spread like a drumbeat over the island in the succeeding hours. News of ship arrivals, illness, every beating and death.

She looks forward to seeing Celine, Lucien and most especially Bamadille, knowing each of them will pick her out for a special greeting, or to pop a warm treat into her mouth.

Sometimes, if he wasn't in their courtyard, she meets Samuel on the path and wonders if maybe he has followed her, or anticipated her, and she wonders if he will get in trouble with his master for it.

"You're like those dancing doves," he says in Soninke, his voice a low murmur, like the doves' of which he speaks. He reaches out to touch her and she pulls away, his fingers were hot irons. She squeezes her eyes shut, to obliterate the image of the vile sailor in the putrid hut. She tries to control her breathing, her pounding heart. She opens her eyes and looks at him. His beautiful eyes, the scars on his temples that match her own. Something has changed between them since that first day. Now there is an electric charge that terrifies her. He looks at her quizzically, a gentle smile lighting his face. He will persist. She will resist. But a little of the deep core of the ice inside her is beginning to melt.

He comes to her door one night. Stooping below the lintel he enters. She jumps up from her mat in a quick motion of unfolding and tries to push him out, but he pulls her to him and breathes into her ear his warmth. She is trembling violently, trying to push from her mind the vivid memory of violent rape that has flooded all her senses. He holds her silently and rests his cheek against hers for a long time, releasing her only when she has grown calm. "Terrible things have happened to you," he says. "You must be healed." He puts his lips to her forehead and is gone.

Four nights of variations on this ritual, and the ice in her has turned to fire. She has trained her mind to smell him and not that other, to feel the softness of his touch and focus only on that. She lets him touch her breasts and put his mouth over her nipples, his gentle sucking makes his penis hard against her leg and she is hot, confused by her body's powerful desire. He slides into her easily and rocks her gently into a blinding joyful light.

She cannot keep this from Maria. Does Pierre do this to you, she wants to know. "Well, not exactly," is the answer.

Akila wraps Maria in her arms. Her chin rests on the top of Maria's mass of curly hair. They are in Maria's bedroom, and Akila can see the masts of ships bobbing in the harbor and hear the gulls arguing over the trash. The heat vibrates the air. "Perhaps it is something you learn," she says. "You know in my village I would by now have been made a woman in the ceremony of Irua," She presses her knees together and grimaces. "I suppose that is one good thing that comes of leaving Africa…because after the cutting there is no pleasure for the woman." She begins swaying gently and a steady humming noise rises from her throat.

"Come dance with me," she whispers to Maria, and she raises her arms, her wrists bent, and circles her hands slowly. The motion undulates down her body and she closes her eyes, moving to an imaginary slow beat. Maria watches and then begins to imitate her. Akila closes her eyes to the sights of the harbor and breathes deeply, making a throaty noise, abandoning herself to motion, her body stretching, her arms turning slowly. Gradually she increases the speed of her turning and the sounds from her throat grow more intense, until she is moving in a frenzy, as if possessed. Maria stops to watch her, and suddenly Akila stops, too, and drops to the floor laughing, sweat dripping from her chin.

"All the women of my village used to do this together. It is the way of our people. It does you good. I'll teach you."

Maria dances this undulating dance again at Akila's marriage to Samuel, later that year. She had insisted that Pierre buy Samuel from the Von Beverhoudts, who are very loath to see him leave, for he is a slave with great capacities and influence on the other slaves. They drive a very hard bargain. The minute the purchase is completed Maria begins planning the wedding.

"No, no, no." Akila shakes her head adamantly. "We will do this ourselves, in the way of our village."

"Well, let me at least provide some food."

Akila rests her chin in her hand and looks at Maria for a moment. "That would be very generous, and we thank you. And you must come yourself, but only you. It will be a great, wild party and now that you know how to dance you will fit in." She winks.

They are married at sunset in a field behind the bakery. A huge bonfire is waiting to be lit and slaves from around the island trek through the hills to be there, bringing an assortment of food, and gourds and sticks to make music.

With the acquisition of Samuel, the La Salle household has four slaves and one indentured servant, each of them with their own peculiar, very sad story. Maria considers this far more help than she can possibly need, and indeed they have more slaves than any of the other villagers. But each of their slaves has attracted Pierre's attention and sympathy as he is one of the first to inspect the slave ships, and thus has first pick. Marcus attracts his attention for his good humor in the face of all the hardship and travail he is living through. He has a way of turning the wailing to song, and giving strength to those around him. He is a handsome, well-built man and Pierre quietly pays a good price for him, and keeps him at his side in the Fort until their home is ready.

Anna is one of the indentured from Copenhagen, a small, sad blond woman who looks as if she will not survive the climate. She was one of the desperately poor of Copenhagen who had been caught stealing to survive. Pierre sees at once that she is too fragile to survive the labor she would be forced to do if assigned to one of the planters, so he puts her to work in the kitchen of the Fort, figuring that he will take her into his own household to do the cooking when he is married. But when that time comes, he finds he has an extra mouth to feed. She is now the mother of an infant girl fathered by one of the Danish soldiers in the Fort, though none would claim the honor. The child is called Cate.

Jean-Baptiste is acquired shortly after their marriage, attracting Pierre's attention because he is so skinny that Pierre cannot imagine he will last a week. Something in his bright, feverish eyes catches Pierre's attention, and he pays almost nothing for him but brings him home to be ministered to by Akila and Maria.

At the bakery one morning Bamadille puts his arm around Akila. "Did you hear about Mette?"

"Why would I ever want to hear about Mette?" she replies.

"She is to be whipped and her husband hung for trying to escape the island in a Company boat."

Akila spits in the dust. "Too bad." She has watched this woman for a long time now with an aversion that has not ebbed. She slips away from Maria on the day of the hanging to witness the event at the base of the Fort. She edges as close as she can get, through the jeering crowd who have come for this delicious public entertainment. She is close enough to hear the man's neck snap. The sound of the lash on Mette's back brings Akila a strange, warm, pleasurable sensation, as if her own wounds were being healed with every laceration.

Mette rises slowly at the end of her ordeal and looks at the swinging body of her husband. For the next month eagles and buzzards will tear at his flesh until nothing but a skeleton is left. She looks out at the turquoise expanse of water. Then she wraps a rag around her shoulders and pushes her way through the jeering crowd.

After that, Mette is not much sought after as a servant and passes through several households until she lands in the household of Maria's cousin David Bordeaux. As new arrivals the Bordeaux have no idea of her history, and Pierre does not bother to inform them. He has not warmed to David, even though he is now linked to him by marriage, for the Brandenburgers are a constant thorn in his side, operating as they so often do on the wrong side of the law, trading with pirates, failing to plant their fair share. So it seems somewhat fitting to him that Mette ends up on the Bordeaux plantation.

But she does not last long there. One day David Bordeaux spies her spitting in his soup. He whips her himself with a passion rarely seen in him, and sends her off with nothing but the bloody chemise on her back. Her period of indenture is almost at an end in any case, but the beating gives him great satisfaction. Down the dusty road she goes, a plan fully formed in her mind. She spends a few nights in town walking out with a few sailors. A blanket she has plucked from a clothesline on her way into town serves as a temporary bed in the brush. She has deep knowledge from her childhood of the use of sponges to protect herself, and these are easily found on the beaches.

It does not take much to establish a lucrative little business. Within a fortnight she is able to buy her own slave, a young Wolof girl with a racking cough and a docile nature whom no one else much wants. But she is good enough to use the blanket in the brush, good enough for the sailors. Mette shows her how to use the sponge and very quickly she has doubled her money. She names her Caterina, after a girl who worked with her mother and was kind to her as a child. She buys a pair of scissors from the Company's mercantile shop and clips Caterina's hair close to her scalp. After a week, the two of them walk out of town and bathe on a secluded beach, where Mette scrubs Caterina 'til her skin is a purple shade of mahogany. She picks all the lice eggs out of her hair. Then they walk up onto the hill above Careening Bay.

"The view is fine here," Mette says. "You can see the traffic in the harbor. We will find that very useful." Caterina coughs and kicks the dust, not understanding a word. "We will build here, out of the way. It is land no one will want for planting. It is close to the town, but not so close that we will be much noticed." Mette lays out the footprint of her house with sticks and stones. She goes to town and hires two men to help her. Her house gets built. It is a simple affair, wattle and daub, with two rooms, not unlike Maria and Pierre's. All the houses of St. Thomas are like this at the time. Shelter that will likely be blown away in the next hurricane season, but easily replaced. She pays the men in cash, but in her Caterina currency as well, to spread the word. Advertising, as it were.

Chapter Seventeen: The Doctor's Assistants

Copenhagen, November 1770

Two weeks have passed since my confrontation with Dr. Struensee and I have calmed down a bit. Dr. Struensee has now sent a message to my uncle and aunt saying that he would like us to assist him that week at the vaccination station that he is setting up in the town.

I think surely Johanne must be able to detect my pounding heart but she just says "Zooks! What an idea."

"It is noble work, Aunt Jo. Important work. I want to do it. And so does Phebe. I know that Dr. Struensee will see that we come to no harm. We have had our vaccinations."

"But who knows if they actually work."

"The doctor does. He is entirely confident. And whatever else you may say about him, he is no fool."

"I can see there is no stopping you. But you must have your lessons too, and not neglect them." I smile at her thinking that it is not so much the lessons as the time I spend on deciphering the diary that will be foregone. But the diary is such slow work I don't mind taking a break from it.

We ride with the doctor in his carriage on the first day.

"It's not a long walk," he says, "so some days you can just meet me. I may have other business in town."

A woman is standing in a puddle of sunlight waiting for us between two columns of the church portico. She has a baby in her arms and two small children dash up and down the pavement.

"Are you the doctor? They say you know a way to stop the pox from coming," she says, wringing her hands together. "I have lost two babies to it."

Struensee bows his head. "I am so sorry. There is no need to convince you then that this is a terrible disease. I will explain the vaccination process to you, so you can tell others that they do not have to die of it." Struensee goes under the portico of the church and begins to set up a station for administering the vaccines. He and Phebe hang a drapery to make the corner private. When all is ready, he beckons to the woman to bring her children for their vaccinations.

"Summy, you go stop people and talk to them. Tell them about the vaccine. Persuade them that it is safe."

I fidget with my gloves and look at the ground. Phebe is watching my face. She comes over to me and whispers, "Pretend something. That you're an angel on a visitation, or a carnival barker. Whatever you feel like. And try not to mind the smell. That woman and her children, they must never have bathed in all their lives."

I look at her in horror. "I don't think I can do this. I'm feeling sick."

Phebe's eyes flash. There is anger in them, something I have never seen before. "Get yourself home then, mistress."

After a long pause I say, looking off over Phebe's head at the church steeple, "No, I can do it. I will. You go with the doctor. Leave me."

I begin with the nicer-looking people. And first with the ladies. Though there are very few of them on foot. But I find one and engage in a conversation.

"The King's doctor, you say? That Struensee man? A scoundrel, my husband shouts at him in his sleep. I dare not have a vaccine at his hands."

"As you wish, Madam, but consider the possible consequences. Your husband need not know." She looks at me, weighing this idea, and finally shakes her head and walks away.

The next woman is of a lower order and has heard of him too. "Come to save us, he has, that doctor. They have to pay us now, they does, thanks to your doctor there. If he's givin' a medicine, I'll have it." And she plants herself at the entrance to the portico and waits.

I instinctively begin to hone my approach based on the apparent means of my target. The vaccinations are given in the portico and I get snippets of the conversations.

Phebe helps Struensee in his preparations, and smiles and talks to keep the patient calm. Curious, they watch her flashing white teeth and listen to her strange lilting Danish.

I hear Struensee say to Phebe, "What a tonic you are to their suffering souls. You have a gift. And gifts must be made use of." Even through my own jealousy, I can see the lift that this little bit of praise gives her. Her gloom begins to fall away. She is no longer acting with her patients; she really looks like a ministering angel, and a glow rises to her cheeks.

Out in the cobblestone square I am trying to take on the soul of a circus barker, but my upbringing is standing in my way. I have rolled up my sleeve to show my own small vaccination scar, and hung my coat around my shoulders so that I can illustrate the procedure more easily. They are cold, these Danes. They step around me as if they don't even see me. I watch the passing crowd for a likely candidate.

"Excuse me," I say politely to a man in a green cap who looks passably intelligent. "Are you aware that there is a serious epidemic of smallpox in the city?"

"How could one fail to know that, Missy?" His stare is severe.

"Do you know there is a way to be safe from the scourge of it for the rest of your life?"

"And how might that be, pray tell." Now the edge is sarcastic.

"By taking the tiniest dose and making yourself forever immune. Do you see this small scar on my arm?" And now I whip my arm out from under my coat and hold it under the man's nose. "The doctor gave me a small dose of the disease, a very measured dose, mind you. I felt a little unwell for a day and now I am safe from it forever. The King and Queen, and even the little Prince have had it. The doctor is here now, vaccinating people who wish to be safe.

I hope you will be one of them. Do it now, and do not put it off because I expect there will be many others in this line in the days ahead and you might have to wait for hours."

My little speech is so effective that lines begin to form, and the portico of the church fills with applicants. I interview each of them to make sure that they are not suffering from another ailment, for the doctor says that is important, and if they are they must wait until they are recovered fully before taking the vaccine.

I run under the portico periodically to talk to Phebe. "Hold your nose when you get to that one," I whisper and roll my eyes in the direction of a man in a filthy blue navy pea coat. I have seen a lot in my life in St. Thomas, but the poverty here is of a colder brand, the filth is layered on and people are drinking alcohol to warm themselves, which seems to rot them from the inside.

One day a gaggle of women appear, all laughing together, wearing low-cut gowns under their cloaks. "We have a royal order for vaccinations," says the blond woman, who appears to be their leader, with an appraising laugh at the doctor. He vaccinates them all, and when they have departed he says to the two of us, "That last one there is Støvlet-Cathrine, the King's woman. At least she won't get smallpox, though Lord knows what else she may give him— probably the great pox. He is the fly that has flown into her web. She has him quite wrapped up."

There is no more talk of Phebe returning to St. Thomas. We have both been rescued by purpose and the wider world. Where Copenhagen had felt cold and windswept before, it has become more intense and colorful, with real people and personalities to talk about at the end of the day. I am relieved. On the days we are not with the doctor I am with a series of tutors, learning Latin and English, geography and mathematics. Phebe is now coming to all my tutoring sessions and working alongside me.

Johanne complains of the absence of Phebe's services. I give her a look and she is momentarily silenced, but quickly comes back with her retort.

"Who are you to get all high and mighty? She's your slave. Why don't you give her her freedom if you're so bent on helping her?" This is the very thought that has been trying to push its way fully into my consciousness. I feel as if she had shot an arrow into my heart.

We spend two afternoons a week at the vaccination post. One afternoon, when the wind is swirling debris from the street up under my skirt, and I am struggling to keep my cape from flying up like a sail, Heinrich von Brockdorff rides into the square on his black stallion. I think the stallion has recognized me because he stops right beside me and gives a jerk to the reins, tossing his head. I know Heinrich cannot have seen my face. I put my hand out to the horse.

"Hello, Voltaire."

"Summy?" He looks down and a new wave of feeling washes between us, like a watercolor spreading light and form into a liquid pool. "What are you doing here?" And I explain.

"I'll have this vaccine." Heinrich slides off his mount in a graceful single motion and is beside me. "Lead me to him."

"Well, that didn't take much persuasion." I cock my head and smile up at him.

"I trust the man. He is an inspiration. He sees the horizon when others can hardly see what's right in front of them. I mean, he thinks, which doesn't seem to be a common thing in the world. Most people just sigh and say they'll leave it to God." He pauses. "Now I do believe in God. But I believe he gave us our minds and our hearts with a reason. Notice he gave each of us the same basic mental equipment. I presume he expected us to use what we have, not just to follow blindly. Besides, my father will pop his buttons in a fury if I do anything in favor of Struensee." He grins broadly and touches my shoulder lightly. "And that makes it worthwhile all by itself."

I take this in. I like this spirit.

Three days later he comes bounding up to me on foot.

"Oh Summy, you cruel woman, you didn't tell me how horrible I would feel." "Well, I tried to, but you were so waxing eloquent about the doctor, and anyway I didn't want to deter you. I see you have survived….and if I'd told you everything you might have not done it, and then you might have died later. Now you are protected forever."

He leans down and kisses me on the forehead impulsively. "You little minx…" And he turns away and is off down the street.

I am about to say "Wait!" but the word spins unuttered in my head. I want to feel the feeling I have for Dr. Struensee for Heinrich. But the heart seems to make its own decisions.

Chapter Eighteen: Settling In

Charlotte Amalie (formerly Tapphus), St. Thomas, April 1694

Maria holds onto her bonnet as she climbs to the top of the Fort. The last time she had been up here was for the ceremony on the day in 1691 that Tapphus was renamed after the Queen of Denmark, Charlotte Amalie. The Fort had been packed for the occasion and she had ended up here on the upper walkway, looking down on the Governor as he made the proclamation. She decided then that it was her favorite place for the view and the cool breeze.

From there the harbor looks like a Danish staircase, with its welcoming arms, on the east formed by the island itself and on the west by the arm of Orkanhullet, or Hurricane Hole. That hilly west side looks down on Careening Cove, and Maria's heart ticks up a beat as she stares at the spot where Mette has established herself.

From here she can see David Bordeaux's plantation at the far end of the village road. Just a little closer is the thatched house that Isaac and Pundi have come to share, on the west side of the town itself, at the end of the arm of Orkanhullet. She can see the wide green arc of the kapok tree where Pundi has hung his hammock. She loves the inside of this house, which like all the houses on the island has just two rooms, one for sleeping and one for everything else, with the cooking, bathing and latrine out back. Since Pundi generally sleeps out in his hammock, Isaac has the more traditional bed, in the house, in a corner where it doubles as a sofa.

The inside of Isaac's house is a dreamy place, full of treasures from all the continents, items that have brought the world alive in the minds of Maria and Akila over the years. Drums and flutes, beautiful blue and white china bowls, a painting by a Dutchman of a woman in a black and white church. A glass ball to foretell your future. Beautiful carpets that swallow your feet. Best of all are the books: the Fables of Fontaine, piles of chart books and maps, the plays of Molière and the Pensées of Pascal. There is a book on demons and witchcraft, and many writings of the Talmud. Most important are the books on plants, and the medical texts with descriptions of the humors, and pictures of the skeleton and the organs and muscles. Maria closes her eyes and thinks of all the time she has spent over the past six years in animated discussion over these texts with Akila, Isaac and Pundi.

She can picture Isaac's ivory walking stick leaning against the doorframe. And the wall of shelves with bottles and jars from floor to ceiling, all of them carefully labeled and containing dried herbs and elixirs, golden, green, amber and black. The cooking quarters in the back have become a kind of pharmacy, and much that is distilled there comes from the gardens that Maria and Akila have carefully cultivated by the La Salle house. For the wild specimens Isaac and Pundi forage the island.

A group of mostly naked children are playing in the road not far from the house. They have become a particular torment to Isaac because their parents and their African caretakers have filled them with mumbo jumbo about this house. The island is a stewpot of superstitions.

The Africans have decided that Pundi is some kind of holy man, and that Isaac is his personal devil. They have endowed even the doorknob of the house with special powers, and the children of the village dare each other to run up and touch it. One little boy has told Maria that knocking on the door is considered a feat of special bravery. She knows how annoying Isaac finds this, and tried to look gravely at the child, but instead had burst out laughing.

Pundi, on the other hand, rarely hears them as he spends most of his time in the back, distilling medicines or meditating. Every morning early he does his ritual ablutions and says his prayers on a carpet under the kapok tree. He had carefully nurtured back to health a sick calf that came off one of the Danish ships, and all have come to love this gentle cow. In her, all of Pundi's Gods seem to live. He would not dream of eating meat, and carefully steps around insects he sees on the ground. She knows he is trying as best he can to adhere to the very strict traditions of Brahmins, but that much that he would do in India is impossible in these conditions. Nonetheless this tenderness for his fellow creatures has been imparted to Maria and Akila.

Isaac and Pundi are an odd sight as they wander the island looking for medicinal plants: Isaac looks far older than he actually is, with his wispy grey beard and watery blue eyes.

His skin is always fair because he keeps himself covered and wears a big floppy hat, and he is skinny and prematurely bent from searching the ground for medicinal plants. Pundi, on the other hand, is strikingly beautiful: tall and straight, always in white that is as clean as the beach sand. His brown eyes glow like coals, emanating a kind of effervescent joy; his skin is clear and golden and he has long slender fingers and the supple body of a yogi.

Maria's eye moves along the curve of the harbor closer to the Fort. She can see the bakery of Celine and Lucien with its thatched roof, and the two huts behind it. She imagines Bamadille putting a tray of bread loaves into one of the domed ovens in back, and Lucien with his bright red hair, waiting on the people in line. In front of the bakery is a large open courtyard with two lines of patrons, colorful dots in the distance. Next to the bakery at the water's edge are the island's two warehouses, one for the Danish West Indies Company and one for the Brandenburgers.

A mercantile shop is just beyond the line of sea grapes below her, at the foot of the Fort. Run by the company, it stocks most of the necessities of life, and often has other quite unusual things that come off the ships that anchor in the harbor. A barber next door advertises himself as an expert on remedies of all sorts, and does his business with the sailors in the port. Then comes the blacksmith, and the shoemaker across from the Von Bergens. There is an inn and more than one tavern, all along the main street, Konge Gade. Just below the high wall where she is standing, an old grove of sea grape bushes stands sentinel, twisted into tortured shapes by the easterly winds. This has become a town gathering spot, with the gallows beneath which Mette was flogged. It is here that the sightless heads of condemned pirates stand on pikes for weeks until their skulls are picked white and clean. It is a custom particularly repugnant to Maria that she brings up frequently to Pierre.

"What do you expect me to do? Just look at any harbor anywhere and you'll see the same thing."

On the hill just to the north of the Fort she can see her own house. There are quite a few other similar modest dwellings in the town, as the planters like to be close to the Fort in case of trouble with their slaves, or a possible Spanish invasion. At this moment the anxiety among the planters is particularly high because of the scarcity of White overseers for the plantations.

Hidden from Maria's view, her husband Pierre is on the wharf below, arguing with the captain of a ship that has just arrived in the harbor. His job is to inspect the cargo and make sure that any items that come off the ships are duly taxed, but his aim is to acquire a fine sofa for their salon, with matching side chairs, and several bolts of coral-colored damask fabric that he has spied. He has a passion for fabrics.

"But they have been commanded especially," says the Captain. "By whom?"

"Bordeaux. One David. A Frenchman."

"Ah, just tell him you couldn't get them. Perhaps next time." If he could have picked from all the people on the island to deprive of his furniture order, none could have pleased him so much as David Bordeaux, that damned nominee of the Brandenburgers. Even if he is related to Pierre by marriage.

The Captain makes no argument, seeing that argument will only raise the taxes he must pay on the rest of his cargo. Why doesn't he just go on to another port? one might ask. The answer is simple, if harsh. In all the other ports they are likely just to confiscate his cargo, claiming that he is a privateer, or a pirate, or working for a government they oppose; for the wars in Europe are so constant and shifting it is hard not to land in enemy territory. St. Thomas is resolutely neutral, and gaining a reputation as a place where you can at least sell your cargo, though a little palm greasing is inevitable. And Pierre's palm is always there, upturned and first.

"Que c'est magnifique!" Maria will exclaim when a clutch of sailors mounts their hill with the sofa and chairs held aloft. "Mais pourquoi? Why on earth do we need anything so fine in a place like this? Pierre, what are you thinking?"

"I am thinking they are beautiful and I like beautiful things. It gives me pleasure.

One has to get pleasure in life, no?"

Maria looks at him oddly. Who is this man, she thinks. Or is he just a boy? Will he always be just a boy?

"Pleasure? I think the Lord has other things in mind for us, putting us down in this place." Oh, what a scold I am, she thinks, and she goes over and runs her fingers through his curly hair and gives him a kiss, a kiss with just a suggestion of her tongue. Hinting at another kind of pleasure. But his attention is entirely on his sofa.

"I suppose we shall have to take great care not to get them dirty." And she sighs.

They serve their purpose though, those items of furniture. Pierre loves to entertain and now they have what feels like a real salon, even if the house is still something of a temporary affair. Pierre invites ship captains to dine regularly. He considers building these relationships a key part of his work, for he himself is a human hinge in the triangular trade. He has a finger in the slave trade, or perhaps one should say a fist. He is charged with getting the sugar cargoes onto Danish vessels bound for Copenhagen when the Company warehouses are full, and the returning vessels come filled with items needed by the settlers. Vessels arrive from all over the world looking to sell their cargoes, and Pierre helps them find a market, for a small percentage. The neutrality of Denmark in the War of the Grand Alliance allows him to buy and sell at a profit from captains who cannot sell directly to each other.

On this evening they have three captains at their table, Tappan from the Massachusetts Bay Colony, Bardewinkel from the slave ship *Christianborg*, and an Englishman named Montgomery with a mixed cargo from China and India. The table is elegantly laid: turquoise and gold plates from Limoges, silver from London. Candles light the small room, reflecting off mirrors that create the effect of an intimate group surrounded by an infinity of light and space. Still, the walls are wattle and daub, rough and unfinished, and it looks a bit like elaborate camping. All of the family slaves have a part to play in the serving, and they too are multiplied in the mirroring light. Anna has prepared a fine fish stew with conch and turtle. The bread is fresh from the bakery, and the wine a fine stock of Bordeaux. The conversation focuses on Danish difficulties on the west coast of Africa, and Captain Bardewinkel is holding the floor.

"It happened last June, and it couldn't have happened without the complicity of the Accra. So shameful for the Danes, the way they were tricked." Bardewinkel looks down at his plate and pauses for dramatic effect.

"A band of warriors from the Akwamu capital just walked into Fort Christianborg claiming to have come to trade. Their leader was Assemeni, a slave who had run away not long before and who knew the whole fort. They were unbelievably cruel. They quartered the merchant and killed the others. They cut the tendons of Harding Petersen's thighs so he couldn't run away and threw him in the latrine. But he did escape, and dragged himself for two days to the Dutch fort.

"But the amazing thing is that Assemeni behaved as if he owned the place, and ran it just as the Danes had. He put on the commandant's uniform and started hosting fancy dinners, and made people salute him as if he were the governor. He hosted dinners for the Dutch and English forts, and they say the food was excellent. Assemeni had been the cook at an English fort. But I understand it lasted only a few months and now the Danes have taken it back."

"That is an appalling story." Pierre is staring at Bardewinkel in disbelief. "What kind of idiots do they have running Fort Christianborg? How are we to manage this place if we cannot get a good and steady source of slaves? We can produce a modest amount of cotton and tobacco, but sugar is where the money is to be made, and that requires a lot of manpower."

Maria is cringing at her end of the table and cannot keep silent. "But where will it all end? How can you enslave so many and not expect them to rise up and murder you in your bed one day? Is there nothing but money to be thought of here?"

"Oh, my dear, soft-hearted wife. You cannot stand in the way of this. Slavery has been with us since the beginning of time. Look with your own eyes. The Africans make constant war and end up enslaving one another. They used to sell us gold for glass beads, and now they sell us their captives."

"That doesn't make it right. Can we not have any hope for the progress of civilization?"

Pierre sees that this conversation is not headed in a good direction and changes topic to the tensions among the European powers and the likelihood of the falling apart of the Grand Alliance.

"Speaking plainly, war among the European powers only makes St. Thomas a better place to trade," he ventures. "As long as Denmark stays neutral, war in Europe is our making here." At this moment Akila enters the room for the first time. She carries the tureen of stew, and leans in between the diners, smiling at each in turn. When she looks into the face of Bardewinkel she is suddenly immobilized, as if turned to stone. She recognizes the face of her babbling banana-talk captain, the man who saved her…and whom she betrayed. When she comes to her senses, it is all she can do not to scream and run from the room. She clutches the soup tureen with all her strength and slowly straightens up.

"Excuse me, Madame," she says to Maria. "I must excuse myself,' she stammers again, and flees to the kitchen. A moment later Anna emerges with a smile and a refreshed tureen.

The conversation continues as if nothing had happened, though Maria is momentarily concerned about Akila. But she is soon distracted by the conversation, for there is nothing more interesting than the palaver of sea captains. They come bearing nuggets of news from around the world.

"The Ayas in Whydah are becoming the biggest traders in Africa now," Bardewinkel hazards. "They are such greedy bastards they would sell their own wives."

"Well, if we can't get slaves from Fort Christianborg perhaps we'll look to them."

Pierre leans back in his chair and Maria inwardly cringes, imaging the chair splintering under his weight and almost wishing it would. She turns to Captain Tappan and says, "And what is the news from New England?"

"Oh, the Bay Colony has been in a most peculiar uproar." Tappan is a straight-up New Englander, a ramrod of a man with a mop of white hair and a face like a leather fire bucket. "A great hysteria broke out in Salem village, all started by a rambunctious flock of young girls. They accused many in the village of witchcraft and twenty have been executed. It spread like a fire, first one accused one and then that one accused another, and so on, 'til in all there were more than two hundred accused. One man was pressed to death under stones. The doings went on for over a year, with twelve magistrates presiding and witches flying on broomsticks around the court room."

"How astonishing," Maria says staring at him. "I have never heard of such a thing in the Americas. What did you say these witches were accused of doing?"

"Oh, all manner of things. Flying around on broomsticks, pinching the children. In truth, anything the children could think up in a moment, if you want my opinion. But t'was taken very seriously by the justices, as if it were a threat to the colony itself, an invasion of the dark powers."

"People can come up with strange ideas. And none stranger than here on the island.

Here we have such a mix of superstitions that every tree and rock has a magical power to someone. My old tutors are considered to have magical powers by many on the island. One is from Spain and one from India, and between them their knowledge of plants is astonishing…and to some magical. But it is not magic at all, just knowledge, accumulated over a lifetime in seafaring places."

"In places like this there are so many beliefs that they cancel each other out, so to speak," Bardewinkel avers. "But in New England the Puritans are a rigid people who see the devil at work in many things. You give a much more delightful dinner party than any you would find at a table in Boston. I daresay they would see the devil in your mirrors!"

The conversation goes late into the evening, and Maria has almost forgotten Akila when the guests depart. She takes an oil lamp and goes out back to the cookhouse to give her compliments to Anna. Akila is sitting on a stool by her hut. She has her gris-gris clutched in her hand. Maria looks at her, and then at the gris-gris.

"Are you all right, 'Keela? Who are you going to use that on? What happened tonight?"

"How can you invite the master of a slave ship to your house?" Akila hisses. Maria's hand flies up to her face, suddenly aflame. A retort flies into her mind, quickly followed by the image of a witch on a broomstick. "Am I just like all the other slave masters then?" she thinks. "Sliding into the mud of this awful place."

She puts the oil lamp on the ground and squats by Akila, her gown in the dust. "You know Pierre does the inviting. But how did you know that Bardewinkel was a slave captain?"

"He was my captain."

"Oh Lord." Maria gasps as if she would choke. "…oh forgive me Akila. Please forgive me." She buries her face in her hands.

Akila is sitting rigidly, which Maria interprets as anger. But Akila's feelings are much more complex than just anger. She takes a deep breath and pushes the dirt around with her toes. "He behaved very strangely to me. I was near death in the hold and seeing that, he had me brought to his cabin. There was a monkey there, I remember. Oh, I so remember that monkey. It was trying to cheer me up and I couldn't help but laugh. The captain was kind to me. He had me bathed. He fed me when I was starving." And then, as if remembering herself, she added, "Of course, I was starving because of him." She pauses. "But you can see, my feelings about this particular captain are mixed. But they are not mixed about other captains of slave ships, I can assure you of that. I know you can't prevent Pierre from inviting whoever he wishes, but please do not ask me to serve another slave ship captain."

Maria's voice is barely audible. "I don't suppose he recognized you."

"I am sure not. Would you have? Remember what I looked like then? I was hardly alive, and so skinny…"

Maria takes Akila's hand and holds it on her left palm. With her right hand she traces the raised veins that run like rivers on its back, lightly with her finger. The gris-gris lies limp in Akila's lap, a red tangle of cloth with a small head. A little like a child's well-loved toy, but more sinister.

With a great sigh Maria says, "You are so precious to me, Keela…my sister really." She looks up at the stars. "We live in a dangerous place." The cacophony of tree frogs suddenly seems to her a threatening sound. "How strange that a place so beautiful can be so ruined by greed. I fear for us, for our friendship. We must try to make ourselves invisible, or so useful to people that they will have to protect us. And I will make sure you are never exposed to another slave ship captain, or any other hurt that I have the power to prevent."

Akila puts her arm around Maria.

"You are probably the most powerful woman on the island, do you know that? There's no way you're going to make yourself invisible. You are the only one who is living any kind of free life. The rest are either slaves to their husbands or china dolls cared for by their slaves." The shadows dance around them in the lamplight.

Akila sighs and goes on. "But even so, what can a woman do against the forces that are aligned in this place? If it is true that even the Whydah chiefs are involved in this trade, and others too, it is too dark and ugly and evil to imagine, and we are surrounded by it."

After a long silence Maria picks up the conversation quietly. "Well, we have Isaac and Pundi to learn from. That is the big difference for us. Look how much we know about what is growing here. Everyone else is surrounded by it but all they think of is sugar and tobacco."

"Oh Mari, I feel so much guilt at what my people are suffering here. And that I can do nothing." Akila puts her hands on Maria's shoulders as she says this, and looks her in the eye. "You are right, we are fortunate to have Isaac and Pundi, to be able to learn and to cure. But there can be no forgetting in this place that I am your slave. And that we are both women."

Akila throws back her head and laughs, casting an eerie shadow. "But then, I'm not really your slave… You can't even own me. I'm Pierre's." She draws Maria into her arms and hugs her tight for a long moment. Releasing her, she pushes the dirt around with her toes.

"We are like sisters at one level, but at another we are worlds apart, and in my world I must fight against the terrible things I see. Truly, I have no idea how to do it. Seeing that captain was a sharp reminder not to get too comfortable. And I will not let you get too comfortable either. We have work to do somehow, and your Lord and my Allah will no doubt put it in front of us."

Not long after this, Maria pays a visit to Mrs. von Bergen, one of her few real friends on the island. There are only thirty-five or forty inhabitants in the village, and it is naturally a gossipy place. She has stayed in touch with Mrs. von Bergen and times her visits at moments she thinks her son Lucas will not be at home. Lucas von Bergen has grown ever more repellent to Maria as he becomes a bigger and bigger plantation owner. She marvels that his wife can stand him.

Lucas had wed Margaretha von Runnels the same year Maria had moved out of their household and married Pierre. It is a burning mystery to her how Margaretha not only tolerates his grumpiness and violent temper but seems almost amused by his behavior. But then, she and Margaretha are complete opposites. Perhaps he is a good lover, Maria muses with a sigh.

Margaretha lives the life of all the plantation wives of St. Thomas, sitting in her salon, receiving visitors, being fanned by Mimba. She was born to a position of privilege and never gives it a second thought. Maria is quite sure that she feeds the wags of Charlotte Amalie on tales of Maria's wild life of roaming the island on horseback. But they are on friendly terms because of Maria's long relationship with the family, and because Maria is on friendly terms with everyone. She is often lectured by the other plantation women of the island on her shocking behavior, but such chastisements bother her not in the least. On the contrary, she feels considerable sympathy for the constrictions that these women seem to feel obliged to live by. It makes her almost glad that she has had no mother to drill her in the behavioral niceties that tie other women in knots. Celine clucks at her occasionally, but she is too busy and tired with the bakery to do much chastisement.

Mimba's girth has nearly doubled since Maria first came to live with them eight years ago. She lumbers now, and Maria can see the pain in her movements. Clearly Margaretha cannot. She sits in her shimmering aqua silk gown with her blond hair arranged in a waterfall of curls— Is she planning on going to a ball this morning?—and issues commands that keep Berti running back and forth during the entire visit.

"I must show you this gorgeous chest that came on the *Henri V* from France last week. Really, you should take advantage of the prices these days and put in an order."

"Pierre does enough of that for the two of us, I assure you." Maria grimaces at the thought.

"Are you still riding around the island with that slave woman of yours? You are the talk of the town, and I don't mean in a good way. Really Maria, I tell you this for your own good. People are really horrified by the way you go gallivanting about. Wearing pants I heard the other day! How could you?"

Maria put her head back and laughed, a happy chuckle.

"And how could you not? That is what I ask. It is so beautiful, our island. The newborn turtles will be hatching and digging their way out for their walk to the sea soon. And we have another family of petrels being born in Botany Bay. There is so much good work to be done!

Surely God does not mean for us to sit all day and do nothing. So many people need our help. And as to that, where is your mother-in-law? Does she need a salve for her rheumatism? I got a beautiful bright yellow powder from India off one of the ships the other day. It's very good for what ails her."

"She is just rising at the moment, but she'll be along soon. She knows that you are here and would never miss seeing you."

Finally, Maria goes off in search of Mrs. von B. and finds her sitting at her dressing table staring in the mirror.

"You are still beautiful, dear friend. Come join us in the salon. You know I can't make conversation for very long with Margaretha," she whispers.

"Oh, I so wish Lucas had married you, dear Maria," Mrs. von B. whispers back. You are full of God's spirit, and that is in short supply here on this island, to be sure. But I fear for you. There are so many who wish you ill out of jealousy. People are so full of envy. I think they envy your fearlessness."

Maria looks at her thoughtfully. "I will take care. Don't you worry. In any case, I have no choice. I couldn't live my life any other way." And putting her hands lightly on Mrs. von B.'s shoulders, she bends and touches her lips to her forehead.

Chapter Nineteen: In the Stable

Copenhagen, December 1770

I have learned to read the state of Uncle Thomas' mind from the sound of his approach in the hallway. Tonight it is quick and percussive, and when I see him throw down his hat I know he is agitated. I am sitting with Johanne doing embroidery. Phebe is working in the kitchen.

"He has fired Bernsdorff, the head of the Council," Thomas says evenly, with no preamble.

"Who, my dear," says Johanne absently, absorbed in her needlework. "Why Struensee, of course."

"Oh yes, I knew about that. But it was not Struensee. It was the King." She sighs as if in wonderment at his ignorance. "Bernsdorff has ruled the Council forever. He has had his turn."

Thomas stares at her. "You are very well informed." His tone is very even. But he is looking at her in a funny way.

She finally looks up from her sewing. "There was a card game in the Queen's quarters today. She told us all about the King's decision. It was she who was very well informed."

"Well of course she is!" Thomas finally breaks the boundaries of his composure. "She plans these things with Struensee. Together they inspire the King to action. They have become quite the trio. Not that I think much of Bernsdorff, but there is something a little unsavory in the manipulation of our crown by a foreigner."

Johanne pouts good humoredly. "Oh, I don't think it is manipulation…More like inspiration. Bringing us out of the dark ages with the new ideas of Europe. Denmark will be first in this and it will be a remarkable thing. But how astonishing that Bernsdorff is gone."

Thomas slings his scarlet jacket onto the arm of the sofa and sinks into his usual chair. "It is not so easy as that. Bernsdorff represents the rich and the powerful."

I pick up the jacket and hang it on a hook by the door. "Do you not like the Doctor?" I ask as I sit down next to him.

"Liking him is not the issue. He has taken too much power unto himself and he is manipulating the King, and the Queen."

"But don't you think they agree with his ideas?" I hear my voice rising and I take a breath and modulate my tone. "I do. I am sure of it…and honestly Uncle, I think you agree with them too! You have always been on the side of the poor and oppressed against the rich."

"You are quite right in that, Summy." He looks at me for a long moment, pensively. "I am not against the reforms, but I know they will not stand, and there will be trouble. Those who are losing power will say that a foreigner has taken over our government. And they will not be far from right." He sighs and stares out the window at the lights of the city in the distance.

"I see what you are saying, but still, we should not back away from doing what's right."

Johanne inhales loudly and says "We certainly should not! And we should most certainly support our sovereigns!"

My anxiety mounts as I sense the rift opening between them. My uncle must have felt the same way for he exhaled loudly and said, "Well, let's talk of something else. Did you have a good ride?"

"Oh, more than good… a lovely day." I sigh deeply, as if I could exhale all the confusion of that day. My heart is beating so hard I cannot fathom that no one has noticed. To cover it I start blathering, "So clear and crisp, and not too awfully cold. Heinrich put me on his beautiful Palfrey, Cunegonde. He rode Voltaire! Isn't that amusing? We rode along the sea… in and out of the surf."

"Voltaire! I guess we know which side he is on!" Uncle smiles a little absently, and then looks up at Phebe standing in the doorway with a plate of biscuits. "And what did you do Phebe?"

"I stayed here and did the chores that Johanne had asked me to do. You will be able to see your reflection in your spoon at supper." She cocks her head with a little smile. Johanne is glowing, and I am suddenly sure that it about more than polished silver.

After supper Phebe and I retreat to my room. I sit on the stool in front of my dressing table, looking at myself in the mirror as Phebe twists her fingers through the plaits in my hair to release them. She takes the silver brush and starts up from my neck, taking long strokes. We have done this ritual since we were small girls, and I know just how to tilt my head in a well- understood sequence.

We had started the day in her room, a tiny closet of a place. She had done my hair up while I watched the comings and goings on the glass bridge, which could been seen through the slit that she has for a window. Since the sun does not rise until almost mid-morning, I watch a parade of people crossing the candlelit bridge. I am always, at the edge of my consciousness, watching for Struensee.

Phebe and I are to be tutored together that morning by the French tutor, Philippe.

Phebe has impressed him with her quickness…it is all so new and fresh for her. I can see that she gets pleasure from learning, that the balance of her spirit has returned in some measure. I am delighted by this, for I would have felt a terrible failure had she gone home. And I would have been so alone. I have taken Dr. Struensee's chastisements to heart and have tried to be much more attentive to her needs.

"Would you like to go to the stables with me later?" I had asked her. "Oh yes."

"I'll be riding with Heinrich. It might be boring for you."

"I am sure I'll find something interesting to do. Perhaps they will let me groom the horses. It's better in any case than staying here."

Our morning lessons with Phillippe completed, I help Phebe with her chores to speed us along. She helps me dress for riding in my green multi-layered costume with the secret pants underneath. She throws on her black cape over her grey dress and ties a red scarf around her head, knotted in the back. When we step out into the cold, her face and chin glow in the sharp winter light, and I am struck by how handsome she is…and I am fretting about leaving her alone in the stable.

"You know I'm always happy to have you with me. I'm sorry you can't ride too."

She looks off in the other direction and says, "Look, there's ice on the canal. Let's try skating one day."

We push open the stable door and the warm smell of hay and horses envelops us. Antoine, the stable hand, is rubbing oil into a saddle. I had met him the first time I went riding with Heinrich. He is French and an excellent horseman, the assistant riding master. His blue eyes dance over Phebe with unmistakable pleasure as we walk in. Phebe freezes when she sees him. And then her face glows as if she had been suddenly taken by fever.

"It's you!" She gazes at him for a long moment and whispers. "This is the man who rescued me on the wharf that day." Her face is alive with delighted surprise. He comes over to her and takes her hand. For a moment I am speechless.

"Well, this is a pleasure." His eyes are riveted on hers. "I never thought to see you again. Are you going riding?"

I step forward. "It's I who will be riding," I manage to say. "But this is so amazing… that you are the kind stranger who rescued Phebe the other day! If I had only known I would have sent my thanks directly! I am riding today with Count von Brockdorff… We were hoping that Phebe could stay here with you? Maybe help you groom the horses?"

He shifts his gaze to me, as if waking from a dream. "Why, of course…not that she has to do anything. And the Count is already here. Out in the paddock. I'll bring Cunegonde out for you." He leads Cunegonde from her stall, and I follow him out and wave to Heinrich.

"Levez-vous!" Antoine says, giving me a boost into the saddle. I wave back at him as Heinrich and I trot off.

That Phebe should have a romance of her own comes as a complete surprise to me. I am embarrassed to admit this, but it always seemed to me that a Black woman would likely not be attracted to a White man. Though I certainly knew the reverse is not true. And as far as I am aware, Beppo is the only Black man at court. That night as she brushes my hair, the two of us trade secrets and Phebe tells me in some detail of what happened next in the stable.

"I watched you ride away with Heinrich and warmed myself in that beautiful sun on a bench. Then Antoine sat down beside me and I teased him a little.

"'What about all that work you had to do?' I asked him in my embarrassing French.

"'You can help me.' And he took my hand as he said that and held it in his. Such a big, commanding hand and so warm…I felt slightly panicked…little butterflies in my stomach. Then he pulled me up to standing and smiled the loveliest smile. We were almost the same height and for a moment I could hardly breathe. The air was so charged between us I had to break the silence, so I said, 'Let me groom Blitzen, will you?'

"So then I spent time in the stall stroking Blizen's flanks and patting his nose, watching his breath drifting in little clouds in the air. I looked into Blitzen's brown eyes and said, 'You and I are the only ones around here with brown eyes, Blitzen.' When I turned around Antoine was smiling at me—glowing, actually, with a kind of yearning look on his face.

"Then he said, 'How odd the world is, the way we get deposited like pebbles on strange shores, far from home. Do you miss your home, Phebe?'

"And then in a rush he said, 'I love the color of your skin. You are a beautiful woman.'"

"So I told him that it's dangerous to be beautiful if you're a slave. And he replied, very earnestly, that I was safe with him. And I believed him. It felt sincere."

"He told me he had been here since he was twelve. A member of the Danish court noticed him at Fontainebleau six years ago. His father knew an opportunity when he saw it, and indentured him to the man. It was one less mouth to feed, and the chance for Antoine to learn a trade in the company of kings. Antoine said his father was sad to see him go, as he was the least dull-witted of all his children." Phebe giggles.

"He looked so sad when he said, 'Who knows if I will ever see him again? I miss him, but things were not good in France then. People were starving in the countryside and getting a son away from it all must have seemed like a good idea.'

"And have you been happy here?" I looked into his eyes and felt that this was a man I could trust.

"I am grateful to my father for letting me come here, though I miss my family, and France, greatly. The Danes are so cold and tidy. Their food is cold too. But at least they have some, so I can forgive my father for sending me here. Someday I will go back to France, though.

It is a beautiful country. But now it is a terrible place to be. A very few people are very, very rich, and many people are starving. But that cannot last forever. Maybe I will go back and help change it. What about you? Do you miss your home?"

"Yes,' I said, 'I do miss my home, I miss my people, my mama most of all. But so does Summy, we are not so different in that. I told him I envied him the freedom to think that someday returning will be possible, that even if I return home, I will always be a slave."

"'Oh no,' he said. 'I am sure you will one day be free. Change is coming. That Dr. Struensee is bringing it at the speed of Blitzen here.' I was quite surprised that he knew about Dr. Struensee.

"'So you know about him too?' I said. 'And what do you think will happen? Don't you think they will just punish him for it in the end? People don't like to give things up, and especially not their power."

"'Maybe, but once freedoms are given, they are hard to take away. His ideas will ultimately prevail even if he does not, because they are fair and just. And look around you. Here the slaves are called serfs. They are not Africans, they are Danes, and in France they are French. What is happening is the beginning of the end of slavery.'

"'I cannot imagine people giving up their slaves in the islands though. They have bought them with hard money.'

Phebe imitates Antoine blowing out through his lips like a horse whinnying. "'That will be harder. But slaves have feet. They can run.'

"'Oh sure,' I say, "until they cut off their feet.' "Antoine looked down at his hands and was silent at that.

"Then he said, 'It is unimaginable to me, what they do to slaves in the islands. I am glad you are here. You must never go back.'

"'But it is my home. My family is there.'

"'Still it is no life.' He just stood looking at me… Oh Summy, such a look as I have never seen before. Then he puts his arm around me, tilts my head up and kisses me. He is tender, as if he is breathing life into something frail. And I confess I kissed him back. It was a lovely kiss and went on ever so long. Then he finally held me away from him and smiled and said, 'Now let's get you on a horse.'

"So I got to go riding too."

I sit silently for a long moment, smiling at her in the mirror, hoping that the surge of confused feelings rushing through me does not show on my face. Jealousy, love, fear; and yes, just a touch of anger. What is that all about? She is adept at reading my expressions, but this one is beyond us both.

"Are you surprised?" she teases. "That such a handsome man could find me attractive."

"Of course not, you are beautiful. Maybe I'm just a little jealous. Antoine's much handsomer than Heinrich." This is true, but I am startled to hear myself say it out loud. I realize in that instant that while I am enjoying myself with Heinrich, I would never want to make my life here in Denmark with him. And I am truly surprised to learn that Phebe is attracted to a White man…and embarrassed at my own naïveté.

"I know you had fun too," she replies. "You can't tell me otherwise. Your mouth was red as a beet when you came back. And he is handsome, in that Danish way."

I put my hands over my face. "Oh how mortifying." And then I blurt out, "Well, you are beautiful. But be careful. You know you could never have him and he knows it too, so you can't be anything but a dalliance for him." The moment I speak I know it was a mistake. All our comradery is shattered. Phebe's tone shifts.

"Well, a dalliance is better than nothing. Even a slave needs the love of a man." She sinks back onto the bed as she says this. But I hear the edge in her voice and am suddenly flooded with guilt and confusion.

"You won't be a slave forever, dear Phebe." I look off into empty space over Phebe's shoulder, a solid wall of ancestors rising up in front of me. "When I grow up, I will make you free." I utter this with such fierce determination that Phebe turns around, as if fearful that someone is listening. She turns back to me and smiles, sighing deeply.

"You know, what will really happen is that I will belong to your husband." We look at each other, and a gloom starts to settle over us both.

Chapter Twenty: The Hurricane

St. Thomas, July 1694

The sofa and chairs become the center of Pierre's attention in July when a ferocious hurricane hits the island. The terror of the event knocks the fear of slave revolts and Spanish invasions out of every mind on the island, save for the slaves themselves, who long to find a way to capitalize on the opportunity nature's destruction presents.

A violent wind begins in the early evening of July 20th and rages ferociously 'til about ten o'clock, when the eye looks down upon St. Thomas and gives its citizens false hope that the end of the storm is at hand. But then it returns with redoubled fury, illuminating the island with the eerie hot light of rapid-fire lightning, and hurling whole trees and thatched roofs through the air. The air is filled with the screeching and wailing of the wind as it sheers houses right off their foundations. It whirls so it sweeps the ocean up in funnels and dumps the brackish rain in torrents on the land, polluting all the fresh water sources that are not in covered barrels. Lightning strikes the thatch of the roofs and sets them afire, and then the wind takes them like fiery meteors and hurls them through the air.

The La Salle house is under the lee of the mountain, slightly more sheltered than most homes. There are caves in the hills above the town, and many have fled there for shelter. Others have gone to the Fort. But those farther out on the island have fewer options.

Pierre stands wailing over his sofa as the rain comes in sheets through the house. He is so stunned by the force of the storm that his focus on these small possessions is an aberration of his mind, his way of managing the enormity of what is happening. He had meant to have some sailcloth ready for such a storm, but this one came so early, a full month before the usual hurricane season. Maria kneels in the center of the room, her entire attention on the wrath of her Lord. Her mind is whipping through all the things that have happened in this filthy place that have provoked Him. Her cheeks grow hot with shame at the thought that this very morning, she had made an idle prayer to her Lord to send some relief from the tedium of her life. Was this His answer?

She is not alone in this somewhat animist approach to faith. In this ugly moment, every person from slave to sea captain is seeing the hand of whatever devil or divinity they conjure, to be directly at work. Their own sins rise before them with awesome clarity, as the world they have known comes tumbling down, and their possessions fly through the air to bash a neighbor on the head.

Maria pauses in her prayer long enough to look up at Pierre.

"Oh, Lord love you. Leave it, Pierre. It is only an object. How can you be so attentive to a sofa when the Lord has you in the palm of His hand and is shaking you to your very boots….and all the rest of us. What must we have done to provoke this mighty fury?"

Maria gropes for Akila's hand as she says this, but Akila is holding Jean-Baptiste in her arms. The man is shaking so she can hardly hold him. Anna has wailing baby Cate held tightly in her lap with her hands clapped over the child's ears. Beside her Marcus is alternately muttering in Wolof and keening in astonished terror. Only Samuel is silent in the tumult. He stands as if bronzed, his eyes wide staring at the debris swirling around the house. He has gone to the spirit world to bargain.

Maria pauses in her prayers to shout over the wind. "What about Celine? Isaac and Pundi? Do you suppose they have found shelter? Pundi would have insisted on taking in that cow of his. Oh… There are so many ill-protected."

She is thinking that truly, this place is damned for its evil, for the enslavement of human beings, for the piracy and theft that goes on, for the ugliness of warfare all around them and the profiteering done from it. As if in response to her thoughts, a bolt of lightning strikes close to the house with a light so blinding and a noise so deafening that she thinks they are on fire and gone to hell.

When at last the wind stops howling and the rain abates, there is an ironic resumption of sunshine, complete with a rainbow, as if all the various gods that represent this small populace have conspired together to mock it. A sense of relief floods every living soul that sees the daylight. Indeed, as human beings will, many decide that they are among the select to have been spared death.

But the daylight illuminates a most appalling scene of destruction, the bodies of the unfortunate are washed up on the beaches in a jumble of splintered ships. Others are lying in the streets. Hardly a house is left standing or a ship left at anchor. The roof has been sheared off the Company warehouse. The living bury the dead as quickly as they can dig graves, for the fear of pestilence is powerful. The bugle is blown at the Fort signaling the need for the able-bodied to present themselves, and Lorentz puts Pierre in charge of organizing them into work crews.

Celine had been hit by flying debris as she tried to cross to Bamadille's shelter to help him. She died instantly from the blow. Maria is devastated. She folds herself into a tiny ball and sobs uncontrollably for an hour at the news. But then Pundi appears and sits beside her and puts his arm around her.

"Talk to me about her. She is the last remaining person from your childhood, an important person."

"Oh, if only I had spent more time telling her just how important she was to me. Do you know, Pundi, in those last months in France she must have been preparing me for the idea that I would have to leave. I know she had many long talks with my father, and I rather think she loved him. She began to play a game with me, a game about going on a trip.

"She would declare that we were going to pretend we were going to a very cold place. And we would go to the attic and find all our winter mufflers and capes and mittens. I would try them all on before the glass and admire myself, picking the softest, snuggliest things I could find. 'Isn't this the most delicious color, Cici?' I would say, swinging my rose cape around me. That's what I always called her when I was little, Cici.

"'A lovely color Mimi, 'she would reply, 'but do you think it is quite warm enough for the land of ice and night?' She always called me Mimi in those days. We'd then discuss in a very grown-up fashion the relative warmth of all those items, until we were satisfied with my wardrobe. Then she would say something like, 'Do you think perhaps we should bring presents to give to the people we might meet along the way?'

"And I would exclaim, 'Oh, yes. Let's bring them some of our honey. 'Perhaps a pot of mustard too.' She would add, 'And some lavender soap? I think perhaps we should pack some herbs from the garden and some tinctures, in case anyone gets sick.'

"'And my dolls? We must make room for them, too, and bring some very warm clothes for them.'

"'Of course, but we cannot take them all. You must pick the one you love most. And I will show you how to sew our gold coins carefully into our clothes so we will always have some money to spend, but no one will know where it is. We must keep it well hidden.'

"And so each day we picked an outfit in which to sew our coins. This went on for many afternoons and at the end of the day, the trunk would be packed and we would go downstairs and have hot cider. Then, in the evening Celine would empty the trunk, putting all the warm clothes away to one side, but keeping out those items in which the gold and diamonds had been sewn. She sat by candlelight and reinforced all my wobbly stitches so that all the treasure was secure and well hidden. She had one of the manservants make leather belts for us with hidden pockets, also filled with gold coins.

"And then, the next day she would declare it was just the sort of day for a tropical island and she would describe the sandy beaches and waving palm trees that she had heard the sailors on the coast describe.

"And I would say, 'Oh I would so much rather go there than to an icy place, Cici. I suppose it will always be like summer and I shall pack my prettiest chemises and slippers, though perhaps we should have to take some warmer things for the evening. Do you think there will be parties there? Shall we take our party clothes?'"

Maria's voice cracks and she looks at Pundi, wiping the tears from her eyes. "And here we are on this cruel tropical island."

"She loved you so much, you know." Pundi gently sweeps a stray curl out of Maria's eyes. "She would want you to be strong. Now you must breathe, in and out, and move quietly into action. There is death all around us and much more waiting if we do nothing." He rises from the couch and gestures to Maria to follow. "Come with me. Bring Akila and Samuel. We have important work to do. We must set up a place for the injured, of which there are many. And there will be much sickness to follow. I know it well from the typhoons of my own country. One thing follows another like night the day. We must bury the dead first, for there are many others besides Celine, and then we will set to work."

Samuel, Bamadille, Marcus and Jean-Baptiste working together dig a large grave in a shady spot just west of Maria's house on the edge of the town. There is no time for individual graves; they must work fast in this climate. The soil is rocky and the digging difficult. They dig first with shovels and then lift bucket after bucket out of the deepening hole, until Maria signals them to stop. Maria and Akila have together washed Celine's body and wrapped her in the soft white cloth in which she will rest in the earth. They have prepared the bodies of four men as well, soldiers and sailors far from home and family. The soil replaced, Maria puts conch shells in the shape of an angel on the earth above the grave, for Celine had loved their shiny pink interiors.

In the meantime, a hospital camp is set up on the beach to the east of the Fort. Canvas tents are strung up among the palm trees at the edge of the beach, made from the salvaged sails of ships that have gone aground. A work crew from the Fort is assigned to help bring the injured from across the island to the makeshift hospital. The patients come with broken limbs and infected wounds that threaten to become gangrenous if not treated properly. The four of them, with Pierre and Samuel in regular attendance, will be many weeks at the camp.

A routine is gradually established. They rotate their night duty, sleeping in four-hour shifts. Pundi goes down the beach for an hour each day and sits quietly, meditating, and then does a series of yoga postures. Maria watches him out of the corner of her eye as she struggles to make her huge tangle of hair behave. It is as curly as an African's, though quite different in texture, and she can make it into a variety of architectural wonders when time permits. But for now it must just be tied up and put in a turban. That done, she fetches wood for the fire, and mangos and papayas for breakfast. Many islanders bring baskets of food for their relatives, which are shared around.

Each new morning the sick and injured stream down the winding dirt path to the beach. Each afternoon brings a torrential fifteen-minute rain; nothing ever dries completely. They treat everyone who comes, slaves and planters, the young and the old, all lying miserably on their canvas cots under the open tents that spread from palm tree to palm tree. From the first moment, they have to decide whether to separate the slaves from the planters and soldiers. Maria wants to put each new patient in the next cot to the last, no matter what the race. "They are all mortal, and no different in the eyes of God, surely."

Akila is of a different opinion. "This is no time for teaching lessons. It's a time for healing. The Africans will be miserable among their masters, and I daresay the same would be true of the planters." They all look at Isaac.

"Well, that is for certain" he mutters, "so I will decide the case. We shall separate them. Do you agree Pundi?" Isaac looks out across the glitter of sunlight on the water as he says this, as if he expects to find Pundi walking there.

"Yes, we must certainly separate them. Everyone is always separated in India and it keeps things from spreading one to the other."

"That makes no sense, since they are all sick, but I am outnumbered." Maria lifts her skirts and walks into the waves lapping the white sand. She turns back to go to work as another cart rolls onto the beach.

Pierre de Malleville is among their first patients to be treated. Unable to walk, he is brought in a cart in terrible pain by two of his slaves. Isaac gives him a shot of rum and moves the bones around to see if they make the grating noise that indicates a break. Despite Pierre's screams, it seems a clean break, to Isaac's relief. Pundi readies a splint and Maria, the bandages, and they all go at him, Akila holding him as still as she can.

The next day Anna Magdalena Morgen, in a feverish state of forgetfulness of her miserable marriage, begs Pundi to lie with her there on her cot and relieve the itch of her body and soul. Maria, tending the woman next to her, pretends to be looking for something under the cot to hide the laughter exploding inside her. Pundi, with deadly seriousness, tries to calm Anna, who clings to him.

"Help me here," he whispers to Maria urgently. "She won't let go." And Maria, with the air of the nursing angel, comes to the rescue, removes Anna's hand from his wrist and takes it in her own, sitting down beside her. She rummages in her satchel for her Bible and reads some psalms quietly to the weeping woman, thinking all the while of her own marriage. "Nothing is perfect…or maybe we just don't see God's perfect plan," she says to Anna, and then she adds, "Think of all your beautiful children." Maria inhales deeply to quiet her own heartsickness. She has so far not been able to conceive a child…and has had very little opportunity to try.

She murmurs, "Pierre is quite adorable compared to Adolph Morgen. It is probably I who am at fault. He is not tempted by me."

One August day, just as the sun is setting in the bay, a Dr. Galanos, the surgeon from the Portuguese galleon *Santo Antonio*, which lies in the harbor, appears in the camp with two precious gifts. The first is a bottle of opium, extracted from Indian poppies.

He bows before Isaac. "I have great sympathy for the disaster that has befallen you here. We were just far enough away to have escaped the worst of the storm. As it happens, I have an ample supply of opium on board and I think it may be of use to you, so please let me offer it. A pity you do not have the plant here." Looking into his handsome Sephardic face, Isaac is flooded with gratitude, and a longing for his own people.

He smiles broadly at the man, and scratching his beard says, "Oh no, it would be the only thing they'd grow, and we'd have that on our conscience as well as all the other iniquities of this place. My friend Dr. Pundit grows a little ganja and we are experimenting with its properties. Quite remarkable…"

Dr. Galanos waves away a swarm of mosquitoes. "There must be an abundance of medicinal plants here on St. Thomas," he replies, spitting out a tiny bug.

"To be sure. I would be pleased to show you some of them if you have the time. I am hoping one day to make preparations to be used in Europe, and to develop my own shipping business."

It is the first time Isaac has voiced this thought that has been rumbling around in the back of his mind. The surgeon cocks his head and smiles. "You could have quite a business. I'd be delighted to help you if you need shipping connections."

The second gift is a pair of carrier pigeons.

"I hope they are not too burdensome. They don't eat much, but I think you will find them very useful here on this mountainous island where transport is so difficult. If you have need of regular communication with another place on the island, where your women assistants are located, for example, you can set up their food in one location, and their nesting cage in another. They will fly back and forth, and you can attach messages to this little clip on the foot. They are very trainable, and this pair will mate and produce offspring."

Isaac's impassive face breaks into a wide grin and he shouts to Pundit. Moments later the three of them are gathered around the cage, looking at the beautiful iridescent birds.

Isaac bows deeply to Dr Galanos. "You cannot imagine how valuable these will be to us. Please join us around the fire for a while, and perhaps something to eat."

"Let me have a look at your patients first." They walk around to each of the tents and inspect the sick together.

Later they sit at the fire long into the night, talking.

"It is evident that the Africans are much sicker than most of the Whites," Dr. Galanos observes.

"It is chiefly because they have so little to nourish them, and they are worked so hard.

In truth it is remarkable that they survive at all, given their circumstances, but then few of them live until their thirtieth year. Yet they do seem to get fewer of the fevers than the planters."

"Tell me about yourself, Isaac. How do you happen to be in this strange place? I am sure there is quite a story behind it."

Isaac looks into the fire and is silent for a long time.

"My story is one you will know well enough. Simple and sad, and common enough among our people. I come from Majorca, where my family were among the Conversos for generations, somehow surviving through all of the spasms of the Inquisition, until the one in 1673. I was in Spain at the time on business, but my wife and two daughters were in Palma. A pestilence swept through the city and the Converso community was blamed. You know how it always is." Isaac lowers his head, looking at his hands, which seem to be moving by themselves, clasping and twisting together.

"My wife and two daughters were burned to death. In the public square. I heard about it a week later in Salamanca." His eyes glisten in the firelight. "I have never gone back. I came here soon after that, just when this island was being taken over by the Danes. I worked with the native Arawak tribes, and tried to save them from the devastating diseases that we had brought.

But there was nothing to be done. There are only a tiny number of them left, and they are treated so badly, I am sure they wish they had died with their people."

"That is a terrible story." Galanos looks into the fire and they are silent for a long time. Finally the doctor says, "Do you suppose there are enough Jews on the island for a minyan? Tomorrow is the sabbath…"

Isaac looks at him thoughtfully. "Well, there are four right here in the hospital tents, and the two of us, and I think I can find four more among the merchants of the town." The two men lean in towards each other and shake hands solemnly. And the next day the first Jewish services on St. Thomas are officially held, greatly relieving Isaac's soul, for he is obliged, like all the white inhabitants of the place, to attend the weekly Sunday Lutheran service in the Fort.

Chapter Twenty-One: The Queen

Copenhagen, January 1771

I notice that Johanne is in particularly good cheer of late. She has a new routine visiting with the Queen and the Queen seems to have taken a liking to her. Many women of the court look down on the Queen's Englishness, find fault with her Danish and whisper about her behind her back. But Johanne is of a simpler type and deeply honored to be in her company. She wants to please. And she plays a good enough game of cards, though she loses more than she wins. Dr. Struensee had wanted the Queen to get to know women of lesser classes, and she has found this one to her liking. I am a little puzzled by this but I put it out of my mind.

Johanne has taken to ringing for Phebe when she wakes, which makes me cross, but I dare say nothing. Her new association with the Queen is giving her airs. Phebe reports that she finds her still under her plump, warm duvet. Thomas's side of the bed is always empty, as he goes long before sunrise to the barracks.

"Phebe, get my blue silk, the day dress." Phebe does a perfect imitation of an imperious Johanne voice. I know Phebe: she has her way of humming a little interior tune in her head when the urge to swat someone comes over her. A trick her grandmother taught her when she was very young. She sings it sometimes at me. Always the same little hey nonny nonny kind of tune. I know to keep my mouth shut when she starts to hum. And I know she is humming away as she helps Johanne with the dress and pins up her hair.

When Johanne moves on into the salon, I join her at the table for the dark bread and cheese and a small cup of beer that Phebe has assembled. We all speak in monosyllables, mapping out the day ahead. Then Phebe and I go off to be tutored, and Johanne sets out across the bridge into the castle. From all her reports, I can picture the scene perfectly.

The Queen would be sitting on the side of her bed in her nightdress with four or five of her ladies-in-waiting fluttering around with various garments to apply to her in succession.

"Johanne! Just the tonic I needed this morning! Come sit by me." Thus addressed, Johanne feels a paroxysm of delight wash over her, serenely unaware that above all she is a curiosity to the Queen, a specimen of a class she has never encountered at close range before.

"Did you sleep well, Caroline?" This is one thing that Johanne has perceived: of her two names, the Queen prefers to be called Caroline, and most of the ladies in waiting call her Matilda, a name much liked in Denmark.

"Not so well, I'm afraid. The baby is beginning to kick. But I am glad it is so active. The good Dr. Struensee will give me something for tonight." The Queen is in her fourth month of pregnancy and there has been a great deal of gossip about it, for she and the King do not sleep together. But there are witnesses who swear that they did so on one occasion four months earlier.

The ladies-in-waiting parade in with various undergarments and the Queen then submits, standing passively, as they layer her bare skin with white damask and slide a soft grey silk day dress on top. She sits in front of a mirror looking at her own round, china-doll face with its grey blue eyes, while Sophie von Bulow piles her hair high and pins it with little flourishing curls. All the while talking to Johanne about the day ahead. They will visit Prince Frederick in the nursery, the daily custom of the Queen, and she will confer with Struensee and the King on some issues of state.

In the afternoon they play whist, the Queen's preferred game, which she has taught Johanne. Johanne gets distracted, loses track of the cards and is not very successful when she has to play the hand. Her partner is Sophie von Bulow, and she taps her fingers impatiently at Johanne's mistakes.

"Stop that tapping, Sophie. Are you trying to signal something?" The Queen smiles at Johanne, who is now flustered.

"For heaven's sake, hush, I am losing track of things," Johanne sighs deeply. She is still learning this game, and though confident that she will improve, she does have a certain dread of asking Thomas to cover her losses. She is thinking that he is so sanctimonious. His pay is an embarrassing pittance, though she knows his family fortune from their sugar plantations is not. He has so far not made a fuss because he sees that she is very happy in her relationship to the Queen. What he is alarmed about is all the new legislation. The aristocracy will not stand for it, he says to her repeatedly. The Queen Dowager is in a rage. Take care what you do and be ready to step back.

Far from stepping back, she is now being included in some lovely dinners. Thomas generally is in the Guardhouse anyway, and taking me along with her makes it impossible for him to complain. I love the dinners as much as she does. I am getting a wonderful education and I like to think I am becoming a very polished young woman, just as my parents had intended. I can see that Johanne is proud to be the conduit for all this, and she knows that it is harder for Thomas to complain if I am along with her. She is actually teaching me how to flirt and she is quite proud of it. I admit I was a little clumsy at that initially. But now I have Heinrich and I am quite content. I can see well enough that Johanne is delighted at the attentions of Frederick Karl von Warnstedt, probably because she can't stand his wife. I can't imagine that she would ever be truly disloyal to Uncle.

Uncle Thomas often comes to pray with me at night and almost always peers into the Missy Box and picks out a treasure to examine. I have been very slowly decoding the diary and the life it reveals has made me question so much that I have always taken for granted. The codes of behavior towards our slaves were just being established. That my great grandmother so resisted them makes me proud, and yet what have I to be proud about? I myself am guilty of simply accepting the society I was born into.

Chapter Twenty-Two: Caterina

St. Thomas, September 1694

At the beach hospital, at Pundi's insistence, Maria and Akila boil endless big pots of water over fires on the beach. He has brought his supply of cinchona bark to the camp, and they distill it into a slightly bitter liquid.

"For our feverish patients…this will lessen their misery. Whatever else we have, we'll always have fever in this miserable place. Boil everything you put on their wounds," Pundi commands. It is a mystery to Maria and Akila why he demands this, but they obey and produce yards and yards of boiled cotton to wrap the wounded.

Then, as Pundi had predicted, the sickness begins in earnest. The hospital is flooded with new patients, most with uncontrollable diarrhea, which is most unpleasant to deal with.

Akila prepares them all a kind of face mask from two squares of cotton with sprigs of lavender between the layers.

"I wonder if it is the water they are drinking. It has perhaps been polluted in the storms." Pundit announces. "We should boil it." This was a way of his family in India, the way of a Brahmin. They had always been healthy in a place where health was a rarity. Stomach ailments were a plague there just as they are here, even in good times.

But now they sweep over the island population like wildfire. Many die of dehydration before they can seek help. The soldiers at the Fort are among the most afflicted, being too lazy to boil the water. Pierre is briefly among their patients. He cannot keep his food down and lies despondent on his cot, periodically propping himself on his elbow to watch his wife ministering to the islanders.

"Where did you learn all this?" Pierre asks Maria. "You were quite amazing at keeping Rasmus Krabbe in hand while Pundi was setting his bone."

She looks at him in surprise.

"Do you really think so? We used to spend hours studying the human body at the Von Bergens'. Those were the books Isaac had at the time, so that's what we studied. I never imagined we'd ever use what we learned. I just thought it was for fun. And we learned about plants and what you can make with them and how they affect the humours and the body. And we tried things out ourselves." She looks around at the ground and plucks up a sprig of artemisia. "You see this weed? Keela and I put it in everything, and mix it with different things. We eat so much of it that I cannot help but think it is what has kept us from getting some of the fevers that are so common here. But I don't really know. I just know I'm going to keep eating it…and feeding it to you, of course. We mix it with different things and write down how it makes us feel. It makes the world ever so much more interesting to know about all these things you see in nature."

One day Mette appears in their little hospital, dragging a young girl behind her.

Akila recognizes Mette instantly and retreats to the farthest end of the beach and begins fiddling with firewood. Maria is momentarily paralyzed, for Mette is now the island's most notorious woman, having been publicly whipped beneath her husband's swinging corpse. Standing in the sunlight, her hair glistening a greasy blue black, she wears the common tunic of the island, pinched off a clothesline, still clean. Oddly enough she is also wearing an exquisite pair of earrings, and Maria can hardly keep from staring at them. They appear to be sapphires with tiny diamonds and pearls, set in gold. They set off a slow-motion avalanche of thoughts in Maria's mind. First there is the creeping memory of Mette's lust for her modest silver medallion on the ship all those years ago. Her taste was modest then…it must have burgeoned into new realms.

And how might she have acquired them? Did she wrench these off some blind widow's ears? Maria forces her eyes away from the earrings, looking instead into Mette's face directly. The same sallow, slit-eyed look of many years before, mocked, almost, by the lovely earrings. Maria unconsciously puts her hand to her throat, touching her medallion.

Mette gives Maria a long, appraising look and says, as if delivering a challenge, "My girl here. Caterina. She won't stop coughing. I heard you had this camp here for fixing people."

Maria looks at the girl. Coughing seems the least of her problems. Her ribs protrude beneath her dirty chemise. Her eyes are like those of a dead person, though one of them has a lively oozing sore on the lid.

"Leave her with us for a few days. We will find something for her cough. She looks as if she needs rest, and some regular eating."

"But she is needed at home. Can't you just give her something?"

"She needs more than a little something. If you do not leave her she is likely to die, and then you won't have her at all." Maria feels her anger rising at the thought of restoring this child to health only to turn her back to this vile woman.

"I'll be back in two days then."

"Don't come before a week if you want her well."

Mette stares at Maria angrily. But she leaves then, without a word.

Akila insists on tending to Caterina herself.

"Keela, there are some much sicker than this one. Why are you doing so for this child?" Isaac says impatiently two days later.

"Nobody did for me, so I do for her. It heals me inside." Maria hushes Isaac and, suppressing a pang of jealousy, picks up some of Akila's tasks. But she watches Akila out of the corner of her eye and sees that she has a special connection to this child.

"Caterina is a sad child. Sick certainly, but the sadness possesses her like a demon." Maria speaks this quietly into Akila's ear.

"I will tell you one day." Akila turns her head away from Maria. "When this is all over," and she sweeps her arm in the arc of the beach camp, "we will deal with Caterina's case."

Caterina stays her week and goes off with a supply of cough tincture, trailing after Mette, but she stays vivid in Akila's mind.

The injuries and sickness fall most heavily upon the slave population, and Akila takes charge of that section of the camp. One old woman, Mina, the cook from a plantation in the West End, is brought in on a cart one day. Her legs are too swollen to carry her, and covered with oozing sores. The overseer, a Scotsman, has brought her.

"She is precious cargo, this one. The best cook on the island. Take care nothing happens to her."

Akila thinks of her mother, of how she too would have been old and round by now and scarred by time if she had lived. She quickly gathers shells and places a circle of them, tiny and perfect, at the head and the foot of Mina's cot.

"To keep your soul with us," she whispers in Soninke. Though she is Muslim, Akila has great belief in the power of the spirits found in every object of nature, and knows that Mina does too. That done, she makes a poultice of yarrow and charcoal from the fire.

Their days are grueling. The fevers take their toll, and many are buried in the cemetery near the Fort. The death of soldiers at the Fort has made fear grow among the White population. The planters barricade themselves in their bedrooms at night and argue among themselves about how to defend against a Spanish attack from Portorico. The hurricane has polluted the water supply of the entire island, and left pools of standing water everywhere.

"Do you think our lives will ever return to normal?" Maria asks Pundi one day, swatting a mosquito on his arm.

He smiles and says, "No, I do not think it will ever be the same again. We have done our work too well to be left in peace, I am afraid."

"Oops, too late," she says, looking at the bright red splotch that has bloomed on his arm. "You have lovely bright blood, Pundi."

Maria and Akila both have their deep faith and their regular habits of praying in this place where death is always walking. The camp is a solemn place. Family members, for those who have them, gather around the sick on their cots doing what ministrations they can.

But laughter is good medicine, and Maria and Akila can still giggle together, and they sometimes do so at the odd practices of their "professors". The very privileged cow in particular sets them off, though they love her dearly. But their faiths do not divide the four. On the contrary, Maria captures all of their thoughts when she says one day with a little laugh, "Between us we must be communing with all the Gods and Spirits of the earth, don't you think? Monsieur Pascal would be very pleased with us."

The whole island meanwhile has been engaged in slowly rebuilding. Pierre has organized his own family's operations, procuring the supplies for the rebuilding of the bakery and then their house, this time in brick. But it is his former manservant Lucien who oversees the daily work, laboring in the stifling heat alongside Jean-Baptiste, Marcus and Bamadille. The finished house is bigger than before and it is one of the first in Charlotte Amalie to have two stories, which Pierre regards as important for keeping wildlife out of their salon and bedroom.

The lower story will for the moment be for storage. Maybe later, he thinks, for renting out to shopkeepers. The cookhouse is an outbuilding in back and the slaves have their simple quarters there too. Water is collected in rain barrels from a network of guts cut through the hills..

While the building is going on, Akila and Maria sometimes surprise their men with a visit. The work at the hospital camp is exhausting, with never a moment of privacy, so each of them sneaks off occasionally, hoping for a private moment with her husband, but if no husband is to be found, at least a nap at home. It is October, the air is heavy, and Maria looks off at the thunderheads on the horizon.

"Storm coming. Hope it's not going to be too windy." They are used to the bucketing rain of an afternoon. Nothing is ever completely dry in this season and it seems as if the mold has little tiny feet, scurrying all over everything.

"I'm going to run up to the house before it comes. Take a little nap. Fetch some clean clothes. Shall I bring you anything?"

"No, nothing for me. You get a good rest."

The house seems quiet as Maria comes up the path. The mournful sound of a dove comes through the trees and the air smells of the rain that is to come. She goes up the steps at the front of the house, a small white figure with her hair tumbled upon her head in a curly mass that Akila fashioned that morning. She walks through the house, listening. She hears a little moan at the back and moves toward it. It's coming from the rear of the house, where they have a kind of shower rigged up. She peeks around the corner where the soft moaning is coming from. Marcus is standing, legs spread. The muscles in his buttocks glisten and move, heaving in and out. A mass of curls that is unmistakably Pierre's is moving in front of him and Marcus has him in a firm hold. Maria stands dumbly, mouth open, watching as the two men writhe in rhythm, Pierre's breath coming in short gasps of gutting pleasure. Slowly, fearing that the banging of her heart will give her away, she backs out of the room and runs silently into the woods.

She sits for a long time on a rocky ledge in the forest, in the clamor of tree frogs and crickets, her head like a pit mine after an explosive blast. A kind of paralysis comes over her, a feeling as of carrying something so heavy and dark that she is unable to lift her limbs. And then the rain comes, like a waterfall so strong she can hardly see through it. She raises her face to the heavens and feels the embrace of God in the torrent. She sits as the rivulets pour down her as from the rockface of the mountain. The rain slows and stops. The trees drip, and still she sits.

Finally she rises as if in a dream and goes back to the hospital camp.

"Good Lord, you are a sight," Akila says softly, holding Maria at arm's length and examining her closely. "But I am so happy to see you. I was beginning to worry. Didn't you get any clothes? No matter, we have a horrible case."

She is in a frenzy over a field slave, whose legs are so infected by the needles of the prickly pear fence that Isaac fears gangrene. The sight and the stench of the man's swollen bloody legs is so unnerving that Maria is abruptly and mercifully captured by the duties the Lord has given her. Under Isaac's supervision, they put maggots on the wounds, wrapping the foot in banana leaves. And then Maria goes behind the camp and vomits.

In the evening a few slaves whose long day in the field is finally over have come to tend their sick and bed down beside them. The White visitors have long departed. Akila sits on the beach by Maria as the moon rises.

"You are very quiet tonight," Akila murmurs, idly making a swirling design in the sand with a stick. Maria's voice, when she speaks, has a tremor of anguish.

"It seems a very long time ago that we arrived here. I can no longer remember the sound of my father's voice. Can you?"

"No, but I can bring the image of him to me anytime. And my mother too."

"I can still see my father standing on the beach in the early morning sunlight with his black cape flying in the wind." The tears begin, and Akila puts her arm around Maria and pulls her close.

"It's all gone now," Akila murmurs. "I wonder what has become of my father.

Whether he ever tried to find me. Or seek revenge. Or whether he too may have been captured and is somewhere on this side of the ocean in misery. Alone." She looks at Maria directly. "Thanks to Allah I have you, and not some other horrible master."

Maria looks into her eyes and melts into sobs. She bursts forth with the story of what she has seen today. When it is finished Akila holds her close and whispers, "It's not so uncommon, especially here in this place where there are so many men, so many sailors. It doesn't mean that he doesn't love you. It's just his nature. You will find joy in other places, other things. But oh, my sweet Maria, I am so sorry. Let us pray that it is not discovered. That would be ruinous for both of them."

The following week Casper Rysberg is brought into the camp delirious with fever. He is well known to them all, a sullen and angry man when conscious, and now simply an ugly heap upon the stretcher, his face grey and fuzzed, as if a thousand caterpillars were crawling upon it in the dancing sunlight. He stinks, but they are used to that now. Maria says under her breath to Pundi, "Here's one to test our faith."

A planter with one hundred and twenty slaves and a large plantation in the East End, Rysberg has many enemies who would be delighted at his death, but he slowly recovers. He lies on his cot day after day, his eyes like leeches on Akila. She is indeed worth watching. Like Maria, she wears an ample white cotton shift and an apron, her hair tied up in a white turban. She is tall and stately, but she is also round and sensuous, her titties move like rolling moons and her backside is just such a pleasure to watch. On the day Rysberg is leaving, he sees Akila bending over a medical text.

"You are not reading that." His declaration has the hint of a question in it. "Slaves are forbidden to read."

"Oh no. Just looking at the picture here." Akila finds herself shaking, whether from anger or fear she is not sure. But gradually she becomes sure. Anger takes her like an earthquake and she begins to tremble. Maria has heard Rysberg's trumpeting voice down the beach and comes scrambling like a terrier to Akila's side.

"And what if she were reading? Has she not just worked a week to save your life? Are you now going to complain of her?" The whites of her eyes flash at the man.

"You threaten me? You are as bad as she is. Someday, someone will teach you your place in the world. 'Tweren't either 'a youse that saved me. 'Twas the Lord's will. Take care. You think she is one of us, but I will show you someday what she is."

He points a long, tobacco-stained finger at Akila, and then he goes off, leaving the two women rooted on the beach. They watch his receding back and finally look at each other. Maria gives a half smile, but unease, like a rolling bank of fog, has quietly enveloped them. This is a place where women and slaves live rigid, constrained lives. Those that do not must anticipate consequences.

"How astonishing that he would turn on the people who have just saved his life." Maria bites her lip. "We've done God's work here. But people have noticed us, where before they hadn't. Let us hope that their gratitude will protect us."

Akila says nothing.

By spring, things wind down at the hospital camp. The island has changed. There's hardly a soul left in the Fort. On the East End a large number of slaves have gone maroon. They are hiding in the woods and fear is heavy in the air. The four healers have been in the camp for nine long months. On the last day of April they will depart, storing the cots, canvas tenting and other equipment in the Company warehouse.

The evening before they are to leave the two women are folding the canvas tenting together, trying not to let it touch the sand.

"I've been thinking a lot about Caterina and Mette." Akila is trying to blow a bug off her arm without dropping her end of the sailcloth as she says this. "When they came here it stirred something up for me, something that's been on my mind a long time, but I had shoved it away. Now I can't anymore…I need to share it. I sometimes feel like I'll die of shame if I don't. We're going home tomorrow, and I don't want to carry this with me alone anymore."

They lash the last canvas onto the pile and walk to the water's edge. Akila sits with her legs crossed under her skirts, Maria beside her. Above the dark blue horizon, radial beams of the sun shine through huge, golden cumulus clouds. They each stare at it, but the display is hardly noticed by either of them.

"You have seen Caterina. Can you guess what is on my mind?"

Maria is pondering Akila's question soberly, her face bathed in golden reflections.

"Do you remember when you first saw me. That Mette was there?" "I do remember. You were a horrible mess…so injured."

"Yes. I was. She had taken me the night before and sold me for the night. If it hadn't been for you, I would be Caterina. She had bribed the guard. The worst night of my life, after the night that my mother was killed." And she describes the whole event to Maria. When she is finished Maria holds her close.

"Oh Keela. That is so dreadful…and explains so much. I think Celine probably knew what had happened, but she never told me, of course." They sit for a long time before Akila speaks again.

"I don't know what to do about Caterina." Akila is looking at her hands, playing with her fingernails. "I have been thinking about it all these months. Men do these things. They do it to their slaves all the time. I think that some of them probably go to Mette's so their wives won't know. Because if they do things to their own slaves, their wives find out. What can we do against the way things are? I don't even know if there's any point to stopping her. So I've turned it around in my mind and decided we should get into Mette's good graces, help her run a clean place, free of disease. Get her to treat her girls well. There may be power in that, that we can use later somehow. She's in an ancient business. Her mother probably brought her up to it."

Pierre looks around his newly appointed living room while he waits for the return of his women. The afternoon sun flickers on the floor as it shines through the swaying palms beside the house. It is quite a different place from the one they left six months ago. Pierre has had it rebuilt with a foundation of stone, a place that they can retreat to in the next hurricane. It is still a simple structure with two large rooms, a salon and a bedroom, but the walls have been somewhat fortified and the back courtyard enlarged.

Pierre has sent Marcus and Jean-Baptiste to help the women with the closing of the hospital and their return home. He sits on the sofa picking his nails and waiting impatiently for their arrival. He is trying manfully not to bite the nails, but he is nervous, he has had this house to himself all these months and he exhales deeply at the thought that he will now be sharing it once again with his wife. Not that he does not love her. He does. With all his heart. Like a sister, she is very precious to him. He means to show it with the wonderful homecoming gift he has for her, which sits before him on the table.

It is a glorious gift, and though he will not reveal its true origins to Maria, a mercurial heat spreads through his body as he thinks of the man who sold it to him. A pirate by God, and oh, the dick on him. He grows hard just thinking of it and tries to calm himself by inhaling deeply. The box itself is exquisite, with many tiers and secret places in it. Beautiful ornate brass hinges, and a mirror on the inside of the top that stands up. A Chinese box, the kind they call a Missy Box. Lined in a glorious velvet. He is not quite ready to give it to Maria yet. He will wait and keep it until a moment when he really needs her forgiveness.

Chapter Twenty-Three: New Understandings

Christianborg Castle, Copenhagen, January 1771,

Phebe seems to be trembling as she drops the yellow gown over my upraised arms.

Her breath is quick and shallow.

You're trembling," I say, trying to twist myself around to look at her.

"Sit down while I do your hair. I'm trembling because I'm trying to get this done!" Phebe retorts.

It's true, I don't want to be late. Johanne's probably waiting. "I
"I wish Mama could see me…and Heinrich."

"Oh Summy, for heaven sakes, get hold of yourself. Heinrich's only a boy. And only your first. Surely you don't want to end up living here."

"Well, I sometimes do, but mostly I don't. But at the moment I am considering it. It's a lot more exciting than St. Croix."

"What about your plan to go to school in America?"

"Well, we'll see. Maybe I could still do that and then come back here. You have to admit, this is an exciting time here right now. Dr Struensee is making it the most advanced country in Europe."

"Yes, but what are the chances he'll really get away with it. You are only hearing what the people around him say. Think of the way people react at home to any talk of taking away their privileges…or giving any rights to their slaves. That kind of change is the most resisted. People will fight to the death for their privileges." She jabs a hairpin into my mass of hair as she says this.

"Achhh…" I duck and peer up at her warily. "Yes, but it's happening right here, right now. We are witnesses to something amazing and he's making it happen!"

Phebe lowers her voice to a whisper. "Do you think the Queen's baby is his?"

"Hush. Of course not. What a little gossip you are." I grin at her in the mirror.

"Well, everyone's saying it. My friend Beppo who is with the Queen Dowager all the time, says that she says it, and that she is beside herself with rage at the whole thing. I think it's going to come out. Be careful."

Johanne sticks her head in the door.

"Are you ready? Let's see you." I jump up and twirl around. "You look lovely. Quite the young woman."

"All thanks to Phebe. Look at what she has done to my hair! She has made me ever so much taller!" I throw my arms around Phebe and kiss her cheek, standing on my tiptoes.

"Oh, for heaven sakes go!"

Johanne and I walk across the bridge together. Uncle Thomas is on duty tonight and so we are on our own. I can feel my Aunt's excitement in the quickness of her step.

As I take my seat next to Heinrich, I scan the table for the King. To my great relief he is well down the table, though so is Struensee, to my sorrow. The King is looking more subdued than the last time I saw him. Slumped in his chair, staring at his soup. I quite pity him. Then I see the Queen's eyes flash to Johanne, seeming to communicate some quiet message. I wonder for a moment what their secret is. But then Heinrich touches my elbow and I turn to him, relaxing into a sensation of pleasant triumph and delight that the evening still has music and dancing to come.

At midnight I come back across the bridge alone, feeling rather cross at Johanne, who had brought my evening to a sudden close after the mazurka.

"Why do I have to go home if you are you staying?" I had argued. "Your mother would wish it."

"My mother's thousands of leagues away."

"And I am your mother in absentia."

Heinrich had tried to help. "Let me escort her to her door."

He bowed to Johanne as he said this, but she was having none of it.

"No need for that," she exclaimed, dramatically pointing at the floor. "You stay right here. She's quite capable of crossing on her own."

I can't imagine why she didn't want him to walk me home, but I can see that there is no changing her mind, so I take my leave of Heinrich and head slowly back across the bridge.

To my surprise, Phebe is still up, doing a bit of embroidery in the salon when I come through the door.

"I thought you'd be in bed!" I flop on the couch beside her. "My hair was the talk of the party…" A slight exaggeration, but I had received some compliments.

"Was it fun? Did the King do something outrageous?" She seems intent on her sewing.

"They whisked him off to bed early…and yes, it was heavenly. I am eternally grateful to my mother for making me study dancing with the awful French prig in Christianborg. What did you do?"

"Oh, nothing much." She looks at me and I can see she is about to explode in a fit of giggles.

"Oh you…what did you get up to?"

"Not much…just a little visit from Antoine."

"NO! Really? Did he know you'd be alone tonight?"

"He seems to have had that information from somewhere…"
"Oh Pheeb…" I giggle. "Did you know he was coming?"

"I thought he might, from something he said last time we were together…but I almost didn't let him in. I was rather afraid your uncle might come home. But then he begged and said he was freezing, so I had to relent."

"And then what happened?"

"Oh, nothing much." She says this with such a sly grin that I know it is an absolute lie.

"Did he kiss you?"

"We snuggled. It was nice. Cozy. And then he went home." She curls her feet up under her on the sofa and lets the sewing rest in her lap. "So you tell me now…what was it like among the grand folk?"

"Oh, you know, everyone watching the King. But they put him to bed early tonight. The dancing was lovely." I am trying to think of a way to ask her if she knows anything about what I read in the diary…what Maria had seen happening between my great grandfather and the man she calls Marcus.

"Tell me Phebe…do you think men can love each other the same way that a man and a woman do…I mean touching each other and kissing and that kind of thing?" I can feel the blood coming to my cheeks as I say this.

"Of course, you idiot!" Phebe draws back and looks at me strangely. "What do you think sailors do on those ships when there's not a woman for a thousand miles? And some of them discover that they like it with men a lot more than they do with women!" She has heard a lot more conversation about those things in the slave quarters in St. Croix than I have in the salon, and I feel a little stupid. But mostly I am sad.

Chapter Twenty-Four: Mo Mo

Charlotte Amalie, St. Thomas, November 1696

The sunlight flickers through the trees. Isaac and Pundi are walking with Akila and Maria in the scrub forest near Mosquito Bay, looking for promising plants. They are watchful of Akila, who is close to the moment of being delivered of her first child. As in all things, she carries the child with grace, like a small watermelon on her tall frame. She climbs over fallen branches with her long legs, smiling back at the others, daring them to follow.

"Pundi and I have been talking," Isaac says to the women. "It is a satisfying life we lead as healers. God's work. We must do it." He turns and looks at the two of them with a wry smile. "For you two it keeps you from turning into the slave and master: a musty, moldering woman rocking in her chair, with her intimate fanning her all day. Lordy what a picture that makes!" He laughs, a dry thumping sound, without humor, and then continues. "But we cannot help noticing that all around us are beginning to improve their lives considerably…making fortunes, in fact."

"Now Isaac, what would you do with a fortune?" Maria is sniffing a mushroom in the palm of her hand. Isaac gives her an exaggerated look of patience.

"Pierre for one." He goes on, ignoring her comment. "He is doing very well for himself, and I daresay for you. But Pundi and I are scarcely paid for the work we do. I see no reason why we can't do God's work and improve our own lives at the same time. I have concluded that it is somehow here in this forest, in these plants that our opportunity will come. I have been thinking of one very interesting plant that has a variety of uses." Isaac plucks a purple flower from a bush with succulent leaves as he says this and holds it out to Akila.

"Guaiacum," she says, taking it from his outstretched hand.

"There is one especially horrible disease that you women may have seen occasionally, but I don't think anyone has sought your help with it as yet. But living among as many seafaring men as we have here on the island, you are bound to be called to treat it before long. And you will find this lovely plant quite efficacious."

"And what might that disease be, Isaac?" Maria says languidly, as if he had cast a spell over her. Though it is in fact the heat that has cast the spell.

"Syphilis." He pauses and smiles at them. "The clap too, but syphilis is far worse, so the rewards will be higher."

"*Dégoutant!*" Maria murmurs. Pundi is listening attentively.

"It first appeared among the French troops besieging Naples in 1495. Note the year: one year after Columbus returned. To me that suggests that the disease had its origin in this part of the world, so it is somehow fitting that we should also supply the treatment." His mouth widens in a grin of satisfaction.

By now they have arrived at the beach, and the four of them sit on a log worn to a slippery golden sheen by the sea. Maria sighs deeply as she looks out at the bands of shimmering turquoise. For a moment everything in her is quieted by the beauty of this island of her exile.

"It is a terrifying, ferocious disease." Isaac is dramatizing his story with contorted facial expressions and abundant use of his hands. "And as you well know, it spreads by physical intimacy."

"Excuse me Isaac, but can you be more specific," Akila giggles.

"The French troops broke out in pustules that were so extreme whole sheafs of skin would drop away. Is that specific enough? In that early time the life expectancy was a matter of months. As the troops departed from Naples they left a trail of cities with the disease. It was called "the French disease" in Italy and the "Spanish disease" by the French. In the two hundred years since, the disease has abated somewhat, and people who contract it live considerably longer…unless they die of mortification. Sometimes the disease goes into a long quiet phase, but ultimately it triumphs, and invades the brain and the eyes in a most horrible way.

"God's judgment," Maria murmurs, still languid.

"Oh Maria. I've spent so much time trying to make you a natural philosopher. How can you say that to me?"

"I have no trouble being a philosopher of nature and believing in God—nor do you, Isaac—and your God is a much more wrathful one than mine."

"Well, Jesus won't cure you of syphilis." He looks out at the hills of the island of St. John across the bay. "But maybe this guaiacum tree can. And maybe there are other, better things here that haven't been discovered yet."

As they walk into the village of Charlotte Amalie, the eye of the sun stares down on the bay. A stench of rotting fish and human waste wafts towards them. It is noon. The heat is intense and the streets are alive with hawkers and sailors. As they pass along they pick up snippets: "slaves" and "hundreds" and "Brandenburgers" rings in the air; until Isaac finally pokes his head into the barber shop and asks what the news is.

"Why, there's news that some labor will shortly arrive," says Cornelius Bastiar. "Two Brandenburger ships from Africa are due next week with more than eleven hundred Negroes. They'll be auctioned on board as soon as they get them cleaned up. There are many more than we can handle here, but St. Thomas will get the choicest…and then I suppose they'll go on to sell the rest in other ports."

Maria mutters, "Pierre will be so angry that the Brandenburgers are getting the profits, not the Danish West Indies Company." The animosity that has grown up between the Company and the Brandenburgers is so acute that many on the island find their disputes to be a source of some entertainment, but since Maria's uncle is on the Brandenburger side, she finds her position a little awkward. Not that she is close to her Uncle David. And the fact that he is the chief importer of these human souls is particularly appalling. On the other hand, her own husband is champing at the bit to get a piece of the slave trade. The slave issue is a bitter point between them, and especially so because he will not allow her to give Akila her freedom.

"Oh Lord, why do we have to live in such times?" She turns to Akila as she says this and sees instantly that Akila is in a state of violent upheaval. She is struggling to breathe, and a great flush has risen into her cheeks. Maria draws her into her arms. She is imagining Akila's distress at the news of the slave ship and she can think of nothing comforting to say.

And then she realizes that Akila is having her baby.

It comes as no surprise that Akila gives birth as a gazelle leaps a fence. Or so it appears to Maria, who has by now seen some very agonizing births, though they have not yet lost a baby or a mother. When she catches the little bundle that slithers out between Akila's long muscular thighs, she feels all the breath leave her body and, in the space where it had been, a rush of other feelings: joy, jealousy, fear and wonder, all in a muddled flood. But joy predominates and leaves her feeling almost as if she herself has given birth.

"A boy," she says softly, and lays him on Akila's breast, still attached to her womb by the cord of blood.

Akila silently cradles the child in her arms, looking into his bright, intent eyes. She is flooded with emotion, and with memories of her own mother. What must she have felt at this moment? It is as if a flash flood were suddenly roaring down the gullies of her heart: she is ripped wide open to all this grief and joy. She starts to bawl.

Maria has a bit of a skirmish with Pierre over the baby's name.

"It is my right to name the baby," he says. "I am the master."

"I beg you to let Akila and Samuel pick the name."

"I don't want an African name. We are in the New World now. These are new times.

And besides, there's enough talk around the island of you and Akila. We let her do things no other slaves on the island are permitted to do. I can tell you a lot of tongues are wagging in the Fort and they are our friends. I can only imagine what some of the plantation owners are saying." He is standing by the open window as he says this, staring at a cartload of slaves being driven down the street. "And no one lets their slaves choose their children's names," he says emphatically.

"They want to call him Mohammed. Her father's name. Please, I beg you, Pierre."

"I'm not an unreasonable person, Maria. I'll compromise. They can call him Mohammed and we will call him Maurice, and we'll all call him Mo, just Mo."

Just Mo becomes Mo Mo as he sucks at Akila's breast and rocks between Samuel's knees, a golden amber child, long and agile, already reaching for the red berries on the tree above him. He is quickly the pet of all in their compound and some beyond. Bamadille and Lucien take turns visiting him, since they cannot leave the bakery at the same time. Anna is still nursing Cate, who is nearly two, and with a little bribery from Maria she is persuaded to suckle Mo Mo occasionally so that Akila can be free to go with Maria when they are called away.

The birth of Mo Mo is wildly unsettling to Maria. Her longing for a child is fierce, but she never has physical relations with her husband. And now she understands why.

"Pierre, don't you want a child of your own?" she says one day.

"I suppose so, though I don't think this is much of a place for a child. I hadn't really thought about it."

She reddens with embarrassment. "How odd, I don't think about anything else." She strokes his shoulder. "Could we at least try?"

Now it is his turn to blush. And looking down at the floor he says, "Why of course my dear."

"I cannot stop thinking of Caterina since Mo Mo was born," Akila says one day. They are in the courtyard outside the special kitchen that is dedicated to preparing medicines. Anna is rocking Mo Mo on her knees while little Cate plays house behind a bush with an imaginary friend. Maria is feeding the pigeons. The original two have become eight, and four are here now pecking at their grain. The others are with Isaac and Pundi. As the Captain had predicted, they have become invaluable messengers between the two households. And at the moment they are providing Maria with an object for her overflowing maternal love.

"The motherless child. Not surprising you'd think about her, I guess," Maria smiles as she lifts a fledgling she has named Albert out of the elegant cage that Isaac has built. She feels the comfort of the bird's quick heartbeat against her breast as he pecks at the grain in her hand.

"I think we should pay Mette a visit." Akila waves away a pestering fly. "A truly unpleasant prospect, I know…but I must do it for Caterina's sake." After a pause she says, "I am amazed that she does not recognize me. I guess to her I was just a thing to be used."

Maria lets out a huge sigh. "I am sure she remembers me though she hasn't said anything. She will not like our coming. She'll likely chase us away."

"Then we must take her something as a present. Something irresistible."

"A basket with some of Anna's baking, and medicinal things perhaps?"

They set Anna to baking her Danish specialties and fill a basket with an assortment of good things: a strong artemisia tea to protect against malaria, along with a sample of the plant so that she can brew it herself. Some acanthosperum, crushed into a paste for open wounds. And some cannabis, which Pundi had taken to cultivating. When they have four or five items cheerfully displayed in the basket along with Anna's delicacies, still warm and aromatic, they set off on foot.

The afternoon is cloudy. They walk along the waterfront by the village and then off to the south toward Careening Bay. They wind up the hill—it's a short walk, no deterrent to eager sailors. They can see Mette's house a long way off, shaded by several huge mangrove trees. It is, they have to agree, a surprisingly appealing place. Two stories, with a veranda on the upper level lined with rocking chairs. Mette has done well in her two years of business here, and has expanded. A man in a red shirt sits rocking and smoking a pipe and as they approach Mette herself comes through the doorway.

She is much tidier than the last time they saw her, and wears the simple white dress of the island. Her hair is washed and piled upon her head.

"Mette," Maria says, mustering some warmth in her voice, and a friendly smile, "you look very well."

"What you doing here?" Mette's eyes narrow with suspicion.

"Come to see how Caterina is doing. Mostly. We brought you some things from the healing work we do. You might find them useful sometime. And some biscuits just baked." Mette moves her head slowly from side to side, as if weighing her thoughts. The man on the porch has stopped rocking and is looking suspiciously at the newcomers.

In a cabin at the back of the house Caterina is at this moment lying rigid beneath a two-hundred-pounder who is rising to ecstasy. Her mind is wandering off to the beach as she awaits the familiar release of hot slime and primal moans. When they come, she makes a little coo of satisfaction to please him and runs her fingers through his greasy hair as if to say, "Good boy." She has faithfully performed her preparatory ritual, sprinkling various powders on the sea sponge she shoves inside herself. Mustafa has brought the required pail of water to her boudoir, for the cleanup. It has all taken less than ten minutes. She is quite numb to it all now, just looking forward to sleeping again when the big lumphead is gone.

Akila meanwhile is out front eyeing the red-shirted stranger in the rocking chair. He has been holding his hand over the side of his mouth in a seeming gesture of contemplation, but suddenly a wasp flies at him and he reacts, waving both hands to shoo it away. Akila spots a nasty looking pustule on his lip. She walks over to him.

"You should get that taken care of you know. It could be something serious. How long have you had it?"

The man is silent, evidently weighing a rude and clever retort. But Akila's commanding look makes him change his mind.

"'Bout a month."

"You probably picked it up in a place like this in your last port of call."

Mette suddenly throws up her hands and bellows, "Don't bring some filthy disease in here, you big lout."

"It ain't no big thing…just a little sore."

"But it might be the clap… Looks like it." She says this in a steely low voice that rasps like fingernails on slate. "I ain't taking no chances. You be off, and don't come back." Mette points to the harbor.

A little smile plays on Maria's lips as she calls out to his departing back, "You might stop in at Isaac Benjamin's on your way back to town. He is developing a remedy for that very thing you've got and would be pleased to see you. It's about the third house you'll come to. Any child can tell you which one."

The big sailor emerges from the back of the house jingling a few Rixsdollars in his hand.

"Nice tight little cunt on that one," he says as he hands Mette her price. His glance stops appraisingly on the two women, and staring at Akila he licks his lips slowly. She turns away, her jaw clenching, and stares out to sea. He makes a guttural half-chuckle and goes off down the steps, just behind the man in the red shirt.

"You're well rid of that fellow," Maria says, breaking a heavy silence. "There are some nasty diseases coming into port. Be careful. You want to take care of your girls."

"Who are you to tell me?" Mette says, her jaw muscles jumping. "I grew up in this business."

"Well, I admit I don't know much about it, and neither does Akila. But our friend Isaac is making syphilis his specialty and developing remedies for it that he's going to sell all over the world. We've got wonderful plants here on St. Thomas to make these medicines. And I think it pretty likely that that sailor had it, or something very near. It's a horrible disease."

"I've seen plenty die of it. No need to tell me."

At this moment Caterina comes wandering in a blinking daze out onto the veranda and, seeing Akila, she squeals and throws her arms around her.

"How you doing baby?" Akila says in a soft, lilting tone.

Caterina just makes a little sound in the back of her throat. She chews her lips anxiously, looking at the dirty floor.

Maria distracts Mette with the medicinal plants in the basket and offers to show her where they are growing around her house. While they are off foraging, Akila goes with Caterina to her cabin and examines her closely. She looks at the pails with their various washing liquids, the sponges, the sheets on the bed layered with sailcloth between, so each customer gets a clean sheet. It is altogether an impressive operation and she feels a certain grudging admiration, but it does not diminish the horror of Caterina's forced submission to all this. The real problem is eternal: the men who desire these children.

"She's planning to buy two more girls from that slave ship that's due in," Caterina whispers. "She gonna put 'em down in that shack down there. To break 'em in she says. Don't tell her I told you."

Akila feels suddenly ill, remembering her first encounter with Mette. She sinks onto the bed, putting her head in her hands.

"Muftafta says they be chained, like animals. He's the boy here, takes care of us."

Akila rouses herself. "We want to stay on her good side, so she'll let us come and visit you. It may help a little if she knows we're watching out for you."

"You're so good to me. Praise Allah." This last phrase she learned from Akila at the hospital, for she herself had grown up with animist beliefs. She can feel the evil spirits of this place looming over her, and she's been puzzling over who this Allah fellow is.

Walking back into town Maria and Akila see the sailor coming out of Isaac and Pundi's house carrying a satchel. They idle in the lane to let him get well away and then walk up the path to the house.

"Hey hey," Maria calls out.

"Back here," comes the response in Isaac's baritone.

They find both men working in the plant room, with the cow lying in the dirt outside the door.

"Did you like the customer we sent you?" Maria says brightly.

"Oh, that was you, was it? He certainly has a case. Bought a good quantity of our remedy." Isaac is stirring a pot of a green sludge as he says this. "He'll likely spread the word to his shipmates." He puts the wooden spoon to his lips and blows on it, then scoops a bit with his finger and tastes it. He wrinkles his nose. "Wanted something to heighten his performance in bed too. Can you believe it? I have no doubt he'll go spreading the clap to whomever he can, so I persuaded him to try one of the pig-bladder gloves Pundi has been making. Doubt he'll use it. I refused to sell him what he wanted though…" And he points into the pot. This is my new special formula. With luck his mates will be coming along and I can try it on them.

"Oh Lord, that's just what the island needs: an outbreak of lecherous men." As the words came out of Maria's mouth, Akila has a thought.

"Isaac, if you can make this, can you make its opposite? You know what I mean?"

Akila feels the heat rising from her neck into her cheeks.

"I am sure something on this island can be found to do that, but who would buy it?" Akila gives him a long, slow smile.

"Me."

At the end of the day, the two women go home along the sea path burnished with rosy evening light, through the village full of sailors who've come off their boats to look for some evening pleasure. As they climb the hill to the house, Maria is glowing. She has been devilishly inspired by her visit to Mette, inspired to delay her bedding of Pierre no longer. Her blue eyes shine with determination.

"I must get him to bed one way or another, or I shall never have a child of my own," she blurts out, seemingly out of the blue.

Akila stops on the path and gives her a long appraising look, a smile spreading wide across her face.

Once home, Akila strides out to the work shed to fetch a cake of soap they have made from pig fat and wild roses. Leading Maria to the bathing enclosure in the courtyard, she takes the bucket of water that has been warming all day in the sun and makes great puffs of bubbles by rubbing the soap with a sponge. She delights in squeezing the sponge, making bigger and bigger puffs of suds and then in covering Maria's naked body with the sweet smelling foam. She blows on the soap in her hand and the two of them watch the bubbles drift up and across the back field, sinking into a rare moment of sheer pleasure. Akila rubs Maria down with a bath sheet and wraps her in it. As the sun sets they retreat to Maria's room, where Akila ties up her hair in ribbons and slips a matching cornflower blue chemise over her head.

"You don't need your pantaloons. Just more to take off. And it's hot tonight anyway."

When Pierre comes into the salon, Maria is looking radiant, with a bare leg thrown casually over the arm of the chair, her blue chemise draped enticingly. They retire to dinner and are served by Jean-Baptiste. As Pierre is reaching for a third helping of rum, she puts her hand over his glass, cocking her head with mock coquettishness. He blinks at her in a dazed fashion, as if taking in that there is no way out of this.

"Let us retire early, my love," she murmurs, taking his hand.

In their bedroom, she stands him in a pool of moonlight and begins undressing him, putting her hands softly on his hips, and then fondling his limp penis playfully. He responds by putting his hands on her shoulders. She kneels and takes his penis in her mouth, sucking on it, until it begins, first with a quiver, and then with a bit of a jolt, to harden. Pierre stares up at the ceiling, arching his back expectantly…until Maria pushes him gently toward the bed.

"Oh my love…" she murmurs, as he falls back onto the bed. She is moving faster now, getting him in position. She springs lightly onto the bed and pulls up her chemise, straddling his legs, performing dazzling maneuvers on his penis with her lips and tongue. A little gurgle in his throat is her signal. She lifts herself on her knees and positions herself over his hard penis and slides it inside, moving on it, and to her complete astonishment she feels her entire body turned to a golden liquid.

In the morning when Akila flutters into their room, Maria opens her eyes and whispers, "What a good instructor you are…" She stretches. "Now it is up to the Lord to do the rest."

"Well, you know it doesn't always work the first time…"

From Pierre's side of the bed comes a somnolent snort, and Maria puts her finger to her lips. She rises and goes with Akila behind the curtain. Their riotous mood of the previous afternoon is now in that bank of memories of intimacy and affection to be cherished through a lifetime. Akila silently takes a sponge and gently washes her, lifting her arms and her breasts, and tapping her knee to get her to put her foot on the stool so she can sponge between her legs. Maria is passive and silent.

Chapter Twenty-Five: The Dowager Queen

Copenhagen, 1771

The day following the dinner a tiny black African appears at the door. I know immediately that this is Beppo, the dwarf slave who belongs to the Dowager Queen. She has sent him on an errand. Phebe opens the door, and I can tell by the weight of the silence between them that they know each other. But Beppo is being very formal.

"An invitation from the Dowager Queen. For Miss Summy. And you too," he says with a little bow, handing Phebe an envelope. I go to the door and stand beside her. Beppo winks. I giggle.

"Thank you, sir," Phebe says, returning the bow. Still smiling, he turns and disappears down the hallway, across the glassed-in bridge, his head bobbing along at the level of the windowsills.

"So that's Beppo." I murmur.

"Yes, that's Beppo. I don't know him well, but we have exchanged words occasionally in the hallways. The poor man. As if it isn't oddity enough to be an African in this place, but to be a dwarf too. I think it's sickening how he is treated like some kind of pet animal. But I truly admire his spirit."

I find myself flushing…is it mortification for my own race? That terrible feeling of helplessness in the face of the vastness of this injustice? I touch her arm and hang my head.

A word about the Dowager Queen, Julianna Marie, the consort of King Frederick, Christian's father. The word is jealous. She is jealous on behalf of her son, Frederick, who at this moment is eighteen. He is a somewhat peculiar-looking man. In his childhood he was sickly and stunted, with a bit of a hump, but he is growing slowly more normal as he attains his full height. Unlike his half-brother Christian, he has his full mental powers. Julianna quite naturally believes he should be King, not Christian. After all he too is the son of Frederick V. She imagines that this should be quite an attainable goal, given the deteriorating state of Christian's mind. But Struensee and the Queen have rescued the monarch from his ineptitude, and they stand in the way of her objectives. I am sure Julianna has invited me because she knows about the friendship between Johanne and the Queen and thinks I might have some chatty observations of my own to share. I suspect she has invited Phebe so that Beppo can pry out of her any observations she might have.

It is an awkward afternoon. I instantly dislike the woman, most intensely and immediately, because of the way she treats Beppo. "Isn't he adorable?" she asks me.

"Well, he is rather handsome, I think." I grin at Beppo, who pulls himself to his full height and smiles broadly into the distance.

"One of our sea captains found him for me. They are hard to come by because they have become quite the fashion all over Europe."

"Oh," I hear the lameness in my own voice, like a deflating balloon.

"Your people in St. Croix are very prosperous I believe. I suppose they have many slaves?"

"I am afraid so. More than three hundred when I left a year ago. The plantation is large." I feel my face get hot with shame. I am hating every minute of this conversation, trapped as I am between the reality of my life and background and my newfound sense of justice. But I know that above all this woman expects me to be thoroughly obsequious, to bow down before her.

We play cards, joined by two other older women. Johanne has been teaching me whist, but still, I am horribly nervous. Gradually it becomes apparent that I have a far better memory than any of these old women, and my confidence and performance at the game grow. The Dowager has a question for me each time the cards are shuffled.

"You must be enjoying all these evenings at the royal table with your aunt. I hear she has become quite a favorite of the Queen. I am not!" Her tone is arch. "But you are probably aware of that."

"Oh no, I haven't heard anything to make me believe that." I am wracking my brain to think of something more positive to say, but nothing comes to mind.

"I suppose Dr. Struensee is always there. Does he sit next to the King? Or the Queen? "Well usually between the two of them." A nervous giggle erupts from me as I say this. "The first time I was at such a dinner he sat next to me and we had such an interesting conversation." I stop short of praising his advanced ideas, because I am all but sure that the Dowager Queen would disapprove of all the Struensee reforms, but I hope to convey quietly whose side I am on.

I have wondered at the beginning of the afternoon whether I might meet Frederick, and see for myself whether he was malformed. But there is no sign of him, nor any mention. At the end of the afternoon I feel quite proud of myself for parrying all the attempts at information that the Dowager had challenged me with. But there is one piece of harmless information that I offer the Dowager: that my uncle Thomas is not a particular fan of Struensee. I think it placates her a bit.

Midway through our card game Phebe and Beppo have disappeared; then, as if on cue, they reappear just as our game is ending.

"So where did you go?" I ask her once we're on the bridge.

"As soon as the Dowager's attention was completely engaged in the game, Beppo signaled me to come with him, and we went down the backstairs and into a garden shed just around the corner. The most curious and adorable place, you wouldn't have believed it. There was a little stove in it and it was just so cozy. Inside were three other Africans, from different families in the city. I was so surprised to see them all sitting there having a fine time gossiping together about their families! I had no idea they lived in the city. I wonder if their families keep them kind of hidden."

The two of us pause on the glassed-in bridge, both arrested at the same moment by the light. The sky is the color of dark delphiniums, a purple-blue streaked with orange rays of the setting sun. We lean on the window ledge, only slightly aware of the shadowy shapes in the street below.

"And do you know, I know every one of their families back in St. Croix. They all come from there, and they knew mine, and yours too. One of their friends had recently escaped to Greenland. Can you imagine that? After growing up in the tropics to end up in Greenland?

And you'd never see your family again either."

When we get back to our rooms there is a letter waiting for me from my mother. A little chill runs down my spine…of excitement tinged with fear. St. Croix is not an easy place and I am always afraid for the people I love. I sit down on the bed and open the envelope, breaking the wax seal unceremoniously. Phebe sits beside me. I can feel that her breathing has almost stopped.

But the news is mostly banal. Except for the sad news that my sister Elizabeth and her husband, John Rogiers, have lost another baby. Their third child to die. She writes of Phebe's sisters and brother too. One with diphtheria who has finally recovered. There was a dance at the Big House. They hung John MacAllister for murder from the gibbet by the Fort and left his body there for a month. A tropical storm sank two ships in the harbor. Phebe and I look at each other when I have finished reading the letter aloud. I take her hand.

"I miss them all so much," Phebe says. "But what a hard place it is." I nod.

"Let us pray for the baby's soul." And we kneel by the bed and each say a prayer out loud for the baby and all those we have left behind. I am planning to work again by candlelight on the diary tonight after Phebe has gone to bed.

Chapter Twenty-Six: The Churprincessen

St. Thomas, 1696

The distant sound of a conch summoning slaves to the fields wakes Maria from her daydream. She has been absently watching Akila dandle Mo Mo on her knees in the back courtyard.

"I am going to ask Pierre to go out to one of those Brandenburg ships and get a girl who can serve as a minder for Mo Mo," Maria announces. "Anna can nurse him occasionally, but she cannot interrupt her other chores to give him the attention he'll need as he grows older. And we have our work to do."

Akila looks up at Maria and takes a deep breath. She smothers a hot spark of anger and leans forward touching Mo Mo's nose with her own, sinking into motherhood. She sighs.

She is suddenly in another place and time, sitting by the well in her village dandling a newborn baby on her knee while their mothers chat. The longing in her heart for her mother is fierce.

"I hardly knew you could love anything so much as this," Akila presses a knuckle into the corner of her eye. "Do you suppose our mothers loved us so? I had never imagined feeling like this. I love caring for him myself."

She passes her hand softly over his head. "But you are right. There are others who need us, and we are so often called away. I will feel better if there's one person who can take charge of him. Part of me wishes we could go ourselves to select someone. I would so like to see if I know anyone on those ships. But I know I couldn't bear it."

Akila looks out towards the harbor. In St. Thomas, slaves have come to be sold directly off the ship in the French manner, not in the kind of slave markets that the English are developing in their ports.

Maria looks thoughtfully at Akila. "They'd never let a woman on board, much less a slave woman. The stench must be unbearable. We get the occasional whiff even from here. I cannot imagine…" Maria's voice trails off as she realizes what she has said.

"I can," Akila says softly, "only too well. But you never get used to the smell."

Maria covers her face with her hands. "Forgive me Keela. Sometimes I'm just stupid."

"Never mind…But maybe we can ask Pierre to see if he finds anyone who fits my father's description."

When Maria proposes getting a nursemaid for Mo Mo off the slave ship, Pierre shrugs.

He is a man inured to bigger surprises from his wife. The request seems modest enough. "If you wish. I am going anyway to get some laborers for a bit of land I'm going to plant tobacco on." Pierre yawns self-consciously; he knows this is incendiary.

Maria feels herself blush to the tips of her ears. Surprise? Mortification? Shame?

Fury? She wonders how long he has been planning this.

"So you're going to become a planter?" She turns away from him as she says this, hoping he will not see her flushed face or hear the tremor in her voice.

"The Company has yet to get any revenue from this island. There's a lot of pressure to make it productive. I can hardly be pressing others to plant if I don't do it myself." His tone is defensive. Whiney. "Don't worry, I'll get an overseer. I'm not going to try to handle slaves right off a ship myself."

"Oh, Pierre, it is one thing to have slaves to help in the house, but it's something else to have them doing such back-breaking work to make money for others, work that will likely kill them. No good can come of it. It is surely against the Lord's will."

"Well, my dear, sugar is the business this island is in and as an employee of the Company I am expected to be in it too. I think I have been a good master to our slaves." Maria turns and looks at him squarely, trying to chase away the image of him with Marcus.

Pierre sighs and pats her on the shoulder.

Unable to speak for frustration, Maria shrugs his hand away. The realization washes over her that what she really feels is fury. As a mason builds his house one brick at a time, Pierre is going to select the first bricks of his plantation, the first generation of slaves to labor in anguish building the wealth of others, entwining her family in a cycle that will go on for who knows how many generations. She sees it all in a wordless flash, and stands looking at him, immobilized by a feeling of helplessness, knowing that he is unmovable.

"Once you do that, you know, we'll never leave this place. I had so hoped that we might go to a more civilized place. New England perhaps…"

"Let us take advantage of the opportunities here for a while. We can make a fortune, and then we can go. There's nothing for us in New England. Besides, they're burning witches in New England. And there are no French there."

She knows it is pointless to argue, so she determines to let it go, thinking of her own immediate objectives.

"Why don't you take Bamadille and Lucien with you. I know they need more help in the bakery." She also knows that Bamadille would recognize Akila's father if he happened to be on board, but she keeps this to herself.

Pierre says pensively, "I don't know that Lucien has the stomach for that errand, but Bamadille would be good. He could talk some to whoever we thought looked promising. He's a good man. I trust him."

As Pierre says this, he is thinking, *Marcus is good for some things, but he can be crafty sometimes, and jealous. Bamadille is older and respectful.* The thought of going out to the slave ship makes his stomach clench, and he is tempted to send Bamadille and Lucien as his proxies, but he wants to see the Brandenburger operation for himself.

"Bring Bamadille by to talk with Akila before you go. She will want to tell him what kind of person she wants for Mo Mo."

He complies with this request. Bamadille and Akila sit together in the courtyard, two people deeply attached by their shared history and suffering. In Soninke Akila says, "See if you can get news of our village, and of my father. I pray he is not a captive, but if he is, let Allah bring him here to me. Be watchful, Bamadille. Find a fine woman for my Mo Mo. If you can, bring someone of our people. But most important, a woman who you think might have good cheer when she is finally out of that terrible ship. Remember how terrified we were? How we thought we were to be eaten or made into leather shoes? It is not easy what we have suffered, but it is not as bad as we had imagined, though you and I fared better than most. I know you will choose well."

Bamadille looks down at his gnarled hands. He turns to face her, and a whisper comes out of him. "I feel terrible dread at the thought of boarding that ship, dread as only you can imagine. The spirits that linger there must be fierce with anger. I will take a gris-gris to protect me. And I will look carefully for anyone from our village. I will find a good soul for your Mo Mo."

They go the following morning. It is November. The hurricane season is over. The sky is a pure cerulean blue. A sailor from the Fort has been drafted to row them out to the *Churprincessen*, registered in Emden. Alongside it is the *Frederick III*, also from Emden.

Between the two ships there are 1110 souls aboard. The terrible smell reaches them before they have gone a hundred yards out into the harbor, and the sailor rowing excuses himself to tie a bandana over his mouth and nose.

"You don't have another do you?" Pierre asks him anxiously. He shakes his head in reply. Bamadille reaches into his pocket and takes out a clean white handkerchief and hands it to Pierre. There is a moment of hesitation and then Pierre snatches it from Bamadille's hand and puts it over his nose and mouth.

As they approach the *Churprincessen* the air is filled with a cacophony of sounds, from singing and chanting to wailing. Pierre's throat constricts with terror. Bamadille sits like a statue, staring straight ahead. There is a rope ladder over the side of the *Churprincessen*. Pierre gives a shout that they are coming aboard, and the captain appears at the rail.

"Pierre La Salle here. My wife's uncle is David Bordeaux of the Brandenburgers."

"Come ahead then. You are welcome. We have a big cargo here and can sell you as many as you need."

"Any aboard who could serve as an overseer?"

"My men are all sailors. Even if they wished to change professions I cannot part with any until we are done with discharging this cargo. We have other ports of call to make here in the West Indies. St. Thomas is far too small to handle so many as we have aboard these two vessels."

Pierre and Bamadille climb aboard, leaving the sailor in the skiff.

Hundreds of dark bodies slick with oil are on the deck, sitting, standing, clinging to each other. Pierre presses the handkerchief over his nose and mouth and wishes he had more hands to cover his ears. He fixes his eyes on a sailor throwing a bucket of water over a woman to wash the waste she is sitting in through the gunwales.

"Oh my God," he says under his breath.

A shadow falls over him and he turns to see a tall bewhiskered man beside him. Red- faced, redhaired and wearing a red shirt, he is backlit by the sun, and to Pierre's eye he looks almost as if he were on fire.

"Pardon, sir," he says in a low voice. "I could not help but overhear you ask about an overseer. Rufus MacAllister here." And he gives a little nod of the head and sticks his hand out boldly. "Though the Captain may not be keen on it, I am ready to be off this ship. I am the second son of a Scottish laird and not a seafaring man by choice. I'd be quite willing to serve you as an overseer, and I know these buggers here and can help you choose some healthy strong ones."

Pierre looks at Rufus MacAllister thoughtfully. The aura of light around him is otherworldly. Is he a devil or an angel? For the briefest of moments he wrestles with his conscience; the captain has been very explicit that he cannot spare any of his sailors. But then, he is working for the Brandenburgers, not the Danish West Indies Company. All the better to be weakening the competition. The question is just how to go about it.

"I can read your mind," MacAllister says, smiling genially. "I'll just give you a nod over one group or another here on board, and then I'll meet you later today in town. The Captain won't have an inkling as to where I've gone off to."

"Come to my office at the Fort this afternoon. Pierre LaSalle is my name. Arrange to deliver the slaves I am about to buy." Pierre nods curtly at MacAllister and moves along the aisle of slave merchandise, trying to look in command of himself.

Bamadille moves beside him rigidly, his stomach roiling. His head feels like it will explode as he tries to hold himself together. He has moved a third of the way down the ship when he sees a woman from his village. He cannot remember her name. MacAllister leans against the forecastle. Bamadille can feel his gaze as if it were a branding iron.

Touching the scars on his own temple, Bamadille turns to Pierre and says, "This girl has the marks of our village. Let me speak to her." And he launches into a stream of Soninke that makes Pierre smile for the first time all morning.

In a matter of minutes Bamadille knows that Akila's father is not on board.

According to this girl, whose name is Kansoleh, he is most likely still chief of their village, or was when she was abducted many months ago. She had grown up with the story of Akila. It was told again and again as a caution, she tells him. The chief had sent a search party after Akila, but they had either started too late or had gone on the wrong trail. The whole village had mourned the death of their chief's wife and the abduction of his daughter. She looks up woefully at Bamadille and adds, "They mourned you too." But he does not believe her. He knows she is saying that as comfort to him, but he likes her for saying it and thinks immediately that she is the one to care for Mo Mo.

Then she asks, "What is this fearsome place we have landed?"

"A most primitive place. Run by White people from Denmark who plan to make a lot of money from plantations of tobacco and cotton and sugar. They need slaves to work the fields. But this family also needs help caring for the babies. We will make our rounds, but I promise we will return."

They continue down the line of slaves and Pierre watches MacAllister out of the corner of his eye. Occasionally he gives a nod of assent as Pierre comes to a male slave.

Pierre then turns to Bamadille. "What do you think?" What tribe is this one from? Can you speak to him?" Bamadille speaks in Soninke and the man answers in another tongue.

"Yoruba," Bamadille says to Pierre. "Not a language I really know."

"He looks strong." Pierre's voice is muffled by the handkerchief. Bamadille looks at the man's bloodshot eyes and sees his terror and confusion. "Yes." Bamadille looks away.

Within a half hour they have identified ten strong men, and Bamadille has persuaded Pierre to buy Kansoleh for Akila.

"She is young and teachable. And they speak the same tongue. That is better when there is a child. Less confusing."

Pierre just wants to get off the ship. He pays the captain in Rixsdollars and arranges for the cargo to be delivered later that day, except for the girl Kansoleh, whom they will take with them now.

As he goes over the rail, Pierre catches MacAllister's eye and they both nod. Rowing back to the wharf they pass Casper Rysberg in a dory on a trajectory to the *Frederick III*.

"I hear he's killed most of the slaves he bought in '92. Worked them to death." Bamadille says this in a low voice, tight with control.

"He's one of the few who've produced anything at all for the Company though. The fevers get them too," Pierre says in a defensive tone. His mind is racing now, thinking ahead to his meeting with MacAllister and to the work of clearing the land for his plantation.

Chapter Twenty-Seven: Hirscholm Summer

Copenhagen and Hirscholm, March 1771

I have been struggling with Maria's diary, cursing the scrunched, abbreviated words on the page, when Phebe knocks. I had been working on an entry that read: *pd vst Brdx plntn myslvsw fvrs*. It had taken some time to figure out the letters, and when that was finally done, I had to puzzle over their meaning. After some thought I had decided that it meant "paid visit to the Bordeaux plantation many slaves with fevers." I groaned with disappointment. How very dull. The diary is a strange combination of extraordinary revelations mixed with banal daily reports. And oh, the lists of diseases and medicines! Despite spending every spare moment alone trying to decipher it, I have made very little progress. I have nonetheless kept the treasure to myself, wrapped up in a nightie I never wear, tucked in the trunk.

I shove the diary and my transcription pages under my pillow, sit down in front of the mirror and take up the hairbrush nonchalantly. "Come in."

Phebe swings open the door.

"What have you been up to?" Phebe asks, cocking her head with a little half-smile. "Are you going to take your hair down and brush it?" Her eyebrows go up, and I realize that I look ridiculous, that she's seen right through me.

"Oh nothing. Just daydreaming," I reply lamely. I can feel the pink flush of the lie traveling to the tips of my ears. But she has other things on her mind.

"Johanne sent me on an errand and I stopped in the garden shed with Beppo and his friends on my way back. It's so tiny…like a dollhouse. Madlane was there. She works for some rich sugar family here in Copenhagen… and Polidore. He works in the kitchen in the castle.

Beppo told us all about Mr. Brandt giving the King a beating after he threw all the furniture out the window. Beppo said he beat him like 'he was one of us'." She attempts a laugh, but it comes out as a snort.

"I can't think how Brandt would get away with beating the King."

"Nor I, but he seems to have. Oh, but it's cold in here. Your fire's almost out."

"There's no more fuel."

"I'll fetch some."

I stare out the window while Phebe goes down to the courtyard to fill the wood basket. I'm wondering what Struensee thinks of Brandt, who seems to me to be his opposite, a hothead to Struensee's cerebral calm. But they are most certainly colleagues.

When Phebe returns, she stokes the fire and pulls her shawl around her shoulders. "Really, what have you been doing all afternoon? I am beginning to worry about you. Have you been stalking Dr. Struensee? Trying to find his secret meeting place with the Queen? You should get him out of your mind. He's not paying the least attention to you."

I am miffed at this suggestion, and at the implication that Phebe is suddenly the mature one who knows best.

"Oh Phebe, you sound like Mother! What's going on with you? You're so different all of a sudden."

"Your mother?! Lord preserve me." She exhales a long breath that hangs like an exclamation point between us. "How can we not be different in a place like this? It's so different. I feel like a plant that's been put in the wrong soil, though you seem right at home."

"What do you mean? I feel like I don't belong anywhere," I say. Phebe sinks down on the bed and I stare out the window. "Do you want to go home?" I look down at Phebe plaintively.

"No. I'm not sure that I ever want to go home. Maybe that's the problem. It's all very confusing." She sits very still, looking down at the floorboards.

Though I had long ago decided that I never wanted to see St. Croix again, I feel an ugly voice rising in me. Is it the master voice? Is it my mother's voice? I open my mouth and close it, appalled at what almost came out. Crimson flares in my cheeks and I feel the tears welling. I turn away, overwhelmed by the weight of secrets, between us, around us.

I know I am flustered because although neither of us wants to return home, I am the only one with a choice in the matter. Yet I am confused by the choice. And no place seems like home anymore. Denmark seems now to me a world where everyone is wearing a mask.

The one I most desire to unmask is Struensee. I cannot stop thinking of him and the moment he kissed me. What was the meaning of that? To silence me? To make me loyal to him? Could he have been attracted to me? I dissect the moment of his kiss slowly, reliving each sensation in my mind, until I have difficulty breathing and have to bring myself back. But now everyone is saying what I may have been the first to observe: that the Queen and Dr. Struensee are in love. I have seen the Queen on more than one occasion cross over the glass bridge into our side of the castle grounds, the side where Struensee lives. Where do they meet? I wonder.

I cannot help myself. I keep my eye on the glass bridge, hoping to see the Queen slip across. But the Queen is now heavy with child and not moving about very much and I am disappointed. Struensee attends her in the palace as her doctor. Not much of a surprise there. But I do see Johanne on occasion walking with Frederik Karl von Warnstedt. And I think that's very odd. I thought he was Sophie von Bulow's lover. I ask Heinrich what he thinks.

"Oh Summy, you know this place is just a snake pit. Everyone's busy betraying everyone else. It's like a sport. You know, that's why I like you. You are such an innocent, sincere and honest. It's the rarest thing you can imagine in Denmark."

"Well, my Uncle Thomas is just like me and I'm sure he would be astonished if his wife were…" I find myself unable to finish the sentence.

"Don't worry your pretty head about it. People get so bored at court, flirtation is like fencing, a game. Mostly it is quite harmless. Have you seen Ove Hœegh Guldberg in your spying?" Heinrich laughs out loud. "He's probably spying on you. He watches everyone like a hawk. Do you know who I mean?"

"The little ugly man who looks like an ancient gnome?"

"That very one."

"He is often with the Dowager Queen, though never in public."
"He is a plotter. Wait and see. Something will happen."

"'Something is rotten in the state of Denmark,' " I giggle at my own wit. "I can't even name it. In St. Croix the evil of the place is quite obvious: slavery and all the horrible ways that slaves are worked to death. But here everyone is so polite, but you have the feeling they'd just as soon stab you in the back the moment you're not looking."

"No one would stab you in the back, sweet Summy. You are the bright light in our dark winters here. And I cannot resist pointing out that even though slavery is not much in evidence here, the wealth of the country is built on it."

Late in the spring the court moves once again to Hirscholm Castle. Heinrich manages to accompany us, and Antoine comes along with the stable crew. Beppo, as always, is at the side of the Queen Dowager. We are back in our old quarters and the shadows of wisteria blossoms dance on the floor of my room.

"She is plotting something with Guldberg," Phebe says, stroking a brush through my hair. "I just know it."

In early July the Queen is delivered of a healthy baby girl whose tiny face is scrutinized by all who see her, with a single thought. Does she look like the King or Struensee?

"Can I see the baby, Aunt?" I twist a strand of my black hair around my finger, a nervous habit I have developed in the past weeks.

"I suppose you want to see for yourself who the little mite looks like, just as everyone else does." She is inspecting her own face in the mirror as she says this, as though looking for some surprise resemblance there herself. "Come with me this morning, if you like."

The room is startlingly beautiful, with high ceilings plastered with cherubs, and shadows flickering on the parquet floor from the sunlight stippling through the trees. A soft morning breeze flows through the wide-open windows. The Queen, resting on a soft grey brocade chaise longue, is the centerpiece, with the baby nestled in the crook of her arm. The Queen's face is flushed and puffy, as if she has been crying. I am flooded with sympathy tempered with curiosity. I start to creep forward to see the child. Johanne puts a restraining hand on my shoulder.

"Caroline, I hope you are well this morning. I have brought my niece. I hope you don't mind. She so wanted to see the baby."

"No, of course not. Come ahead."

"Your Majesty," I say uncertainly, curtsying. And then I peer down at the child. "Oh how lovely she is." I put my hand to my mouth as if to cover my awe at the tiny face staring back at me. I look for some resemblance to either Struensee or King Christian. In truth, both of these possible fathers have rather long noses, and the baby's is just a baby's, snub and short. I cannot decide. But I feel the blood rush to my face nonetheless, as if my thoughts had been read by the Queen.

"She is just perfect. A little beauty." This much I can say with no equivocation. The baby is named Louise Augusta.

In the days that follow, Johanne is much with the Queen, and reports that she is exhausted, crying and laughing alternately. "Mothers are often very emotional after they give birth," she says. "If that's what it's like I am in no hurry to have children." And under her breath: "Not that that's very likely in our case." She sniggers, as if this thought must out, but doesn't really want to be heard.

But I do hear, and I've always remembered the comment, though it didn't have much meaning to me at the time.

I don't wonder for long, however, for the summer has many distractions and my spirits have lightened. The days are long and dreamy, lingering into a foggy twilight. There are parties almost every night that go 'til the dawn breaks into a fierce daylight. Sometimes there are small card parties, sometimes there is dancing. The men sit in small groups talking politics, watching the women dancing or waiting to be asked. I like to listen to them…to watch them to see whom they are eyeing.

On this evening I flip open a fan, a manoeuvre I have been practicing in my room, and lean against a pillar. The room is a soft grey and white confection, alive with candlelight, which brightens the evening light still seeping like a fog through the windows. I watch the dancers and listen to the men sitting at a card table nearby. One of them is the ugly toad of a man, Guldberg, who sits silently listening.

"There are six hundred of them and they are tearing the town apart. The crown has paid no wages to them at all, and they were brought to Copenhagen to build ships and get paid. They all expected to be rich by now and they are in a rage to be so treated. I hear that every tavern has been turned upside down."

I feel a hand on my shoulder and I wheel around, startled.

"Oh good," I whisper to Heinrich behind my fan. "Perhaps you can explain to me what I have been hearing from these men. Something about Norwegian sailors and Algeria."

He blows out his lips and says, "It's too boring for words. I will spare you." I make a face but acquiesce, offering him my arm and heading for the dance floor.

Heinrich is much by my side throughout the summer. We ride, we picnic. Always in a group. Always laughing. I am now taking care not to be alone with him as I was on that first ride in the autumn. But the summer has its way of making me feel languid. One night in August he takes me out on the lake in a rowboat and we drift. I lean back against him. He puts his hand on my breast, a barely noticeable swelling at this stage, but sensitive nonetheless. He plays with my nipple and suddenly I can't breathe. He leans down and kisses me, and I feel a strange little earthquake inside. I sit up abruptly.

"We'd better go in." I can almost hear my mother's voice whispering in my ear.

Phebe and Antoine have their own little nest in the stable, though Phebe complains that it affords them little privacy. Antoine is responsible in the course of each evening for the horses that carry the guests to the parties. For those who come in carriages, he must put up with their drivers, who are eager to get up a game of cards. He has his own room in the back and Phebe slips in unseen and awaits him. She brings her mending for those moments when he is occupied. But when he can get away, they cuddle together on his bed, fully clothed, for fear of the need of his leaping up, or of their being discovered. But she has confessed to me that she does not mind his hands roaming over her breasts. Or his mouth. In fact she has shared things that have made me blush scarlet, but I cannot help but be fascinated. She tells me how she has discovered ways to make him exquisitely happy with her hands and her mouth. A chair rests against the door so no one can enter easily.

Morning lessons are suspended for the summer. No one gets up very early when their nights have been so long. When the sun is reaching its zenith Phebe comes into my room and chastises me.

"You're wasting a beautiful day."

"I'll get up," I murmur with a sigh.

"Good party? There were certainly lots of people. It was busy down at the stable."

I lie back on the pillows. "We went out in the skiff. It was so lovely. But you feel like everyone can see you. I cannot ever get used to the light here."

Phebe goes over to the window and looks out at the courtyard. "There was a lot of gossip about Dr. Struensee last night in the stable. And about the Norwegian sailors, who are in a fury. I can hear all the grooms talking through the wall while they play cards."

"Yes, the Norwegians seem to be on everyone's mind… Don't you think it's grand that the King has made Johan a count?"

"Oh Summy, open your eyes! Everyone was outraged about it. They were objecting that he proclaims himself a man of the people and then becomes a count. And he's not even Danish, and he doesn't speak the language. At least that's what they were all talking about." She frowns at me. "Don't you at least think that it is a little odd?"

I feel a surge of anger at her tone. I prop myself on my elbow and look at Phebe. "You shouldn't gossip."

Phebe looks as if she'd been slapped. She turns and leaves the room.

It is days before our relationship begins to heal. Phebe has been distant, not in a distracted way, but with deliberation, and I have been arguing with myself, back and forward: "You shouldn't have said that to her," comes one little voice of reproach. "But she shouldn't gossip. You were quite right to tell her so," comes the echoing reply. I distract myself with the diary, poring over it for hours. I've made it about a third of the way through, and the work is going faster. I am in awe of Maria, her boldness and especially her relationship to Akila. I feel proud to be named for her. But I am a little puzzled by the intimacy between Maria and Akila. It is hard to imagine that relationship today. I love Phebe, but I could never entirely forget that she is a family slave. Akila doesn't seem to be a slave as much as my great grandmother's closest friend, almost a sister. How do these attitudes get baked so thoroughly into us?

In the end, I cannot bear Phebe's frostiness. Reading the diary is making me think differently about my relationship to her. If these feelings of "superiority" have been baked into me, what attitudes have been baked into her? Hate? I realize we have gone into dangerous territory.

"I'm sorry I spoke to you like that. It was wrong of me. You have every right to your opinion. And I cannot bear for us to quarrel. You are my dearest friend."

Phebe looks at me for a long moment. "You are forgiven." She smiles lightly. "Now tell me what you are doing with Heinrich. I'm dying to know."

"Well it's not very exciting…"

Uncle Thomas is much occupied with his duties despite the fact that we are in the country, reasonably far from the turmoil that is reported in Copenhagen. He paces in the evening and tells us that tensions across the country are rising. The harvests have been bad two years in a row. Struensee's proclamation giving freedom to the press the previous summer had unleashed a flood of pamphleteering that has not abated. Word has spread like wildfire of the King's elevation of Struensee to Count and worse, that he had given him the authority to issue cabinet orders with the force of royal authority even without the King's signature.

At the bottom of the social ladder are the Norwegians, who are incensed that Denmark seems to consume all that Norway produces, while the Norwegians grow poorer and poorer. The contingent of Norwegian sailors in Copenhagen is focusing its rage on Struensee. Thomas has kept the guards on high alert all summer, fearing a revolt that might spread to our summer idyll.

One afternoon in late August, Phebe and I find him sitting in the Guardhouse. I bend down and kiss him on the cheek.

"Uncle, how are you faring? You have been preoccupied lately and have not been to see us. We sit down on either side of him and I take his hand.

Chapter Twenty-Eight: Comfort

St. Thomas, December 1696

The rippling effects of Mo Mo's birth are still being felt in the La Salle household.

Maria's emotions are like her hair, unruly, tightly coiled and overabundant. She has developed an arsenal of distractions to keep herself under control. She spends hours pounding herbs; she goes determinedly to the waterfront looking for interesting wares off the ships in the harbor; and when all else fails, she rides Cibonie at a gallop on the beaches. She is both jealous of Akila's having a baby and of the baby itself, for Mo Mo seems to have stolen all of Akila's love. She has almost forgotten her night with Pierre two weeks before. He had finally awakened with seeming amnesia and never spoken a word about it.

Akila raises an eyebrow at her. "You know it is only natural that I should love my child. I love you none the less for it. And I know you love him too." It is true, he is an adorable creature and Maria dotes on him, but somehow that only deepens the pit inside her.

On the morning that Pierre has gone to the slave ship Maria rides Cibonie out of town along the beaches, trying to quiet her roiling emotions. She finds she cannot quite get her breath whether she is active or still.

She rides into the waves and feels the tension slowly ease. She is almost at Isaac and Pundi's. She slows the mare and walks her toward their house. She jumps off in the yard, leaving Cibonie next to the cow.

"Anyone home?" She calls out.

"In here, Maria." It is Pundi's voice.

Maria puts her hands up to her hair, fussily rearranging the strands that have flown loose on her ride. She finds herself hoping that he is alone.

"Oh Pundi. What are you doing?" She comes into the workroom and stands beside him looking down at the collection of plant materials he has on the counter. She watches his beautiful brown hands meticulously separating the greens.

"Where's Isaac?"

"Well, I'm doing this and that, and Isaac is foraging as usual. His favorite pastime."

"Oh Pundi." She sighs and realizes that she said this a moment ago. She is so confused. Tears start welling in her eyes.

He scratches his head, looking at her. "Maria? Are you all right? What's going on?"

And she begins to sob. He puts his arms out and she falls into them, pressing her face into his crisp white shirt. It smells so clean, like the sun, she thinks.

"Come, let's take a walk and you can tell me all about it. I need to get out into the day." He puts his arm around her comfortingly and leads her outside. He takes a clean cloth and dips it in the barrel of rainwater and wipes her tear-streaked face. Maria shuts her eyes and basks in the tenderness of the moment. She feels like a starving creature being fed manna. The animals contentedly graze on the meager pickings of the yard.

"It's just everything, Pundi. My life has unravelled. Akila is wrapped up with Mo Mo. Of course he's adorable, but it has changed our life so. And Pierre has this dreadful plan to start a plantation. This very morning he's hiring an overseer and has bought a lot of field slaves off that Brandenburg ship. It's going to start us down a terrible road." She stops and looks at him for a long moment, debating whether to tell him the worst bit of all.

"And my husband doesn't love me." The words sound so melodramatic and stupid she puts her hand over her mouth and stares at Pundi.

"What can you possibly mean? Of course he does. He's devoted to you. He's always got his arm around you. He's always bragging about you and how brave you are. It's just a matter of time 'til you have a baby of your own, Maria." She looks up at him, hesitating, the breath gone out of her. What has she got to lose?

"He loves men, Pundi. I mean he makes love to men. He doesn't make love to me." Pundi stares at her for a long moment and takes a deep breath, exhaling dramatically.

He says very quietly, "Well now, that's another thing entirely." There is a long silence between them, and he continues. "But how do you know? I mean the men part."

"I know it with my own eyes. When we had the hospital. I went home one day to take a nap and saw him with Marcus. Oh my God I will never get the sight out of my head. He didn't see me. He doesn't know I know."

"Oh, my sweet Maria! I am so sorry. You know, Pierre is a handsome lad, and he was just that when he first went among sailors. I am sure that is what happened. Sailors are a bawdy lot, and there are a few who just prefer men to women." Pundi pauses for a long moment looking at Maria, and then he gazes down into the dust. "Have you ever been lovers?"

"Well not exactly. Oh, he's attempted it maybe three times, but without much success. At least Akila tells me that is not how it is supposed to be."

Tears begin again trickling down her cheeks and Pundi puts his arms around her.

They are by a stream.

"Let's sit here and rest for a few minutes. I will teach you to breathe in a way that will calm you." They sit cross-legged, facing each other. He demonstrates holding one nostril closed and breathing through the other. She tries it. They sit for some minutes doing the breath exercises.

"You're a master already. See how it relaxes you? And energizes at the same time?"

She smiles and closes her eyes, and leaning forward, offers him her mouth. After a long moment she feels the touch of his lips on hers. A light, gentle touch at first, she responds slowly with the tip of her tongue, running it over his lips. The sensations flowing into her body overwhelm her and she feels as if her mind were far above her, departing to some other realm. Its last murmuring is, "Let Him lead you like a lamb." And then the mind is gone, along with her will. Her body is some melting thing, hot and flowing, and the will to stop has just spilled out somewhere. He pulls her to him, cradling her in his arms and she lets his tongue explore her mouth. She can scarcely breathe for the pounding of her heart. His eyes are closed but his face is flushed and she sees that he has been overtaken just as she has. His hand moves up under her chemise and caresses her breast. The sky opens up above her and she feels herself floating in a lavender field. The bees are making honey and honey is running through her entire body.

He licks her nipple and takes it into his mouth, sucking, awakening a life force within her that is like fine hot gossamer filaments stretching from her groin to the top of her head. Instinctively she reaches down and touches his penis, reaching her hand into his dhoti. She has a moment of intense surprise. It is hot and hard and she realizes in a flash that Pierre has never desired her this way, has never hardened like this for her. She grasps it with a powerful sense of fulfillment and rightness. This is the gift that God has asked her to be patient for, the gift He has been waiting to give her.

"Stand up," he murmurs, and she obeys. He unbuttons her pantaloons and as they drop to the ground she steps out of them, lifting her chemise over her head. Her abundant hair has sprung loose from its chignon and she stands naked before him. He kneels and buries his head in the curly mound between her legs, licking her with his tongue. She arches her back and looks up through the trees at the wild expanse of the heavens, and moans. Then she pushes him down gently and with one tug unties his dhoti, revealing his penis, like the gnarled root of a great tree, pulsing with a love deferred. She sits astride him and he puts his hands on her waist, looking at her as one who has just let an ocean of feeling wash through a dam that was never meant to withstand such a force. They roll together gently until she is under him, and she flushes with ecstasy as he slides in and out, controlling his own orgasm with exquisite care to give her pleasure. They make love in every way they can think of, on top and on the bottom, from the front and back, alternately laughing and crying. She marvels at God's inventiveness and that they have waited so long and doubted the other's love.

Pierre sits behind his desk in the Fort shuffling his papers from pile to pile. He is sitting in his cool dark lair, in his white linen shirt with its flowing sleeves and tiny monogram under the collar. He bites his nails, impatient for MacAllister. The weight of the moment stretches to an eternity. He is not without his fear of God, and in this decision to buy field slaves he intuits a weighty shift in the balance of righteousness. But it is the business of this land, the business he is here to promote, and he shoves his discomfort out of mind, setting to work on thinking of names to call his ten new slaves.

He will do it alphabetically he has decided, from the tallest to the shortest in the hopes of keeping them straight. He will name them after towns in France, like Malo and Rochefort. He begins to make a list and realizes that many are the names of saints. So be it. Perhaps it will make them saintly. In the end it is only a matter of two hours before MacAllister appears in the courtyard of the Fort, visible through the open door in the hot sunlight, with his coffle of slaves. They have been given the customary pantaloons of island slaves and look around the Fort warily.

"Ah, there you are," Pierre calls from his dark office. He jumps up, nearly overturning his chair, and strides into the sunlight, shielding his eyes with his hand. For the second time that day he assesses MacAllister, who is looking less like an angel of mercy now that he is on Pierre's turf. A big man whose most noticeable feature is his skin. It has been so burnt by the sun as to make him look as if he'd been flayed.

"At your service, Mr. La Salle. I have brought you the best of all those on the ship. It's been a long voyage and I have had time to come to know them a bit. None of the troublemakers are in this group. And we even have a bit of common language developed over the voyage, though it is limited to be sure. Among themselves they speak some Mande language, same as your man there," and he points to Bamadille.

Pierre walks around the group of men, looking at them curiously, his heart pounding and a strange mantra running through his head. *They are mine, I own them…mine.* He silently commands his cock to stand down.

Despite their emaciated appearance, some of them are strikingly handsome, he thinks. He raises an eyebrow at one who seems no more than twelve, and smiles broadly at a giant of a man, with skin like cocoa and a broad flat nose. The whites of their eyes glow with an uneasy mixture of fear and curiosity, as they stare back at him and steal glances at the Fort. One of them keeps his eyes almost closed, as if sleeping on his feet, but Pierre catches his glance. He makes a mental note. The third tallest, he decides.

"Well, they look a good crew. You'll have your work cut out, for we must make a forest into a field. But they will be motivated enough, I dare say. There will be nowhere for them to shelter if they do not work. Nor anything for yourself. I have tools and a cart and supplies to get you started. They are ready to go. And I will pay you well." He names a healthy sum and smiles beneficently.

"'Tis acceptable." Some of MacAllister's surly countenance falls away with the realization that he is not going to have to negotiate. "I am most glad to be off that infernal ship and the sooner

I vanish into the hinterland the better, for the Captain will be on the lookout for me, to be sure."

Pierre orders the crew in the canteen at the Fort to feed and water his new slaves. They squat on the dirt floor of the courtyard around a pot of cold fish stew, cassava and plantains, reaching their hands into the pot and stuffing the food into their mouths as fast as they can. Pierre watches them with a building anxiety. He had not thought about how much ten men eat.

Pierre and Rufus bounce along on mules alongside the slave cart up through the village and along the coast. Pierre has had the bright idea that Marcus and Bamadille should ride in the cart with the slaves and keep them calm, get to know them. They are a strange pair, the gentle old Bamadille, who's been a slave all his life, even in Africa, and Marcus, who might better have been named Narcissus, and who has all the arrogance of one who is master of his master.

"Give them hope," Pierre instructs them, "hope for a new life that will be hard at first but not always. When they have cleared the land and built shelters and got things going, we will bring women for them. They will make a life here, a good life. And please explain to them that there is no point in trying to escape. There is nothing but sea surrounding us. Better to settle down and make the best of it."

The distance they are travelling is not far, the entire island being only some thirty square miles, but their entourage moves slowly along the dusty path. Pierre has selected a prime spot just west of town, next to the plantation of David Bordeaux, Maria's uncle. He has calculated that the Brandenburgers may not last long here, and that the Bordeaux estate might one day become his, one way or another.

As they ride along, Pierre focuses his attention on Rufus MacAllister.

"So tell, what mishap in your life has put you here among us? I can think of no virtuous possibility, but perhaps you have one up your sleeve," Pierre chuckles at his own insight.

"My older brother inherited my father's land. I got nothing. A common enough story for a Scotsman. How I ended up in that black hole of a slave ship is just a series of misfortunes… and an offer of pay I could not refuse, but which I will now not collect, since I jumped ship. But no matter. It was intolerable. And I can see that this is a place of opportunity just in its infancy… and on dry land."

At the back of Pierre's mind there are little murmurings of doubt that this is the entire story. But he does not doubt that he will one day know the whole, for this island is in an odd way the center of the world, and information is one of its main commodities.

Pierre punctuates their passage through the town and adjacent countryside with bits of enlightenment on the inhabitants of the community.

"There are but little more than four hundred of us on the island, and half of them are children. White folk I mean. They're from all over and speak all kinds of languages, but what counts is that they're White. Before your ship came in, we had some five hundred slaves working the hinterland. That will rise now with this cargo. Perhaps by as many as four hundred. We need the labor, but to be so outnumbered is making people jittery. Runaways, what we call maroons, are a problem. They can hide in the hills indefinitely. But let's keep that from this crew…"

They pass the house of Isaac and Pundi, and Pierre points it out. "A most unusual pair live there. The island would fare poorly without them. A Sephardic Jew from Spain and an Indian doctor.

The Jew was my wife's first tutor and they have taught her and her slave woman most amazing things. They saved many people after the big hurricane in '94, and now the four of them provide most of the remedies on the island."

"And what does a man do for women hereabouts?" Rufus inquires.

"Funny you should ask at just this moment." They are passing the turnoff to Hurricane Hole and Pierre points up the hill.

"When you get horny you can go visit Mette there. The men hereabouts use their slave women freely, but for those without, Mette provides. As you might imagine, there is a shortage of women on the island, so she does a real service."

They ride in silence for a time and then, as if he had been mulling the question of Mette, Pierre says, "There's a Company rule that you have to attend church on Sunday at the Fort. You'll be fined if you don't, but since no one knows you're here yet you have a little grace period 'til your ship's departed. Best not to show your face in town 'til you get this land cleared."

As they pass the plantation of David Bordeaux and go into the scrub beyond, Pierre turns his mind to the tasks at hand.

"We've some sailcloth for tents with us, but you'll want to build shelters. For today we'll get your camp set up. In a day or so I'll come back and we will walk the perimeter of the land. Then you'll set this crew to digging trenches and we will burn this forest. It is the fastest way to clear the land. There is much talk of sugar being the next rich crop here, but no one has had much success yet in growing it, so I think we'll start with tobacco. The real money will be in sugar, and everyone's experimenting with it. We'll profit by letting them go first."

"Here is good enough," Pierre says, climbing down from his mule. "When it is cleared, you'll have a good view of the beaches and the island of St. John over there. One day that will be ours too. But for the moment the English have it. And the French have St. Croix. The Catholic French, that is. My wife and I, we are Huguenots. More the pity, because St. Croix is much flatter than St. Thomas and better for cultivation."

Marcus jumps down from the cart and stretches.

"And now," says Pierre, "I will tell you the names I have selected for them. Line them up in order of their height."

The planets on this day in 1696 must have been in peculiar positions. If one imagines the La Salle household as a dollhouse, it was being turned upside down and shaken. More modest but still momentous shifts were taking place all over the island. The population, for one thing, was doubling, as the slave cargo was slowly unloaded. An odd combination of greed and fear was sweeping the White population. Among the Blacks there was intense curiosity. Would they hear news of their village? Would they know someone? How would these new arrivals change the structure of their lives, the pecking order?

Mo Mo is in a basket beside her as Akila waits impatiently in the back courtyard in a clean white dress for Bamadille's return. Finally he appears, his hand in that of an emaciated child with running sores around her eyes, wrapped in bedraggled burlap. Akila guesses she is about twelve years old. The terror and distress of the child are easy to read in her solemn, wide- eyed face, and for a brief flash Akila is reliving this moment in her own life, remembering what a bloody wreck she was when Maria rescued her. She looks at Bamadille's soft brown eyes welling up and knows he is thinking the same thing.

"This is Kansoleh," Bamadille says softly. "She's from our village."

Akila drops to her knees and puts her arms out to the child. She takes the corner of her apron and wipes Kansoleh's eyes.

"You are safe now. Do not be afraid. We will care for you," Akila whispers in Soninke. She wraps her arms around Kansoleh and hugs her for a long moment. Then, sinking onto a bench, she pulls Kansoleh onto her lap. She is big for lap sitting, but Akila holds her tightly, rocking back and forth. Kansoleh begins to cry, great sobs suddenly wracking her as she clings to Akila.

Bamadille grins broadly. "That's good. She is letting some of that horror out… She says you are a legend now. That they prayed for you for weeks and months. She says they prayed for me too, but I'm not sure I believe that."

Akila feels a great lightening of her spirit to think that she is remembered, that this child before her comes like a gift from her father. A picture forms in her mind of her father on his prayer rug in the dust of the village square, surrounded by other men of the village, all facing east saying their prayers. She knows it will always be this way and she takes comfort that she too can still pray. But she is overwhelmed in that instant with a sense of loss, of the life she might have had in the comfort of that familiar, loving community. Her eyes are suddenly brimming with tears, tears for all three of them.

"You are part of the legend too, Bamadille. How would I have survived without you?"

"Allah would have preserved you."

Akila smiles and thinks to herself, "Right now, there is only one way to soften this child's despair." And she leads Kansoleh over to Mo Mo's basket. She lifts Mo Mo into Kansoleh's arms.

"This is Mo Mo. He will ease your suffering… though I know it is great. Praise Allah you have survived that dreadful voyage." She presses her fingers into her eyes as if she could shut out the pictures that are there. "It is a miracle that you are alive. We will care for you now and give you a chance to recover a little. We are like our own little village, Bamadille and I, and now you. And our mistress is a most unusual woman, unlike anyone else you will meet on this island."

Akila pauses, musing. She crouches down and cups the girl's shoulders gently in her palms, their faces close together, Mo Mo between them. "I will not lie to you. Life on this island is harsh. We are among the fortunate in the family and work we have, but we are still slaves, and very likely we will die slaves. But I will make sure no harm comes to you. You will be little Mo Mo's guardian, and I will be yours."

Kansoleh is rocking Mo Mo, a movement that comforts them both. Tears make muddy streaks down her cheeks. Mo Mo reaches his little hand to her face.

Akila takes a deep breath. "Come, it is time for prayers. Bring Mo Mo." She leads her across the yard to her hut and spreads out a second mat beside her own. "You will sleep here, next to me. We come from the same village and share our belief in Allah. He has brought us both here together for a reason."

"Get to work, man," Pierre calls out to Rufus.

"This is my work. To make sure they work, and don't run." Rufus has a slight smile as he says this, as if daring Pierre to contradict him.

"Well, you are very…" Pierre searches for a word. "Stationary… Perhaps it would be better if you set an example. No one seems inclined to run away at the moment. We have all the food and water, for one thing."

Rufus looks at him assessingly, taking in Pierre's stance and carefully arranged working clothes. Under his breath he mutters, "He's a molly, by Jesus." Though the utterance is *sotto voce*, a look passes between them that is well understood by both. Rufus prolongs the look but then reluctantly puts down the whip and sets to cutting brush with his machete.

"That's the idea," Pierre mutters after a few minutes. "Show them the way…"

The men work at varying paces, but all of them have been sick and malnourished on the voyage and their pace is slow. Rufus soon gives up working and starts yelling. "You there… pick up the pace." The man called Lussant falls and sits in the undergrowth getting his bearings. Rufus raises his whip and growls. "Get to your feet…" He continues in the role of angry monitor for the rest of the day, until there is a camp of sorts established.

As the afternoon wears on Rufus says, "Do you mean to leave me here alone with this crew tonight?"

Pierre sighs elaborately. "That would be the idea. We've all got our work. I've got to get back to the Fort and the governor. Bamadille has the bakery and Marcus is my manservant. You'll have to figure out who is the most reliable of these fellows, someone you can give extra rewards to now and then, to be the boss when you're absent. I'm sure you know how this game is played, and if you don't I'll take you over to Casper Rysberg's place for some lessons. When you run out of supplies you can come to the Fort and we'll get you reprovisioned. Now let's walk the boundary of my plantation, so you can begin to get it cleared."

As they walk Rufus' mind wanders to Mette. He can see her shack up on the hill across the bay, and he knows just who she is. She was shopping aboard his ship. And her two selections were very much to his taste. Though why should he have to pay for a woman?

Their house on the hill above the Fort looks entirely different to Maria when she returns that afternoon, walking Cibonie slowly up the street. Smaller, confining. She hands off Cibonie to Jean-Baptiste and goes alone into the bedroom. Akila is nowhere in sight, and Maria takes a deep breath of relief. Akila would know her secret at once, and she doesn't want to have that moment witnessed. She goes to her bedroom and lies on the bed, looking at the dancing shadows of palm trees on the ceiling. Eventually she props herself on her elbow and rings the bell beside her bed. In a moment, Akila appears.

She stands at the doorway looking at Maria.

"Pierre bought the nursemaid. She's a mess, no surprise, but she speaks Soninke and will be good with Mo Mo eventually I think." She comes closer to Maria.

"Lordy, what have you been up to. I can smell the pleasure on you. Who have you been with?" she draws a big breath and her eyes grow wide. "My Lord Maria, I hope it was good!"

Maria blushes and puts her hands to her cheeks. "No secrets from you. You're right, but I'm not going to tell who. At least not just yet. I'm still taking it in myself." Akila cocks her head and looks at her for a long moment, smiling.

"I won't press you. You have a right to pleasure like anyone else. But be careful. Do be careful. I'll go fetch some water to wash."

As the sun begins its descent and the cumulus clouds rise like stacks of whipped cream, Pierre begins his return ride home with Jean-Baptiste and Marcus, he on the mule and they walking beside him. They are a weary group, but Pierre is euphoric. His venture is launched. He has spent the day observing his new work crew and on the whole he is impressed with MacAllister's perceptiveness. Pierre is delighted to have found an overseer and congratulates himself on his choice, being all too familiar with the thieves and pirates who generally lurk around the port. He is willing to overlook for the moment that the man himself is clearly a bit of a hothead.

"What do you suppose MacAllister's real story is?" Pierre muses aloud as they wend their way through the village.

"The one you called Lussant said he is a violent man with a quick temper. I wouldn't be surprised by anything in his past." Marcus picks the dust out of his nose with a sweep of his thumb.

"Greedy…but that can be motivating. I think he's a loafer."

They go on in silence and Pierre turns his mind reluctantly to Maria. She will be waiting, he remembers, and his mood suddenly lurches downward. Her morality sits on him like a lead weight, and he feels a sudden flush, a noxious combination of anger and shame as a monologue takes shape in his head. "What the hell are we doing here if not to grow sugar? And you need slaves to grow sugar, and a lot more than ten." A picture of Margaretha von Bergen, Lucas' wife, takes shape in his mind. Why can't Maria be like her? Like a pretty piece of furniture.

He sighs aloud and Bamadille looks at him wonderingly. A wave of guilt washes over him. No, Maria is exciting, even dangerous in a way. Smart and feisty. He feels a swell of pride and a kind of love, though not the kind of love Lucas must have for Margaretha. The key is to keep the peace. She has her own business healing people, and she does it well enough that they overlook her eccentricities, the liberties she gives her slave. And it keeps her out of my business. *Tonight I will give her the Missy Box. A peace offering,* he thinks, as he comes down Konge Gade and sees candlelight shining from the windows of his house on the hill. Just the box for the moment. The jewels will come later. They are the family wealth, after all.

The men wash together in the courtyard and Pierre puts on a clean white shirt and linen pantaloons. Maria is sitting in the salon straining her eyes to read a text on syphilis that Isaac has just acquired. Pierre comes in and looks over her shoulder.

"Good God, what is that? A picture of man's bollocks? What horrible disease are you studying now?"

"You've never seen it? It's syphilis."

He sits down on his beloved sofa and puts his bare feet on the low table before him. "You do have strange occupations, my dear," he says leaning forward and trying to disguise the rising lump in his crotch with his elbow. "Put away the book. I have something for you. Something special."

Chapter Twenty-Nine: The Norwegians

Hirscholm, 1771

The crickets of August have begun to sing in the long shadows of Hirscholm's late summer. I am growing a little weary of Heinrich. But the parties are still fun. Struensee is always there, propping up the King, who has grown surprisingly silent and torpid. The Queen appears some evenings, pale and distracted. She is surrounded instantly by her coterie of friends, including Johanne.

On this night in August, I am leaning against a column in the second-story portico of the ballroom, overlooking the lake. A full moon hangs in the smokey sky, casting a long yellow light over the glassy surface.

"Your necklace is quite remarkable…I noticed it from across the room." Struensee's voice from behind me is unmistakable. In that moment I feel as if the diamonds are radiating heat up to my face. I touch the necklace lightly, as if I could stop the flush from rising.

"It was my great grandmother's. She had a surprisingly shocking life, and this was her husband's attempt to bribe her into submission." I smile at him.

The doctor looks at me steadily, as if assessing something.

"I predict that you will have a most remarkable life, Miss Suhm. You are a bold young woman."

"I will take that as a compliment, and thank you for it, Dr. Struensee."

Even in the flickering candlelight, I can see that he is troubled. He is in trouble, in fact. I have a great desire to comfort him. His popularity is diminishing very rapidly, even with the people whom he has done so much for. That puzzles me. Nonetheless, these evenings are a kind of netherworld far from reality, and I push away the thought and look up at the man.

At that moment a rumbling noise breaks the spell of Hirscholm, and the real world suddenly appears, roaring up the road toward the island castle with picks and shovels. The Norwegians have come all the way from Copenhagen in a fury that is focused on Struensee. The summer night is suddenly filled with a thundering, angry clamor. The doors of the balcony are wide open and the room is engulfed with the roar of the crowd. The music stops and the room is for an instant strangely still. And then everyone is moving in all directions.

Heinrich grabs my arm and tries to lead me out of the room toward the back, but I pull away and stand still, refusing to move, mesmerized by what is happening. I push past Heinrich and move toward the balcony looking for my uncle below. I see him on horseback holding up his hand, as if he could keep this crowd back with a gesture. The guards on their horses have placed themselves in a ring around the entrance to the castle. As it is on an island there is only one approach and I see in an instant the great advantage of that. But I have goosebumps of fear nonetheless. The roar of the angry crowd is deafening and my heart pounds. They are drunk and out of control.

Uncle Thomas fires a musket in the air and it quiets them for a moment. Struensee is propelling the King toward the balcony. The King steps out on the balcony and suddenly the crowd hushes, and then begins a rhythmic chanting: "The King, the King." Struensee stands behind Christian, hidden in the shadows. He is telling Christian what to say. "My good Norwegian brothers, you will have your pay. But only if you go now, back from whence you came. You can rely upon me, your King. You will have your pay." He giggles as though he has just made a fine joke. But a cheer goes up from the crowd nonetheless.

Johanne comes to stand with me.

"They really love him," I whisper to her. "How little they must know about him. Or maybe they just don't want to believe what they hear."

"We need our heroes, I guess. Our Kings to be kingly," Johanne replies.

I suddenly remember Phebe, down in the stable. "Oh, Lord protect Phebe," I say to Johanne. "I must go to her."

"Is she in our rooms? She will be safe enough there."

"No, she is in the stable."

"The stable? What's she doing there?"

"Never mind, but that's where she is."

"Well, you certainly can't go there. She is a resourceful person. She will be all right."

"Can't we at least get word to Uncle to go to her?" I rush to the balcony and look down. He is not in sight, but the grounds are still full of the Norwegians, milling about.

"Summy, you would do no good if you went out into this fracas. You would only endanger yourself. You must leave this in God's hands."

She was right, of course, so I began to pray under my breath.

Perhaps He heard me, because Phebe tumbled into our rooms shortly after I did. She was disheveled but in one piece, and I threw my arms around her.

"You won't believe what happened down in the stable."

"Tell me. It must have been awful."

"Well, this unholy mob of the smelliest, most disgusting men were suddenly all over the stables. Antoine and I were in his room with the door closed and a chair against it. But this giant of a man with a red beard kicked it in. He actually stood there staring at me as though he'd never seen a Black person before….and then this strange grin came over his face and he said, 'What have we here, I've never tasted one of these before.' He actually licked his lips. It was so disgusting. He reached for my arm and got Antoine's fist full in his face. They fell to the ground hammering each other. Antoine got on top of him and lifted his head by his hair and started slamming it into the floor, over and over.

"'Stop! You'll kill him,' I screamed. And he screamed back, 'Yes, that's just what I intend to do.'

"And I grabbed him around his shoulders trying to pull him off. The man lay still. I was sure he had killed him and said so.

"'Oh no, he has plenty of life left,' Antoine said and then he told me to stay there. He took the man by his feet and dragged him out the door, slamming it behind him with his foot.

"I stared at the splintered door, listening to the chaos outside. I sat there for a long time until Antoine finally returned. He had dumped the Norwegian off with his friends, who revived him. In the end the Norwegians left. I bet their roar could be heard all the way to Copenhagen. But I had to laugh when I learned the party guests were left to stumble home on foot because the Norwegians had taken all the horses."

"Oh Pheeb, I am so sorry you had to go through that. But I'm so glad you're safe. I wanted to come find you but Johanne wouldn't let me. I don't suppose I could have done much for you anyway. I am so glad that Antoine protected you." And I meant that. At that moment I was truly happy that Antoine was in Phebe's life and grateful to him for saving it.

"Lordy, Sum, that's the second time Antoine's saved me..." Neither of us slept much that night. Uncle Thomas didn't return until dawn.

The Norwegians had shattered the calm of Hirscholm, and Phebe and I are both deeply shaken. But the thought of returning to the seething discontent of Copenhagen is even more disquieting, and so the royal party will stay on into the fall. Rumors buzz around the castle like bees around the late summer roses. The guards slouch in the corners of the courtyard below my window, flicking their heads towards the Queen's suite and laughing raucously. The kitchen maids below Phebe's window titter behind the sheets as they pin them to the line. That the Queen and Struensee are having an affair is all but common knowledge now. The sheets do not lie. The rumors are about how it will all end.

My brain crackles with it all. My shoulders are knotted and tense. The drama of the court has become like the foggy light of the Danish night, unreal, mystifying. I am retreating into my island world, into Maria's diary, feeling the great orb of the sun beating down on the little village of Charlotte Amalie. Isaac and Pundi and Akila are as real to me as the black cat that mysteriously appears each day to jump up on my lap. I crave time alone. I send Phebe off on pointless errands, and I know that Phebe spends more and more time with Antoine, Beppo… anyone she can find.

I stand at my bedroom window staring out at the gathering clouds of a thunderstorm, feeling terribly alone. I am afraid for Struensee and stunned by what I am reading in the diary. I couldn't possibly tell Uncle Thomas. He had told me that Maria was a healer and a somewhat notorious woman for riding around the countryside. But the story of Pundi is entirely new.

Who's to say whether he might even have been Uncle Thomas' grandfather?

And Maria's relationship to Akila? To be honest, this has really shaken me. They were more like sisters than slave and master. This floods me with shame because even though I love Phebe, really like a sister, it has also been drilled into me deeply that Phebe is my property. This is the way of the world. It is a way that was just beginning in my great grandmother's St. Thomas. She had fought against it…a losing battle. But she had fought nonetheless. I realize that though in my mind I reject the idea that Phebe is my property, I have been too deeply infected by the plantation culture to be entirely free from it. I had never thought about these things…the way ideas get subtly planted in your mind and you don't even know they're there.

I picture Phebe in Antoine's room, staring at that broken door. I know she is hiding from Johanne, who instantly drafts her into the household chores when she sees her. And I have pushed her out, so that I can be alone with the diary. And just as I am thinking this, there is a knock at the door.

"I need to talk to you," Phebe's words tumble out. I can see that she is very distressed. But she has startled me, and my first reaction is to view her as an invader into my inner sanctum. "Why are you shutting me out every morning? What am I supposed to do here by myself?"

There is a long pause and then I feel myself softening. I am ashamed and embarrassed, realizing that maybe my sanctum was losing a bit of its luster. I look at Phebe and think of Akila. I take in the hurt in Phebe's face, grab her hand and pull her into the room.

"Sit down. I'll tell you what I've been doing." I lift the black cat out of the chair and drop him on the floor and motion to Phebe to sit. I settle myself on the bed, twisting the small pearl ring on my finger.

"I found my great grandmother's diary. I fiddled endlessly with the Missy Box and finally I pressed the right place with the sharp end of the key. It was amazingly well hidden, the spot. And then I got so rapt in the diary I just couldn't bear to share it. It was so personal. It turned out to be very difficult to decipher…written in a kind of code, so it's taken me months to figure it out. And I'm a long way from finished." There is a long silence. At that moment I am wondering why I hadn't shared it with Phebe.

Phebe looks at me, waiting for more.

"Do you know," I suddenly blurt out, "your great grandmother and mine were really very best of friends. Like sisters. Kind of like we are, but much freer."

"You mean they didn't keep secrets from each other?" Phebe says, looking at me directly.

I look down. "I'm really sorry. I don't know why I didn't tell you."

"Well, I suppose it would have been awkward if it was full of nasty things about Akila."

"No, it was quite the opposite. I should have shared it with you…" I look out the window and then sideways at Phebe. "Isn't it amazing. A Black slave and her White mistress. Can you imagine what people must have wanted to do to them."

Phebe looks at me, and I can see on her face that this is not a subject she wishes to pursue. But the question hangs in the air between us.

"Well, I can certainly imagine what they'd do to them today… but maybe since they were among the very first to come there, all the rules that control our lives now hadn't been thought of…"

Like cutting off your hand if you raise it to a White person, I think silently, looking down at my own hands. There is an awkward pause between us. She offers a bleak smile. "What do you think Uncle Thomas would think about the diary?"

At the thought of this I panic. "I couldn't possibly tell him what's in the diary. He'd be just horrified. Not at their relationship. He'd be all for that, and I think he understood that they were very close. But at great grandmother's love affair. And that his great grandfather was, well, not very interested in women."

"Ooh…"

"I'm really sorry that I didn't share this with you, Pheeb…that I shut you out. You are my very best friend. I can't imagine what I'd do here without you."

Phebe's face flushes and I instantly know that I have somehow overstepped. She was just on the verge of forgiveness, but I have rekindled her anger.

"Then why do you send me away every morning. Don't you realize I have nothing to do? That everyone here just looks at me like I should be their slave if I'm not busy being yours. I actually have to hide or I'll be drafted into washing the Queen's sheets."

The hairs on my neck are standing on end. I am stabbed with the realization that Phebe is sometimes just invisible to me, when it suits me. I have been so indoctrinated by my upbringing that I have been robbed of the bold heart of my great-great grandmother. I look down, blinking the tears away.

"I am so sorry, Pheeb. I have no excuse, really. Let's pray together. I need to ask your forgiveness and the Lord's. What a world we've been born into. It's so…confusing."

Prayer is one thing we can always agree upon. We have both been raised to pray. We are good Moravians and at this moment praying is the only thing to dispel the tension.

So we kneel together and pray out loud, pouring out our hearts to the Lord and seeking His guidance. In this we are like our great-great grandmothers.

Chapter Thirty: The Missy Box

St. Thomas, December 1696

Maria stares at the Missy Box, mustering with all her might an appropriate look of pleasure and surprise. She is still aglow from the day's encounter, but the gift suffuses her with guilt and confusion. It sits nestled into the folds of her lavender cotton dress and she runs her fingers with an exaggerated absorption over the inlaid patterns of birds and flowers.

"It is called a Missy Box," Pierre says softly. "Chinese. The men hawk them on the wharfs in Canton. They call out, "Box for Missy?" at everyone who goes by, and here we are with a "Missy Box". I bought it from a Dutch sailor last month who told me it's full of hidden compartments. Maybe if we open them all we'll find something surprising. Isn't it quite wonderful?"

Maria tilts her head, looking up at him and feeling as if she were acting in a play. She is thinking that they are all like Missy Boxes with their hidden places. She smiles broadly at the thought.

"Just beautiful. Thank you, Pierre. A very special gift, and it will be in our family for many generations, I am sure. What fun to have something with all these special hiding places."

"There's nothing in it now, but we'll have fun filling it over the years. You can start by putting in the jewels that are left from your father." The mention of her father slams her like a fist. She sits up straight and takes a deep breath. Whatever would he think of the place she's got herself in now?

Akila comes in at that moment and stands beside Maria's chair, looking at the Missy Box intently.

"Look at what Pierre has given me, Keela. Isn't it extraordinary?" She blushes at the secret between them, appraising Akila's face with anxiety. Would she give her away somehow? And then she lets out a sigh. What did it matter anyway? Akila leans in to inspect the box as Maria opens it, revealing the lush purple velvet interior.

"It has all kinds of secret compartments, and a kind of treasure map to show you where they are."

"It must have taken years of work to carve all that and put it together. Hard to imagine." Akila touches the velvet with her finger and then straightens up. "I came to tell you that I want to visit Caterina tomorrow. Would you mind?"

Maria pauses, not sure that she trusts herself to say Pundi 's name out loud. She turns to Akila, away from Pierre.

"We were all going to the Rysberg plantation in the morning to see to their slaves. I can go with them alone. You and I can ride over to Isaac's together in the morning and you can take the beach road on to Mette's." Maria feels a hot flush rising up her cheeks as she says this.

Pierre grunts and sits up straight. "If you're going in that direction, why don't you stop in and visit our own slaves. It would be well to check on their health and take care of anything they may have festering. Leave Rysberg's slaves to another day." Then he leans back again with his hands behind his head and looks obliviously at his blushing wife.

The scene in the courtyard the next morning is of a very impatient Maria alternately standing in the doorway of their makeshift pharmacy watching Akila and pacing over to the wash tub where Kansoleh is bathing Mo Mo. Akila is contemplating their supplies and picking things off the shelves, filling a basket. Maria's head is full of Pundi, but she suddenly takes in the scene before her.

"Do you really think she deserves such bounty?" Maria's voice has a tart note of humor.

"Not in the least. I can think of no one less deserving, but why would she let me in if not for what I might bring her?"

"Well hurry…there's a lot to get done today. "She pauses, inhaling deeply. "Did you hear that Pierre has decided to call our plantation "Work and Rest"?

To which Akila responds with an acknowledging grunt at the back of her throat. She gives it no more thought. She is stewing in frustration as she thinks of Mette and Caterina, stuck between her desire to save the one and to punish the other.

They ride at a trot through the village and on out the dirt road along the coast toward Isaac and Pundi's house, the rising sun warm on their backs. Isaac is in the garden in front of the house when they approach.

"You two made a beautiful silhouette riding up here," Isaac says in his soft voice.

Akila slides off her horse and lands in front of him. She is now taller than he is, and he stretches himself broadly in the morning light and smiles at her.

"Good morning, dear Isaac. I am bent on a mission today. Have you given any thought to the tea I mentioned to you?" Akila asks.

"I thought that would be your first question. Of course I have. It is a simple concoction. I have prepared some for you to take along and will share the recipe." He pauses and smiles. "I cannot take all the credit though. Pundi pointed out that such concoctions are a regular part of Hindu ritual, and the plants to make them grow in abundance hereabouts."

Akila inhales deeply and visibly relaxes.

Isaac can feel the charge in the air. He looks at Maria, and then realizes she is looking at Pundi standing in the doorway behind him. He had guessed long ago that these two were destined for each other, and on this bright clear morning he senses what has transpired. How could a man so sensitive to the human soul, and to all those pheromones, not be instantly attuned to the two who are dearest to him. Pundi emerges from the doorway, shading his eyes with his hand as if saluting them all, and just stands there smiling at Maria. She throws her arms into the air and looks up at the sky.

"Oh, what a beautiful morning! Are you two ready? Have you the supplies packed? Pierre wants us to start at his plantation." She flips her wrist in a gesture off to the west. "'Work and Rest', he calls it…They work while he rests," she mutters, looking off to the horizon.

"We are quite ready," Isaac says. "Let me just give Akila what she needs."

The morning is warm and soft. The clouds look like fat-bottomed geese parading across the vivid clear blue sky above as Akila walks along the beach path. Her heart is racing, not with the exertion, but with trepidation. She had not considered before what it would feel like to face Mette alone. She lengthens her stride, sinking her heels into the dust as if drawing strength from the earth. She can see Mette's compound above her on the hill, and she turns up the well- trodden path, drawing deeper, slower breaths to calm herself. The house is still and silent as she approaches, the rocking chairs on the veranda empty. She stands in front of the house, suddenly relieved, feeling a little stupid not to have realized that they would all be sleeping. They probably went to bed not long ago, she realizes.

She walks slowly around the house and sees that a couple of little huts have been built, just like the one that Mette had forced her into ten years ago on that terrible day. The memory slams her like a fist to the gut and she is roiled with a painful, sick feeling, and then anger. She is relieved to be alone and she keeps walking in a steady rhythm to compose herself, around the main house and the outbuildings and then up the stairs onto the veranda. The place is filthy. A noxious combination of smells swirls around her. Urine, a whiff of vomit, with an overlay of tobacco masking the worst. A pile of chicken bones sits on a rush mat on the floor beside one of the chairs. Something sticky beside it has attracted a column of busy ants. She sits down in the farthest rocker and looks out at the ships in the harbor, a sunlit forest of masts with skiffs loading and unloading assorted cargos. Her mind quiets as the flies buzz around her and the heat of the morning swells.

A skinny African boy with a broom peers around the corner of the house. She senses his presence before she sees him.

"Who are you?" she says in Soninke. He just stares at her, frozen in place.

She gestures for him to come to her. He hesitates and then approaches curiously. "I clean." And he bows and begins to sweep.

"Caterina? Where is Caterina?" Akila asks him.

He points to the back and she realizes he means the outbuilding she had seen. She stands up and he shakes his head vigorously, warningly. She sits down again.

"Big man with her." And he continues to shake his head.

"Will you go get her?"

He shakes his head vigorously, eyes wide.

She rocks for a while, watching him. His pantaloons are tied up with a rope and hang like two big bags around his skinny legs. He is so young. Not more than ten, she supposes.

Caterina comes through the back and out onto the porch. Akila rises out of her chair, looking at Caterina's face. She has a raw fresh bruise on her right cheek.

"Oh Lordy, look at you."

"Pay it no mind." And she throws her arms around Akila, burying her face in the soft cushion of her breast.

"Can't we just get you away from here?" Akila whispers. "Why don't you come away with me now. Now, before she gets up."

"That would not serve us. She would just come and find me, and accuse you to the magistrate."

"I suppose…but we must make another plan." Akila pauses, looking hard at Caterina. "Well anyway, I have brought you something. Maybe it will subdue the brutes." She gets her basket and pulls out Isaac's bag.

She looks for the boy and sees he is well out of hearing. "Isaac has prepared this. It will calm. And a man taking it will not be able to get hard. More likely to just go to sleep." Caterina takes the bag and sniffs it. "You make it into a tea. You can make a pot, make it strong, and then put a little into their rum. It will make your life easier." She smiles. "Just make sure they pay first."

Her smile vanishes as she looks over Caterina's shoulder and sees a big red-faced man in leather breeches emerge through the curtains at the back. He stops, and a slow broad smile comes across his face as his eyes narrow menacingly.

"Now just look at this. This is my kind of woman. Look at the bubbies on you, girl." He takes a step forward, eyes fastened on Akila. Caterina steps in front of her. In a swift motion Rufus moves toward them and flings his left arm into Caterina's chest, knocking her backwards. She falls against a stand that holds a washbasin, which clatters against the wall.

Rufus ignores her and puts his meaty red hands on Akila's shoulders.

"You have bad skin, must be terribly itchy. I could make a cream to cure it." Rufus is taken aback, momentarily distracted from his purpose.

And just at that moment Mette comes up behind him and points a knife into his back.

A long slender stiletto.

"Let go of her. She's not one of mine. You cannot have her. She is your boss's property. Now pay up and get out of here." Her voice is low and steely, her eyes narrowed and angry. He turns and looks at Mette and then looks at the knife. He raises his hands and smiles.

"No harm meant. I just assumed she was one of yours. That you had kept her from me…" He reaches into his pocket and pulls out some silver, and keeping his eyes steady on Mette, holds it out to her. She snatches it quickly from his outstretched palm with her left hand and waves the knife in her right at him.

"Get out."

He turns and walks down the steps. The three women and the boy stand watching him silently. When he is well down the path toward the beach Mette says, "Now you get out too. What are you doing here anyway? Spying?"

"No, I brought you some things. I wanted to see how Caterina was doing. Let me put some ointment on her cheek. I'll leave some for you."

Mette grunts, and Akila decides to take it as a sign of permission. She reaches into her basket and takes out a preparation made with artemisia, a staple for wounds.

"Sit down. I'll put it on you," she whispers softly, seeing the fear and anxiety in Caterina, wanting to ease it. In that moment she determines that, at whatever cost, she must get Caterina out of here soon.

At almost the same moment, Maria follows Pundi and Isaac into a makeshift camp where a small village seems to be taking shape around a fire pit. Maria instantly recognizes that this is the heart of their family's future plantation. She scans the chaotic scene, looking for the man Pierre has described as Rufus MacAllister. He is nowhere in sight. What she sees is a collection of nearly naked black men hard at work building themselves shelter. Several of the men are wielding machetes. She stands very still watching them, a quiver of goosebumps on her arms, crawling up her neck.

One of them stands to the side, directing several others. She looks at the list that Pierre has given her of their names. After each one he has written a little description. Evreux is not hard to spot, and she watches him in awe. Never has she seen a person of such… "Majesty" is the word that comes to her mind. He has so little flesh on his bones that his face has the appearance of a wooden mask, but for the flash of his eyes. Eyes which soon alight on her and make the goosebumps spread to her scalp. She takes a deep breath. Pundi puts a hand on her arm and she instantly relaxes.

One of the men approaches and stands silently looking at them.

Maria holds out the basket of food that she has brought and gives him a lopsided grin. She is thinking that this might be Hippolyte.

"I am Maria La Salle, Master's wife." She bows slightly. "We come with medicines, to look to your health. Where is Mr. MacAllister?"

Hippolyte, for she is quite correct in her identification, gestures toward the ocean. "Away." Maria's eyebrows register her surprise. Isaac has meanwhile wandered over to a group of men working on weaving some brush into what will become a wall of their shelter. He squats down and looks at a fresh wound on the shoulder of one of the men. By the looks of it, made by a whip. He digs in his bag and pulls out a jar and, gesturing to the man, begs leave to apply it. The man pulls back suspiciously. Isaac smiles and says a couple of words that Akila has taught him, which makes the man break into laughter. "Is it my accent?" Isaac says laughing, looking up at Pundi. But a certain barrier has been crossed and everyone relaxes. The tallest man, Evreux, comes over and watches Isaac apply the ointment to the wound. It is the same artemisia mixture that Akila is applying to Caterina at almost the same moment. Evreux is talking to them and gesturing, holding his hands in the air and looking up, then touching the wounded man. Pundi is staring at him.

"He is trying to tell us that this man is their healer. He's the one who knows their medicines and communicates with their spirit gods." Pundi nods and bows to the wounded man.

Hippolyte speaks some of the creole Danish that is a familiar patois of the island. "He must have worked at the Danish slave castle in Accra," Maria whispers to Pundi. "Where do you suppose MacAllister has gone off to?"

"I don't know, but let's get this job done."

"Hippolyte," Maria says firmly, "line up these men so that we can inspect them." She keeps looking at the list Pierre has given her, trying to give names to each one. She determines that the wounded man is Lussant, and wonders what he did to get that wound. Her stomach turns at the thought of the future of these men.

They move on at midday to the Rysberg plantation, stopping back in town to pick up Akila. Casper Rysberg is in a hammock on his porch, asleep.

Pundi holds up his finger.

"Let's leave him," he whispers. "He's a foul one. We can go to his overseer."

Akila speaks quietly. "I have an errand in the kitchen. I'll just go around back and then meet you up in the field."

She looks at the sleeping form of Rysberg, his black beard, like a thing alive, moving as he breathes. She has never forgotten his threat at the hospital when he saw her reading. And she has heard his reputation as a master, and particularly what he does to his female slaves. She walks to the back of the house and stands at the door of the cookhouse, peering in at the three women cleaning up the midday meal. Their chatter suddenly takes her back home to her mother's banter with her sisters. She watches silently, enjoying the moment, and then smiles broadly in greeting.

"I have something for you," she says in a dramatic whisper, holding out a small bag made of burlap. "A tea. A small amount of this will make your master's sugar stick go limp for a good long time, and probably put him to sleep too. Give it a try, but not too much at first. You need to figure out how he'll react. But I daresay you'll sleep better yourselves if you give him some."

The oldest of them stands grinning at Akila, her hands on her hips.

"Well now, how did you guess that that is just what we needed? You some kind of witch, Akila? You just give that here."

"Well, I guessed it by the look of Mattie there," and she points to Mattie, a handsome girl of fifteen, her belly round and her breasts blooming over her dress.

Having delivered her package, Akila climbs the hill to join the others, feeling an airy sense of delight, which is quickly dampened when she meets up with the others, who are talking to the overseer.

"Don't know why you should trouble over them." The overseer is a big, rough Dane, not long ago indentured, but now his own man, working for Rysberg. "They'll die soon enough anyway, the way he works them. Watching the slaves in the field, it was clear enough that none was getting enough food for the work being demanded of them.

"Can their diets not be supplemented?" Maria asks, looking up at the skeletal forms working on the hill.

"You know the rules here. Slaves raise their own food on their own time, in their own plots. But there are some still not in the field," and with this the overseer points to a collection of huts, "with fevers. Miserable bastards, probably past helping, but you can try."

In the huts they find three slaves, emaciated and shaking with fever. They bathe them and administer their remedies, plant substances that will bring the fevers down for a bit. But they all know there is no cure, and silence comes over the three of them as they each retreat into their own thoughts.

Pundi puts his hand on Maria's shoulder and she turns and looks at him. It is only this fresh, lovely face that keeps him from complete cynicism. Wordlessly they communicate their need for each other.

"I'll meet you back at the house, Isaac. See that Akila gets home, will you?" Pundi doesn't need to say more.

They ride away, Maria and Pundi, and search for a place that they can make their own bower. They find it on a low wooded hill: an array of huge grey boulders covered with soft green lichen, looking like a pulpit at the top of the hill, in a bower of trees. From the road below, this spot is entirely hidden, yet high enough to see anyone who might approach. They lie together in the soft moss behind the boulders, surrounded by ferns and orchids. The sun filtering through the trees makes streamers around them. The birds trill and whisper their secrets.

It is not many weeks before Maria knows she is pregnant.

One day a small African child arrives from the tavern to fetch medical help. It is Akila who answers the summons. She follows the child into the cool shadows of the tavern. Adolph Morgen flips the towel he has been using over his shoulder and looks at Akila wearily. She is a forbidding woman, stately and unsmiling.

"What goes on here?" she looks him in the eye, not without sympathy.

"An old sea captain in the backroom. Very unwell. Perhaps not long for this world.

Lord preserve us! What have I done to deserve another death under this roof?"

"Why, you've chosen to run a tavern, man," Akila says, grinning. "And a hostel so that men may not have to die in the street. Show me to him." She flips out her palm in a gesture of invitation.

Morgen leads her to the back and fairly pushes her into the room. Shutting the door behind her he turns quickly and leaves.

The *Fredenbourg* has sailed, but one of its number has not sailed with it. Lying on the bed is Captain Bardewinkel, in the last throes of one of those miserable tropical fevers that are so prevalent that it's hard to tell one from another. He is barely conscious and knows he's not likely to see another sunrise. The innkeeper is distraught that the captain has been dumped unceremoniously in one of his rooms. It's never good for business to have men die on the premises, and especially of these nasty fevers. Akila stands quietly over the captain, looking down upon his grey, damp face. His eyes are closed. His body shakes convulsively. She stands there for a long time. She is a child again, rocking violently in the ship, chained to the floor, looking up through the square holes of the deck, at the streaming sun and the stars. She can smell the human filth. She looks at him, and it is his filth, his sweat. She thinks of the monkey and she is sitting again in that cabin. How strange that he did not molest me, she thinks. I was too young then to know that that was what he must have been thinking about. But he only fed me. And then she thinks of the nail file and of all that happened afterward. How futile it all is, she thinks.

He opens his eyes and looks up at her, and she sees terror in them. Is it of her? Or of death?

"Captain Bardewinkel," she says in a scratchy whisper. "You know me?"

"I will never forget you." "How could that be?"

"'Twas you conducted me here, some twelve years ago."

The silence is thick and heavy. His eyelids droop and he says, "Forgive me then. My life has been a terrible sin." And he looks at her again, or is it through her, beyond, to something else he sees? Something fearful.

Akila sits by him, a great moral storm lashing her. She tries to quiet it, and drawing a deep breath she looks about the room for some distraction. There is a sheaf of papers beside the bed on a table. She picks it up and leafs through it. The name Rufus MacAllister is on every page at the top. Her eyes grow wide in recognition. She begins reading. It is a report of a trial in Copenhagen. It seems that MacAllister has killed a woman in a brothel. She can read just a few words of the Danish, but it is enough to get the skeleton of the story. It is the testimony of the other women, and of the errand boy. With a fire poker, MacAllister had struck her. And for this they had put him, indentured, onto a ship, and he had finally ended up on the *Churpressen*. And in the employ of Pierre.

"He is a murderer, that man. Pierre has hired himself a murderer." She says it out loud and Bardewinkel opens his eyes just as she is putting the papers in her satchel. She jumps in surprise when he looks up at her. But she realizes he has seen nothing.

"Have you something that will end this misery? Please…be merciful, and help me die," the captain whispers.

Bardewinkel has begun to sweat profusely and is writhing now. She sits for a long time watching him and remembering his fingers putting bits of bread into her mouth, the monkey beside her, touching her arm, her face. Inquisitively.

She leans down to the satchel at her feet. She takes out a leather case with twelve glass vials, slips two out and puts them on the bedside table. She takes the mug of water that is on the table and pours out most of it on the floor, leaving just a mouthful. Then she counts out the drops, twelve from one bottle, six from the other, and spills them into the water. She stands and leans over the trembling old man and lifts his head, cradling it in the crook of her arm. She holds the mug to his lips.

"Drink this. May Allah forgive me. And you. For all our sins,"

She watches the liquid dribble slowly into his mouth, his throat constricting as he tries to swallow.

She gently releases his head back onto the pillow and watches. He looks at her, and she sees the shadow of a smile cross his face, and then his eyes close. She sits for a long time watching his breathing become labored, and at last there is a quick convulsion and a rattle of breath, and he is still.

She prostrates herself on the floor and prays.

Akila sits with Samuel that night in the field beyond the house, watching the moon rise.

She has Mo Mo on her lap and kisses him behind his ear. The evening is warm, the air heavy with moisture. The tree frogs are just beginning their cacophony.

"The most remarkable thing happened today," Akila says, very softly. "I was present at the death of the captain who transported me here from Africa. I've told you the story…more than once I suppose. Of his strange kindness to me. So I did him a kindness in exchange." She looks up at Samuel, as if asking his forgiveness. He takes her meaning instantly and puts his arm around her.

"It is part of healing…a kind of healing in itself. You helped him return to his ancestors. He was a man tormented by spirits. And they may be with him still because he did great harm." She looks at the moon as she hears this from his lips, as if it held all answers to all mysteries.

"I took some papers away with me. They make it clear that Rufus MacAllister, Pierre's new overseer, is a murderer. He killed a woman in Copenhagen. So Pierre's hired himself a murderer."

"I daresay he knows it already, don't you think?"

"Do you?" Akila's voice is full of surprise. Mo Mo reaches up and touches her nose and she bends and touches hers to his, and then looks at Samuel. "That never occurred to me. It would make Maria furious if he did."

"Maybe you best stay out of it. Half the White folk on this island are probably murderers. Lots of them came here as indentured servants. Like your Mette. Anyway, wait and see. Maybe there will come a time when the information is useful."

Akila sighs and gets to her feet, lifting Mo Mo up to the moon. "Time for sleep, little one. Let's go see Kansoleh." Samuel rises beside her and they walk silently back towards their hut in the courtyard. She is thinking that this is a secret that will be hard to keep from Maria, but she feels obliged to heed her husband. For the moment she will keep it to herself.

Rufus MacAllister is striding around the growing perimeter of their camp watching each of the men in turn, assessing their value to him. He stops and scratches his beard, grating his dirty fingernails hard into his skin. The itching drives him mad. Then he starts on the top of his head. He is always scratching. The itching is becoming more than he can bear. The sun is unbearable too. He almost longs to be back at sea, where at least there are breezes, and the work somehow doesn't seem quite as endless as this clearing of fields.

"Tedious, that's what it is...," he mutters. "This digging trenches and burning. Hot and tedious." And he fans himself with his wide-brimmed straw hat as he watches the men dig. The ten of them are spread about thirty feet apart, working slowly. "Evreux," he calls out. "Take charge while I go visit the master's house. I'll be back before too long. Just keep them digging the fire trench. Then we'll burn just before the afternoon rain."

Forty minutes later he walks into the back courtyard of the La Salle house. He is looking for Akila, and he finds her. She is in the cookhouse.

He leans on the doorframe grinning at her. "Nice garden you have here. Are those all herbs?"

"In the herb garden, yes. The kitchen garden is yonder," and she gestures with her head to the west. "What brings you here today?"

"Well you, of course."

"Well, I'm busy so why don't you just go about your business," she replies curtly.

"Oh, don't be that way. I just want some ointment for my itchy skin. You got anything that might help?"

By this time he has left his post at the door and has come up close behind her. He leans in, pressing his hard cock against her. She jumps and moves away, turning to face him.

"That's no way to ask." She stares at his smirking face, and the look she gives him wipes the smirk away, and he inhales deeply and stands straight.

"Well, I really could use something. I'm itching something awful."

"Let's start with this cold tea. It's very good for itching." She ladles a cup of cold tea from a pot on the counter into a metal cup and hands it to him. "Drink that down, and then we'll see about an ointment."

Rufus puts the cup to his mouth, watching her intently over the lip. He drinks it all down.

"Tasty. And refreshing. Thank you." He watches her intently as she moves to some shelves across the room and takes out a ceramic canister. She fills a jar with a translucent cream.

"Made from aloe, chamomile and mint, and a few other items. Should help. Use it sparingly. It's very time consuming to make. Now be on your way, please."

A languorous feeling has come over Rufus, and he looks at her dreamily. His lust has subsided into something closer to wonder. A pleasant, sleepy warmth has come over his genitals. And his itching has subsided.

"What about that tea?" He looks intently at the cup in his hand. "Do you have some more of that? It seems to have stopped the itching."

Akila's hand goes involuntarily to her mouth, her eyes widen and a smile lights up her face as if she had seen a heavenly vision on the far side of him. "Oh my, I hadn't thought of that side effect. Of course. You may have all the tea you want." She goes to a corner of the room where there are many small packages made from large desiccated leaves, carefully folded and tied with string. She gives him four.

He bows slightly. "Thank you."

"Think nothing of it," she replies, and her radiant smile follows him down the path through the hedges of rosemary.

Chapter Thirty-One: Return to Copenhagen

Copenhagen, Christianborg Castle, Fall 1771

I had been dreading the return to Copenhagen, but it is inevitable. Hirscholm is not designed for winter. The royal party has put it off as long as possible. A dreadful harvest has put the city in a state of high agitation.

"I miss Hirscholm," I say to Phebe on our first morning back, in the privacy of my room. "Or maybe it's summer I miss…but there is something ominous in the air here."

Phebe makes a distracted little noise of assent. I know her mind is on Antoine. Then she suddenly looks up, my words belatedly making their way to her brain.

"And you don't think there was something ominous in the air out there? What about the night of the Norwegian sailors? And all the little conspiracies you were seeing everywhere?"

My chin is sunk into my palm as I look morosely out the window. "I guess… it just didn't seem so gloomy there."

"There is something about the way the days get shorter…the chill that is in the air. We're not used to that in the islands. Our winters are so beautiful. The world is upside down here."

Gradually we resume the patterns of our former city life. Lessons in the mornings.

Occasionally we help out at the vaccination post, though Struensee no longer goes himself, but has others running the operation. It is difficult to persuade people now to get vaccinated. All the most persuadable have already had it. Nevertheless, I work hard to instill faith and fortitude in passersby.

"What's the point of getting vaccinated when we're likely to die of starvation," one old woman screams at me one morning. I jump, taken by surprise at the emaciated figure draped in black and grey rags, wisps of greasy hair emerging from her filthy bonnet. The hamper of food I had brought along with thoughts of bribery has long since been given away to the hungriest urchins. Phebe had been a magnet to their curiosity, and they swarmed like starving pigeons this morning, curious and afraid at first, daring each other to touch her. After a few tasty morsels they seemed to forget her skin color. But they still would not be vaccinated. Of that they are truly afraid. For their elders the vaccine is associated with Struensee, who is now quite unpopular. In the very first week that we are back in

Copenhagen, Struensee has issued an edict restricting the press. I can well see why he has to do it: he is being lampooned everywhere, and sometimes the Queen along with him.

"Who do you suppose is printing all these nasty leaflets," I ask Phebe, as we tramp over them in the street, leaving boot marks on Struensee's face.

"Well, I suppose any of the nobility would have plenty of motivation. After all, he's shredded their privileges. But the ones with the Queen's face…well that's something else. That might even be the work of the Dowager Queen herself. Beppo says she really hates the Queen."

"And little Frederick even more."

I stop abruptly and look at Phebe incredulously.

"Well, think about it," Phebe says quietly. "Without Struensee protecting Christian, her son might be regent."

"You don't really think she's capable of all this, do you?" I ask, gesturing at the litter. "Oh, she has plenty of help!"

In their quarters, Thomas and Johanne have stopped talking about Struensee. In fact they have almost stopped talking altogether. I admit that it was Struensee who got Johanne invited to the Queen's parties, and that's where it all began to unravel. My heart goes out to my uncle as I watch him over breakfast poking at his food, lost in thought. He must, I think, by now suspect what I am almost sure of: that Johanne is seeing another man, Frederick Karl von Warnstedt. I had spotted them yet again from my post on the glass bridge. I had thought he had been Anne Sophie Bülow's lover, and I am now completely confused. But I am deeply sad for Uncle Thomas. Still, I am not sure how much of his gloom has to do with Johanne and how much with the uneasy state of the city.

Phebe manages occasionally to beg off our lessons with the claim that she has too much to do. Johanne assigns the work, so I have no trouble believing the little white lie. The lessons are dull, and I'd get out of them myself if I could. Phebe's gloom is long gone, so she has not the same need of the lessons anyway. I am pretty sure that she is slipping off to the little garden shed where she can meet with Beppo and his friends, and with Antoine. I think Johanne has been so distracted that she has forgotten to make her usual long list of chores.

Somewhat to my relief, Heinrich has been occupied with other things since our return. I have been dreading the thought that he might propose marriage to me. Phebe had actually said it aloud just yesterday.

"Well, of course he's going to propose. You are a rare one, Sum. I mean, you're beautiful, intelligent, and ever so rich. He'd be a fool not to ask you to marry him. I can't believe he's not done it already, but you are very young, so maybe that's what's holding him back. Anyway, doesn't he have to ask your father first? Maybe he's written to him." I am charmed by her description of me and I beam at her.

"Well, he may ask, but I'm never going to marry him." And then I think I have perhaps gone a little too far, so I add, "I mean, he is nice, but not nice enough for me to live here for the rest of my life."

I am quite sure now that I have no wish to live in Denmark. And I have no desire to go back, ever, to the Caribbean. I will go to America and finish my schooling in the Moravian School in Pennsylvania. Maybe I can even persuade my parents to emigrate.

The only problem is Phebe. I cannot take Phebe to school with me.

Chapter Thirty-Two: Moriah

St. Thomas, 1697

On a Saturday night early in the new year of 1697, there is a spontaneous gathering of slaves in a field between the village and the new La Salle plantation. It starts as the moon is rising, with Samuel drumming on a djembe that Pierre, under the influence of Marcus, had bought from a ship in the harbor. Akila rises in the moonlight and begins her slow dance, her undulating hands just visible in the flickering light, her hips swaying, slowly at first, and then faster and faster. The sounds carry through the night, reaching others who arrive alone and in groups.

A fire is built. Instruments have been created from gourds and sticks…whatever materials are at hand.

Sunday is their day off, though hardly for rest, as it is the day they must work their own garden plots to survive. The great influx of Africans from the two Brandenburg ships has swelled the numbers around the fire, and indeed, the numbers of fires around the island. They crave each other's company, music from home, something to relieve the endless toil. The sounds of the drums and ululation travel over the hills and raise the hair on the necks of such as Caspar Rysberg and Rufus MacAllister, but they dare not interfere. They may have a few muskets, but they are now greatly outnumbered. The drumming grows wilder and the dancing hypnotic, wild. Exhaustion overtakes the revelers, and some rest around the fire, clapping encouragement to the others. They talk as best they can in their many dialects, inventing words that seem expressive.

It is here beside the fire that the idea forms in Akila's head of a hut in the woods.

Omar, one of Rysberg's slaves, says to her, "You must have a place for us to come for obeah. A secret place the boss man doesn't know."

She has known for some time that her people are often beyond the reach of Isaac's kind of medicine. Their sickness, which she has come to understand through Isaac as physical or pathological, is entangled in their heads with their belief in the powers of the spirit world inhabited by their ancestors. She has seen a slave known as Malaka die last month from something that was completely mysterious to all of them. He had no fever, but he was in a kind of stupor or trance, convinced that a jumbie was stalking him. He seemed to die of terror. It had happened so fast that she had not thought to summon Samuel with his Sangoma powers. Malaka had something in his head that no amount of Isaac's medicine could have cured. The Africans called this medicine obeah: a mystical combination of spiritual healing, real medicine and potent belief. They craved this spiritual healing of their homelands, and much of its power lay in the secrecy of its practice.

She and Samuel could make a place in the woods for obeah where they could be undisturbed. Maria and Pundi and Isaac would help them get it started. She sits on a log looking into the fire, and the vision of it takes shape in her mind. She knows the place: a mossy dell in the woods high above the house in the village. It is a place no one would come unless seeking it, a small plateau just hard enough to get to.

Akila goes to the bakery the next morning. The business is thriving, and slave women line up for their masters' bread, chatting in line. She goes down the queue, passing out small packets of her special tea, explaining to each in a very low voice how and when to use it on their masters. There is a great deal of giggling. Lucien comes over with his great smile and a special pastry for her. He has grown a bushy red mustache and she grins at him.

"How elegant you are with your mustache, Lucien! I've come to talk to Bamadille. Is he inside?"

"And here I thought you'd come for me."

She digs her toes in the dirt and looks down with a smile. "…Tomorrow perhaps? But thanks for the pastry," and she takes a bite, leaving a little clump of sugar on her upper lip. She licks it off with her tongue.

"Bamadille," she calls out when she is inside. "Bamadille, I need your help." And she outlines her plan to build a dispensary in the woods.

"It has to feel like home. I know you can do that, you better than anyone. And Samuel will help. He will need to be the Sangoma. We'll make a little garden there too. Remember when you gave me the gris-gris, Bamadille? That's the kind of medicine we need."

Bamadille takes her hands and looks at her palms. "We may be slaves, but we can build our own world here." A sly smile comes over his face. "We can grow things too, on the side, and trade them. We can have our own medicines. And our Sangoma. You are a chief like your father, Akila. Building this will bring our people hope."

For a brief moment both of them are transported back to their village, with Samuel's father, their Sangoma, busy in his hut, the women trading their produce and goods in the marketplace.

The next day Akila sits down and outlines her plan to Maria, Isaac and Pundi.

"We'll only be there a day or two every week, Samuel and I. Otherwise, we'll be working with you. But you understand, there are certain things that cannot be cured by your medicines… A healing of the spirit. Samuel knows it well because his father was the medicine man of our village."

"Do you think that Pierre will object to Samuel doing that?" Maria says gently. A shadow of foreboding has come over her, and she looks down with a little embarrassment, because she knows she's using Pierre as a foil for her own feelings. She knows as well as Akila that he does nothing to keep track of what his slaves are doing unless he needs them personally.

"I doubt he'd even notice, do you? And of course, we'll never tell him, or any other White people on the island. That is very important." Akila looks stern as she says this, and Maria knows there is no stopping her. In truth, Maria is sufficiently distracted in her own bubble of joy at this moment: she is in love and with child. And she doesn't really care whose it is. She sighs and smiles tolerantly at Akila.

In the end they all pitch in to create the little woodland dispensary, Bamadille heading the crew. On a steep hill far from the road, the spot is surrounded by a dense grove of trees, each of which has its own medicinal properties. The genip and kapok trees nearby are well known as places that jumbies will inhabit. Samuel has picked the place because of these trees and because of its inaccessibility. Frangipani and mango trees are in this little forest, providing beauty and fruit. Isaac and Pundi have brought all their most treasured formulations to fill the hut, but when they have departed Samuel goes about adding the necessary spiritual elements, represented by old bones and chicken feet, feathers artfully arranged, and a pile of rags from which little dolls can be constructed…gris-gris. The interior is dark, and filled to the brim, with a corner for a small fire, and a pit of ash where bones can be tossed for telling the future. Samuel sits in the doorway on a three-legged stool and whittles a small female figure, carefully rounding her breasts. He is now the island's Sangoma, even if he can only be there one day a week.

That spring brings new terrors to the island. Privateers have become brazen enough to start seizing ships inside the harbor, including one that held Isaac's shipment of guaiacum products to Europe. Privateer is just a grand word for pirate, and piracy is an old tradition. Maria is particularly irked in the case of Isaac's loss because the pirates this time are French captains, her own countrymen. They hold commissions from Governor Du Casse of Petit Goave, who gaily disclaims them and tells Governor Lorentz to hang them all. Though Denmark is neutral in this war of the Great Alliance, this spring the Spaniards are nonetheless threatening to attack St. Thomas. Much of the population has been evacuated to

Curaçao and some of the Leeward Islands. Maria has refused to go, despite Pierre's daily urgings.

August 1697

Maria lies heavily on her cot with her eyes closed, listening to the street sounds outside. Her mass of curly brown hair is held with a single stick on the top of her head, and she reaches up to make sure it is secure. Her hair in tropical heat is the equivalent of wearing a wool cap, but Pierre will not hear of her cutting it short. His own curls are now quite blond from the sun and she trims them every month.

From the harbor comes a clamor of shouting, a musket shot, louder noises than are usual, but in truth Maria is only half listening, being in her own slow, fecund world. She opens her eyes, staring vacantly at the light dancing on the ceiling; she runs her fingers over her huge belly and feels the child within. The tiny bottom is sticking up…a good sign. She is quite ready to meet this child. But she is also terrified. Of the birth, most certainly. She has seen enough births to have no illusions. Even an "easy" birth is very hard. And when she sees a woman having her sixth or seventh child, she thinks God must make them forget how it was before. Not that they have any choice in the matter.

But even more frightening than the birth is the question of who the child might be. Will it have Pundi's beautiful brown skin or Pierre's white skin? Will people notice? She calms herself for the thousandth time with the thought of the dark-skinned ancestor she has invented, and she begins to embellish further the story in her mind. She has grown quite fond of this great grandmother, so renowned for her smoldering eyes.

Pierre is suddenly standing over her. She has taken in these last months to sleeping in a cot at the end of their bed because she is so hot and restless at night. He leans down and pulls the sheets up over her belly and breasts, as if her nakedness affronted him.

"You're awake. Good. I must be off. The harbor is under threat again."

She looks at him sympathetically. "Be careful... What a world to bring a child into," Maria mutters as she watches Pierre run out the door. She swings her legs to the floor, easing herself to her feet. The house is eerily quiet, but she can hear a great commotion in the harbor. Then the loud rumbling of a cannon. She feels the dribble of a warm, wet fluid down her legs. She knows instantly what it is.

"AKEEELA...!" she uses all the force of her lungs.

Out in the courtyard, Akila is on her prayer mat in front of her hut when she hears the call. It is the call she has been waiting for and she leaps to her feet.

"Anna, get the water boiling. It must be Maria's time," she yells as she runs by the cookhouse.

As with most births, there is a good deal of rushing about and a great deal more waiting to follow. Akila is commanding in her role as midwife, alternately massaging the little round bottom in Maria's lower abdomen and clenching Maria's hand. She washes her hands many times, in Pundi's way, and reaches up inside Maria's womb to check on the baby's passage. She walks Maria around the room; she gets her to squat. Maria howls. Akila chants some peculiar African rhythm that Maria can't understand, but that calms her. Maria pants and howls, staring at a spot on the ceiling that has begun to take on the shape of a bearded prophet. And on and on they go, until the sun dips down over the harbor and the moon rises.

During these many hours Pierre is not seen, but coming home in the evening he finds his house in anxious chaos and no dinner waiting. He peeks in on Maria but quickly retreats from the intensely athletic event that seems to be in progress. Finally, at three o'clock the next morning, the crown of black hair appears. She is a little girl, a very pink little girl with jet-black hair.

"Oh, all babies have black hair when they are first born," Akila says.

"I want her to have your name…Maria." Pierre says it softly close to her ear. "But we will pronounce it Moriah as they do in New England." He sits looking at the two of them. "Doesn't she just look like a Moriah?" He leans forward and takes the baby's foot in his hands. "Did you ever see anything so perfect?"

"Never. She is just a miracle. A treasure given by God." Tears make little streaks down Maria's cheeks. She is awash in emotion from joy to intense sadness, thinking of her own mother, who had died giving birth to her and had never known this sweet feeling. And her father who would never see his grandchild. And that Pundi is not here. "But the only Moriah I have ever known was a ship," she whispers with a smile.

Pierre is a happy man. Despite the chaos that reigns in his own harbor, or perhaps because of it, he has become a wealthy man. For every Rixsdollar the Company makes, he quietly takes his cut. Protected by his friendship with Governor Lorentz, he is sanguine in his dealings. Much of his fortune has been the result of the European wars. Denmark's neutrality has made St. Thomas a haven for trading. That will soon end. No matter. Now he is a plantation owner, and his plantation has just produced its first crops of sugarcane and tobacco. He has taken a hands-off approach to it all. Maria and Akila have monitored the health of his slaves so closely that he has not had to deal much with Rufus MacAllister. And as

MacAllister's pay is dependent on the production of the plantation, he has no worries about his motivation. All in all, it is a fine arrangement, and though he has yet to see any profits, he knows they will come and provide well for him in his old age.

Chapter Thirty-Three: Winter Secrets

Christianborg Castle, December 1771

The days in Copenhagen grow shorter as winter descends. From our quarters across from the castle I can see the candles being lit, one by one, as a servant passes through the rooms. As if in some kind of dance of synchronicity, Phebe appears at that moment in my room with fresh candles. She sets them in their holders and begins the ceremony of lighting them.

"Am I interrupting your studies?" she giggles. I lower my chin and grin. "This winter is so long and dreary. I never thought I'd miss St. Croix. Do you suppose boredom is just the lot of women everywhere?"

Phebe snorts. "No. Most women have to work endlessly, washing, cooking, cleaning, sewing, tending to babies. They are too exhausted to be bored, believe me." That silences me for a moment.

"There must be more purpose than that to a woman's life, don't you think?" The door suddenly opens and Johanne comes in.

"Have either of you been in my room?" Her tone is demanding, abrupt. "No," I say at the same moment that Phebe says, "Just to clean."

"Well, you have no business there unless I specifically request it. Do you understand?" Phebe nods and curtsies with her head bowed.

"Yes ma'am. So sorry. I ran out of things to do and thought you would like it."

"Well come to me when you run out of things to do. I will fix that," and she turns and leaves as abruptly as she entered.

I look at Phebe, whose lips are pursed and eyes glistening. "What was that all about?"

"She has her secrets."

"Yes, she certainly does, but they're not so secret as all that."

"Lord above, this country is just one hotbed of conspiracy and infidelity. Such a place full of secrets I never did see. We do lots of sinning back home, but it's nothing like this. I think everyone in the castle is secretly meeting someone."

"It must be the long dark days. They need something to cheer themselves up with," I giggle.

"I overheard your uncle in quite a temper the other day, when you were out with your count. Johanne's been gambling with the Queen and her companions and has lost quite a lot. And he's furious with her. I didn't notice anything in her room, but perhaps that is what she is trying to keep secret."

"Oh, poor Uncle. I think her relationship to the Queen puts him in a rather awkward position."

From this point on I begin to track Johanne's movements carefully, timing her toilette (forty-five minutes) and watching her assignations from her viewing spot on the glass bridge. I have my eye out for the Queen and Struensee too, and catch a glimpse of them once slipping into an apartment on the barracks side of the bridge. But their affair is such common knowledge now that I no longer feel particularly privileged to have figured it out before anyone else.

I am disappointed in Struensee, and worried for him also. Disappointed because he has gone too far in everything. He should have been more discreet with the Queen. And he went too far with his proclamations. He was up to over five hundred new laws, and now the King has given up all pretense of signing them. Even France's Voltaire has taken note! The day the King had received a letter from Voltaire, Struensee had stopped me in the garden and shown it to me.

"We are the leaders of Europe, little Summy. It's time for the Middle Ages to end, and they are ending first here in Denmark." He almost did a little jig. I cringed at his use of the word "little".

I am struggling. Heinrich comes each day at the end of my lessons and I dutifully walk with him into the city.

"Is there any more beautiful place on earth?" he says to me as we walk, his arm arcing over the twinkling harbor lights glowing all around us. I want to scream at his blandness, his obliviousness to the drama that is unfolding all around. He has no interests beyond his horses, as far as I can see. I am trying to figure out how to break off with him gently. I wish my mother were here to counsel me, but in my heart I know just what my mother's advice would be. I can almost hear her saying: "Men are like that, you can't expect too much from them. Just be grateful if they take care of you. Some of them are truly brutes. Just try and get a nice one, who treats you well. And has money." The last would go without saying.

I look in the window of the tavern we are passing by. "Let's go in," I whisper to Heinrich.

"Don't be ridiculous. Women like you don't go into a place like that. Nor men like me." I know it is the end of the discussion.

I want more than this European life of convention. I want the kind of passion my great-grandmother had. Now that I have met my father's brother, Anker Suhm, I suspect that my father was a lot like Heinrich. General von Beverhoudt, my stepfather, has always been puffed up with himself, a caricature of the country gentleman. I can hardly take him seriously. But he has taken good care of my mother and her daughters, and I suppose that is all my mother really wants.

Phebe tells me at night about her evening with Antoine. She waves a hairbrush around, gesturing happily. I suddenly think of Akila and Samuel and little Mo Mo, and I feel my great grandmother Maria's loneliness like a bleak fog wrapping itself around me.

At breakfast Uncle Thomas sits silently in the flickering candlelight, preoccupied. I try to draw him out. "Do you think this unrest in the city will spread, Uncle?"

He looks at me almost as if he hadn't noticed that I was there. "Pardon me?"

"The riots…do you think they will spread? Should we be alarmed here in the castle?"

"No telling if they'll spread. But you'll be well protected if they do. No reason for alarm." And then he looks down at his untouched plate and goes back into his own thoughts.

I stand behind his chair and wrap my arms around his shoulders, hugging him. I want to comfort Uncle Thomas, but I don't want to reveal that I know about Johanne's affair. I want to tell him the real story of his grandmother, but how do you say such things to your own uncle? It would devastate him. I have made it about two-thirds of the way through the diary. The work is painstaking and best done by daylight, of which there is little at the moment. But I struggle on. The rewards are great, and it is the only thing at the moment that is worth getting out of bed for.

Chapter Thirty-Four: Malo

St. Thomas, January 1702

Maria is sitting quietly rubbing her bare foot against the cat under the table, wishing the company would go home. Casper Rysberg's presence at her dinner table has ruined the evening for her and had been the subject of a most unpleasant argument with Pierre.

"Well, you can just shut up about it," and he had slammed his hand flat on the desk as he said it. "I'll invite whoever I want to my table and it is really none of your business. Because that's just what this is: business, and it's important that I not be seen as excluding any of the planters. Don't forget, I work for the Company." She had thought at that moment, what a hard man you have become in this awful place. You never would have spoken so cruelly to me before. But she just touches his arm lightly and smiles at him, a calming smile. "I understand. It will be as you say. But I will not have him next to me. He hardly bathes at all."

"No, you must have him next to you. I cannot offend any of the guests by putting him next to them…unless he is also next to you."

The candles are beginning to gutter. Marcus and Jean-Baptiste stand at either end of the table fanning the company with large palm fronds. They look as if they are ready to drop, and Marcus was already furious that he had been assigned the task. Too bad for you, Marcus, she thinks to herself. But it is time. She has had quite enough of Caspar's monosyllabic conversation, and the palm fronds do nothing to disperse his odor. She gives Pierre a smile with urgent meaning, but he is holding forth on the subject of pirates.

"If the Brandenburgers can profit from trading with them, I don't know why we shouldn't. Most of the time the English are none the wiser."

"It's a dangerous line to cross," Lucas von Beverhoudt murmurs. "We don't want their warships bearing down on us. Not worth the risk. Our money is in sugar and now we've begun to see real profits. And England's a big market."

At that moment Kansoleh enters the room with Amalie, Akila's newborn, in her arms, and Moriah and Mo Mo trailing behind. They are four and five years old now, devoted playmates. Kansoleh is silent, as Moriah goes to her mother. Maria lifts the child into her lap and smothers her playfully in kisses, smoothing her ink-black hair back from her forehead. She is a strikingly beautiful child, with the blue eyes of Sèvres porcelain, Maria's eyes. Mo Mo squirms uncomfortably behind Kansoleh.

"Off with you now to sleep," Maria whispers to Moriah, setting her down and putting a hand lightly on Mo Mo's head.

Casper Rysberg turns in his chair and hooks his arm around the ladderback and stares at Mo Mo.

"And who's bastard is that?" he mutters under his breath. "That slave woman of yours? Best not let him get as uppity as his mother. Nothing good'll come of it. I say this for your own good, Maria. People talk, and they're none too happy to see slaves take on airs. It's catching, like a disease."

Maria stares at Rysberg, her eyes wide and her nostrils flared. Her mouth is open as if to speak, but she is so angry that she is for the moment speechless. Pierre rises quickly from his chair as if to foreclose on the speech he fears she might utter.

"Perhaps some brandy, gentlemen? Shall we adjourn?"

Akila and Samuel are walking in the moonlight on this night to the Sangoma hut in the woods above the town, carrying supplies for the long day to follow. The lines will begin to form before dawn and will continue all day. Akila will examine people who wait outside the hut for illnesses that she can treat, but she knows that it is really Samuel who will heal them. He will treat their minds, instructing them in rituals to bring their bodies and their minds into spiritual harmony, calling on their ancestors and the spirits of the natural world. In return, they will bring a variety of offerings for Samuel's services, a yam, a head of cabbage, precious foods for those who have only one day to grow their own sustenance. Most times Samuel will tell them to keep their food, for he can see they need it more than he does. But then they bring other kinds of offerings. Buttons they have made from seashells, string, the little precious items of daily living.

Akila and Samuel will sleep here tonight, together in their private nest. They will make love and murmur to each other until they fall asleep in the moonlight. In the morning they will be wrenched by the things they will see, but tonight they are at peace. In the morning they will do what they can to help their people. But it all must be in deep secrecy, for practicing obeah is forbidden, and they would be brought before the magistrate and punished severely if they were found out. The Sangoma hut is well hidden, camouflaged by the forest and idle during the week, except for the visits of Maria and Pundi, for this is their private place too. It was Akila who suggested this to Maria, but she has not told Samuel about Maria's special relationship.

Not so far away as the gull flies, but a messy tangle of thicket if you had to walk it, Rufus MacAllister is sitting on the veranda of his two-room cottage at Work and Rest, looking out across the sugarcane fields to the ocean. The moon glows the color of corn silk, casting an ever- widening ribbon of shimmering light on the sea. He lifts a jug of rum to his lips, one of the great side benefits of working on a sugar plantation…an endless supply of this lovely mind numbing by-product. To his right is the sugar mill, to his left the foundations that have been laid for the new great house, Pierre's pet project, though Maria swears she will never live there. He loves to see the way she thwarts Pierre at every turn.

From behind him comes a steady drumming and mournful wailing, the sounds of the slave camp, a village really, for now there are more than two hundred slaves working these fields. He has tried to forbid this strange music; he has whipped and starved and even tortured to put a stop to it. But still it goes on, like a heartbeat. He has always wondered if those drums carry messages. Or are they just a tormenting noise? He moves himself on to happier thoughts.

"I picked well, he should be damned grateful," he says aloud as he squirms around to get a good purchase to scratch his groin, sticky with sweat from the heat. As Pierre had promised, women had followed soon after. One for each man, though which one for which was anyone's guess. But they are most all pregnant soon enough. And so it goes on, buying and selling and mating 'til now there is a village full, and four assistants working with him to keep it all in order. Punishments? You can't be lenient. This is a life-and-death sort of game. Lots have died of course. The work itself is killing and the fevers constant. But these slaves get special attention from Maria and her healers. They fare better than most. And he has had to carry out the direst punishment only three times: chopping a foot off for attempted escapes. He smiles to himself remembering Maria's horror at that.

Below him on the spit of land is Mette's place, a dim glow of candlelight marking the spot. He thinks of Caterina and scratches some more. He is itchy in a different way now. Life is becoming too predictable; he feels almost domesticated. Yet he has none of the elegant life of Pierre, despite the fact that he does all the work. He swats a mosquito hard on his leg. "Damn the man," he murmurs aloud. He pictures Akila, her melon breasts, her round ass, and scratches harder. "And a wife like Maria he has no use for. Someone should show her how it's done." And he chuckles at his own cleverness, though he's been saying this to himself for five years.

Isaac and Pundi are under the same moon, listening to the same drumming, each in his own world. They have built a second house near the first, so that they have their own private quarters. Their pharmacy is a cookhouse, with work and storage space between the two buildings. In it they have a store of medicines they have concocted. Their main export is their guaiacum extract. But they have preparations from many other things, including artemisia, which helps with the malarial fevers, and when they can import the bark from the cinchona tree it is even better.

The cow stays in the cool of Pundi's yard, under the acacia tree, indifferent to the bickering of the chickens and the cooing of the pigeons in their roost. They have become wealthy men in these five years; their medicines for syphilis are much in demand in Europe. Isaac now owns a frigate that he can depend upon to take their products to market and bring back what his heart most desires: books. It sits now in the harbor almost fully loaded, ready to depart for France when the winds are right.

Isaac sits now in the beautiful, glowing room he has created for himself, with Turkey carpets and a large mahogany inlaid desk from Ceylon. He sits in a plush red velvet armchair, surrounded by his treasures from around the world, listening to the drums. He has been studying them over the years, and he can hear that this combination of rhythms is saying that a slave has gone maroon. It has the sound of "run, man, run", he muses to himself. Across the way, Pundi is cross-legged on the floor in a pool of moonlight, meditating in his simple quarters. He prefers white. Even his cow is white. Despite the soothing repetition of the drums, he is having trouble concentrating, emptying his mind. Maria is always achingly there.

Out in Hurricane Hole, Mette has a houseful of customers. She now dispenses rum for a price, hardly a scarce commodity, but it is forbidden to bring it here. You must buy it on the premises. Whale oil lamps cast puddles of amber light on the veranda, and waiting sailors sit rocking in the shadows. One plays a melancholy tune on a tiny flute. Mette surveys the sailors for one that appeals to her own tastes. Although it is brutally hot and humid, she shivers for a moment. The fever never seems to leave her completely, and the chancre in her vulva is alarming. The tincture that Akila brought her is almost gone and she is trying to stretch it out, for she doesn't want that woman around. Mette has concluded that she must be a witch. But whether a good witch or a bad witch, she is not sure.

Little Joe, now a silent, well-muscled man, waits to serve rum behind a makeshift bar.

In a back room, Caterina has just lifted a layer of canvas off her bed, smoothing the next layer carefully for the next customer. The ritual calms her. She has tried to interest her customers in Akila's tea, but it is always rum that is on their minds. In other matters, however, she has followed Akila's instructions with care, and quietly taught her sisters tricks that Mette herself knows nothing of. She has an elaborate fantasy life in her head, and her chief fantasy is that Mette will soon be covered with ugly sores and die a horrible death.

Across the inlet in the village of Charlotte Amalie, Bamadille and Lucien stand side by side in the bakery kneading loaves of bread in an identical rhythm. The rhythm of the distant drums. Press down, fold, flip. Again and again. With his foot, Bamadille operates a pedal fan made from large palm fronds that serves to keep the mosquitoes out of the bread and off the bakers. With his hands he mixes the dough. They are lonely bachelors, much beloved on the island for their wonderful bread. But there are just not enough women on St. Thomas to go around. Bamadille is still Pierre's slave, but he operates almost as a free man, though the profits from the bakery are all Pierre's.

In the slave quarters of Work and Rest the drums and the singing have changed. At the beginning of the evening the sounds had been festive. Music for dancing. But they have taken on an urgent, anguished tone. A woman is crying.

"Malo is gone," she wails. "Malo, Malo, come back," she calls out, a high wailing in the still night. Others have gathered around her, singing and chanting, a small sound at first that grows powerful, commanding. Are they trying to protect him with their incantations? It is a haunting, eerie sound, as if they were chanting, "Run, Malo, run." The singers know that there is little chance that Malo will escape for good. There are always roving bands looking for maroons, and though some stay in the woods for months, most are caught in a matter of days. They are surprised that Malo has run. He is one of the original slaves and he has never run before. He has had a lashing from Rufus earlier in the day, but there is nothing unusual about that. Their chanting takes on a mystical quality, as if on the breath of their singing they could carry him far, far away.

In the bush, Malo's heart beats wildly, as if responding to the rhythm of the drums. All his instincts tell him to go up, to climb to the highest point he can find on the island. The moon is full, but he is deep in the darkness of a thicket, moving slowly, pushing branches aside. He is terrified of snakes and tarantulas. He stops and forces himself to breathe deeply. He is wearing only a loincloth, and his skin is scraped and bleeding from thorns. He fears the dogs even more than the snakes, and they will smell the blood. But for this moment he is free, he is his own man. The night sounds of tree frogs and the crashing of surf on the rocks below drown out his passage through the forest. After a time, he realizes that he is on the secret path to the Sangoma hut. The wild beating of his heart slows down. Tomorrow his people will be coming in streams to this place, for the very reason that it is well hidden. As he gets closer he hears the low murmur of voices and recognizes them as Akila and Samuel. He knows that people will come here even before daylight. He finds himself a spot deep in a thicket nearby, from where he can watch and remain hidden. He makes himself a bed of sorts with leaves, and lies down to rest, but images of snakes keep rising in his mind. He thinks of his mother and how she always used to say to him, "they are even more afraid of you than you are of them" and he repeats the phrase over and over until he is asleep.

He wakes up because he is hot, and he realizes that he has slept well into the morning despite the murmuring sounds that are coming from the Sangoma hut. He dares not creep out of his hiding spot. That was another thing his mother always said to him: "if you can see them, they can see you." He distracts himself from his hunger and his thirst by trying to identify the voices he is hearing. With each one he wonders if they would betray him if they saw him. You can never be sure what is in another man's mind, how the information might serve his own ends. At last the sun begins its descent and the air begins to cool. He closes his eyes and imagines the spirits of his ancestors roosting in the trees around him, protecting him. He knows that Samuel picked this spot for its powerful trees and their spirits. He says a silent prayer. Darkness falls quickly and the night air fills with the screeching sound of tree frogs.

When he is sure that everyone is gone, he creeps slowly out of his hiding spot and goes to the Sangoma hut. It is empty of people, but he can feel the powerful presence of spirits, and he falls to his knees before them, praying. He looks around the hut furtively, looking for food. And he finds it. They have left a basket of fruit. Does it mean they are coming back? He takes two mangoes and runs back to his hiding place and devours them. All the next day he explores deeper into the woods, going slowly in circles through clouds of mosquitoes and butterflies. His plan is to stay in the woods for as long as he can, and then go to the coast to try to steal a boat and get off the island. He has heard you will be free if you get to Portorico, though he has no idea where that is.

Pierre is in a good humor as he unties a dinghy on the Company's wharf. He's about to inspect the cargo of a schooner that came into the harbor the night before; and that is always a lucrative moment for skimming a bit off the top of whatever deal is happening. He turns abruptly when he hears his name called. Caspar Rysberg's overseer is in the road, a hulking man with an expression that could only be read as sanctimonious.

"Did you hear that one of your field hands went maroon last night? One of my women heard it in the bread line an hour ago."

"Ah, *merde*." Pierre spits on the ground in fury. "Do you know who it was?" "One called Malo."

"Malo?" Pierre's voice is incredulous. "He's one of my best men, one of the first field hands I got five years ago. I wonder why he ran after all this time?" Pierre looks past his informant, absently.

"Look man, you better get a search party out, and fast. It's like a fever around here when one of them breaks loose. Get on with it. And make sure he pays with a limb when you find him."

Maria is tending to Mrs. von Bergen when Mimba comes in with the same news. "They're getting together a party to search for him," she says. Her large frame is bent over, and she shakes her head back and forth with gloomy foreboding. "Some party," she mutters under her breath. "Wonder why they call it that."

"Malo," Maria puts her hand to her mouth. "Are you sure it was Malo? I wonder what Rufus did to him that made him run after all this time. You've got to be desperate to run on an island this small. So few really get away. And I can't imagine that Malo can swim."

"Why, you sound like you want him to get away, Maria," Mrs. von Bergen says in a voice of astonishment.

"Well yes, I do. I really do. Any man who can get away from that awful life deserves to. I'm going to pray for him. But don't you tell Pierre."

When she gets home, she writes a message on a scrap of paper. She clips it carefully to the string harness on the pigeon and opens the trap door and lets him fly. He's well trained to fly to the other roost, the one at Pundi's house. Twenty minutes later Pundi reads the message: "Meet me. Usual place."

It is a message he has both sent and received often enough. Their time is always four p.m. unless the message says otherwise, and at three p.m. he sets out on a well-hidden path.

Maria is sitting on Samuel's stool in front of the hut. She stands when she sees Pundi's white shirt flash through the trees. She has been humming to herself quietly, unaware that Malo is not twenty feet away, hidden in a thicket, watching her, his heart pounding with fear that she will turn and see him. Of all the White people on the island, he would rather be found by her than any other. In truth he loves this woman and her companion, Akila. They are infinitely gentle and kind in their treatment of the slaves, not just on her plantation but all over the island. Still, he is her husband's slave and she would surely have to turn him in. He holds his breath as he sees the Indian doctor come up the path. And what he sees after that: well, that makes his eyes grow wide, and it is all he can do to keep from laughing with delight. For a brief moment Malo forgets his own predicament.

Chapter Thirty-Five: On the Eve of Disaster

Copenhagen, January 16, 1772

Years later I found, among the papers she had saved, Uncle Thomas's letter of January 16, 1772, to my mother.

My Dearest Sister, he begins. I can picture him writing it, chewing his fingernail for a bit and thinking how to put everything to her.

Trusting in the Lord, I pray that you and the General are well and in His care.

I fear that things here in the Court are reaching a point where some dreadful event is likely to occur. It will surely involve the Queen and Dr. Struensee, about whom rumors have grown ever louder. Whatever transpires will be deeply upsetting to Maria, though I know that the Lord will bring us all through this moment of history. I cannot tell you precisely what I am referring to for I do not know as yet, and if I did it would be a state secret beyond my powers to reveal, but it is quite possible that by the time you receive this letter you will know the facts of the case to which I refer. In any event, I think that it is time for Maria to quit Copenhagen for healthier climes. I know that you are fully aware that she is refusing to return to St. Thomas and is determined to go to the Moravian School in Bethel, Pennsylvania. I had rather hoped that she would find a suitable husband here in Denmark, but the young man who has been pursuing her is not sufficiently to her liking, and in truth I think the climate here has dampened her spirits. It has done the same to my own, and I am going to apply to the council for a government position in St. Thomas or St. Croix.

I have written to the Moravian School in Pennsylvania to expect Maria for the upcoming term. Little Phebe can stay here with me until I return to St. Thomas, and then I shall bring her along, unless you prefer that I sell her here, where I am sure she would bring a fine price. But truly, I think she would be better returning to the family.

I trust that you and the General are doing well, and that all the little girls are thriving. I will write again in the next few days.

Your devoted brother, Thomas

I awake on the morning of January 17 feeling buoyant, despite the darkness and the cold. Tonight is the costume ball and I am going as a Viking woman. I have had a beautiful silver gown made, and will have my hair plaited specially. I have only to get through four hours with my tutors. I find them very tedious, but I have to admit that I have learned a great deal in the past year and a half. I can now speak elegant French, English, Dutch, German and Danish, and can read and write Latin. I love learning languages, and feel a different personality come over me with each one. The world seems a place of infinite possibility at this moment.

Phebe comes in and sits at the end of my bed. She has already been up for an hour and done all the chores that Johanne had laid out for her.

"You'd better get up. It's almost time for lessons." She flips the duvet back and makes a mock bow, gesturing me out of the bed.

"I HATE THIS COLD!" I bound out of the bed and wrap myself in the duvet.

"Did you make any more progress on Maria's diary last night?"

"Oh yes! I'm getting close to the end, and I find that very alarming, because they are so happy, she and Pundi. I am so afraid for them, because there's not much more to read and I'm feeling that something terrible is going to happen. Something that will cause her not to write anymore." I watch my breath form frosty clouds as I say this. "But if it does happen, no one has ever told me about it. But then, they never told me anything about Pundi. Maybe it was always a secret."

I wrap the duvet tighter and look directly at Phebe. "Oh Pheeb, I feel like I'm her. I'm so full of dread. I can't imagine how it's going to end." I drop the duvet. *"Je dois faire pi pi."* And from the commode I say, "I've written to Mama asking her if she knows any family secrets, but she hasn't replied yet."

Smoothing the duvet on the bed, Phebe says, "Maybe my mother knows something that your mother doesn't. There are usually at least two versions of every story…the slave version and the master version."

Chapter Thirty-Six: Malo

St. Thomas, January 1702

In the cover of night Malo has moved to another place on the island. The Sangoma hut has turned out to have entirely too much traffic for comfort. His new spot is in a bower high above the road in the place that is called Maroon Hill. Large rocks and thick foliage offer excellent concealment, a place where he can sleep with little fear of discovery. He stays here for three days. He has "borrowed" a knife from the Sangoma hut and to stay alive uses it to kill mice and other small creatures. He longs to roast them, but cannot take the risk, so he eats them raw.

He is restless and bored. He imagines finding a boat on a beach and setting out for Portorico. He has seen such boats and is sure he could steal one. But he cannot swim, and his courage has thus far failed him.

For a week, he hovers in this spot, watching the foot traffic below, eating only when his hunger becomes acute. He has made his own cozy burrow, but he knows he must move soon. He is still working on his courage a week later when he awakens one morning, blinking into light and into the faces of six white men.

They drag him in chains behind their horses back to Work and Rest and deliver him to Rufus MacAllister. In his terror Malo has soiled himself.

"Get up, you scurvy slime." Rufus brings his whip down hard on Malo's back.

Malo stands erect, looking off across the sea to the island of St. John, willing himself to be there.

"Bring the axe. You there, Paris, look lively. Get me the axe. You'll see what happens to those who run. They never get away. There is no way off this island.

Malo is still looking out to sea, but he is trembling so hard his teeth start to rattle. "Please, don't chop me." He is whimpering now and ashamed.

Paris hands Rufus the axe and looks away, out across the turquoise expanse.

"Get Lussant and Tonnay. And call all the others from the fields to come and watch." Paris gets the conch and blows it, the signal to assemble.

"No Master, don't chop me. Please don't chop me. I be no use with one foot." Malo is whispering, unable to find his voice, he is so consumed with terror.

"Oh it's just a foot," Rufus laughs with a dry humorless rasp. "You'll hardly miss it."

"I seen something. Something you'll like to know. I tell you if you let me keep my foot. It's a good bargain."

"I don't bargain with slaves…and never with runaways." Rufus is standing with the axe in his hand, watching the slaves stream in from the fields.

He looks at Malo thoughtfully. "Why don't you just tell me your little secret. If you don't, I just might decide to cut off both your feet."

Malo shudders and tears run down his cheeks. I never should have said anything, he thinks with shame.

"I have to whisper it," he says.

"I'm listening," and Rufus puts his right ear to Malo, who leans over and speaks softly into it, his skin crawling at the stink of the man and his own shame. In a very quiet whisper he tells Rufus what he has seen in the Sangoma hut.

Rufus breaks into a broad grin. "Oh my sweet Jesus, is that ever music to my ears. I couldn't have asked for such a gift if I'd spent a year thinking." He looks at Malo and pats him on the shoulder. "You can keep your feet, Malo. With such a gift as that, you can keep them both. Blow the conch, Paris, and get them all back to work." He turns and goes back to his porch and his rocking chair to think about how he will use this information.

The following Saturday afternoon Akila goes alone to the Sangoma hut, taking supplies for the day to follow. The news of Malo's capture is all over the island. She is not surprised. No one ever gets away alive. But she is relieved, and puzzled, that he did not lose a foot. She picks her way carefully through the thick undergrowth, looking forward to her work at the hut. For all the healing work she does with Maria, Pundi and Isaac during the week, it is this work at the Sangoma hut that has the most meaning for her, even though it is Samuel who does the real healing. Akila talks with those who wait for him, looking at their accumulated sores and wounds, and treating them as best she can with her salves and herbs.

On this Saturday she is arranging new supplies in the hut and she hears rustling in the woods outside. She turns to see Rufus MacAllister blocking the light in the doorway.

"And how are you, Akila?" he asks langorously.

"Busy."

"What is all this trash in here?" he says, peering into the smoky darkness. It is indeed a startling sight, with skins and bones hanging and what seems like rubbish everywhere. The air is dead and smoky.

"Wouldn't have any meaning to you."

"Now why are you so unfriendly to me?" he says, reaching out his hand to touch her arm.

"I'm just busy, is all. You go now. You've got no business here."

"Oh, but I do. My business is you." He comes up suddenly behind her and grasps her breasts, and nuzzles his face in her neck, holding her tight. "You are never far from my thoughts, Akila. And I am going to have you, whether you like it or not, so you might as well accept that."

Akila is standing frozen in his vise-like grip, her heart pounding. She suddenly has no voice.

Rufus takes her breasts in his big hands from behind her.

"Oh my. Oh my, my, my. Such lovely things." His cock is hard against her leg and she feels fury rising in her. And then she hears a sound. A click. Rufus hears it too, and turns his head slightly toward the sound. Maria is standing ten feet away with a musket in her hands.

"Let her go, or I will shoot you, you bastard. I should shoot you anyway. You are truly the devil's own. Now get out of here before I do it."

The look that Rufus gives her puzzles her. It starts out menacing and then turns into a smirk, as though he's almost pleased that she's caught him. Or is he pleased at the thought of something else? No matter, she thinks, as he lets Akila go.

Rufus turns and starts to walk away. Halfway down the path he looks back at Maria. His heavy lids are like a lizard's, but the menace of his expression is palpable. She feels a chill despite the afternoon heat.

Akila throws her arms around Maria.

"Praise Allah! What a miracle that you just happened to appear…and with a musket!

How did you happen to have a musket?"

"The Lord works in mysterious ways. I've been thinking of you up here occasionally alone and that it might be well if you had some protection, so I was bringing the musket for you to have on hand. Just in time, I guess."

Minutes later the afternoon rains come, dumping torrents of water from one end of the island to the other. Maria and Akila stay in the Sangoma hut to wait out the rain. Rufus is dripping when he arrives at Pierre's office in the Fort.

"For God's sakes man, don't stand on the rug," Pierre mutters upon seeing him. "What are you doing here?"

"Come to see you. Thought you'd want to know about Malo. I decided not to chop his foot. I thought you'd want to know why. You'll probably hear about it from some of the other planters. He had a tale I thought you'd want to hear."

Pierre is sitting at his desk looking into the light. Rufus' expression is hard to see. But his voice is full of innuendo.

"Well, what is it? What's the tale he told you?" Pierre's tone is impatient.

"He was hiding for a time by a hut that's atop of the hill over by Mangan's. And he saw your wife. She was with that Indian doctor. They were making love in the hut. He saw it all. Watched them through a peep hole. He didn't want to tell me. He's very fond of your wife, I'd make out, but fonder of his feet. It'd be my guess it's been going on for some time.

Pierre's face flushes red, whether from embarrassment or anger is hard to know. "Son of a bitch," he says.

Rufus walks all the way back to Work and Rest, feeling his satisfaction mount with every step. He could tell by the expression on Pierre's face that he would make the bitch pay. He may be a pansy, Rufus thinks, but he doesn't want to be a cuckold.

Chapter Thirty-Seven: The Ball

Copenhagen, January 17, 1771

On that night of the ball, January 17, I am completely absorbed in the idea that I want to glide into the ballroom and make everyone gasp. An entrance. But the minute I arrive I forget all about that. The mirrors make the room appear to be lit by a thousand candles, and reflect multiples of everything, including me in my low-necked silver gown, with my hair braided in a Viking style. I hold a mask to my face and stare at the delightful scene, trying to recognize people in their disguises. I have been given a Tanzcarte. This innovation has come from Germany and is causing titters all over the room. I am thrilled by the stream of gentlemen that have approached to write their names on the little card. Not a dance is left after the first fifteeen minutes. I cast little sidelong glances at the cards of the other women nearby, to see how many partners they have attracted. The Queen has not yet arrived. Nor has Dr. Struensee.

I am feeling light and free this evening, unburdened of Heinrich, who is away at his country estate. I dance a gavotte with a count whose long, unpronounceable name I instantly forget. The Queen is announced at the door as soon as our dance ends. She has a mask, but I cannot figure out what her costume is meant to be. It is simply a beautiful, lush, moss-green gown. My aunt moves quietly toward her, and they bend their heads together in conversation. It is a very long time before Dr. Struensee arrives, and I cannot help noticing, as I suppose everyone else in the room does, the Queen's pleasure as he dances with her. The tenor of the party shifts as the music ends and snippets of whispered conversations bounce around the room. I suddenly regret that I haven't another space on my card, but he doesn't even ask. Everyone seems a little on edge, and I wonder if it is the novelty of the dance cards.

When I get back to our rooms Phebe isn't there. I am surprised. She hadn't said she was going out, but then I hadn't asked. There's a quiet knock at the door.

"Come in." The door opens and Phebe is standing there in her usual grey dress, looking very somber.

"Did you have a good time?" she asks.

"Oh yes. It was very lovely and my costume was a great success. Have you been with Antoine?"

"Yes, in the stable. We played some cards. But he was in a very serious mood. He kept staring at me in the oddest way, until I couldn't stand it any longer and made him tell me what was bothering him. Then he said that he thought something is up at court and that there is more than the usual whispering and conspiratorial talk going on. He thinks your uncle is involved and that there's a chance we will be sent away."

I sit up and stare at her. "Sent away? Really? Back to St. Croix?"

"I suppose. Where else would they send us?"

Later I found out that Antoine had proposed to Phebe that night and asked her to run away with him to France.

"Run away," she had said. "I can't do that. I can't just run away."

"Why not? In God's eyes you are nobody's slave."

"Yes, but what about man's laws?"

"I don't think they really apply in France. The slaves in France are the serfs. In any case, there's every kind of person in Paris and no one will bother us if we're married."

"Married? Are you asking me to marry you?" Phebe had smiled with pleasure, dipping her chin and looking up at him coyly.

"Yes, of course,'" he had said softly. "'I've always assumed we would be married…but that will not happen here."

"Oh Lord, I don't know what to do. What would Summy do if I ran away? It would break her heart."

"Do you really think so, Phebe? Isn't she going to school in America? Don't you think she'd be happy if you were happy?"

"Well, her parents would be furious. You don't know the General."

"Yes, but I know Summy, and I bet she can stand up to any General."

"I will pray on it, Antoine. The Lord will guide me." Antoine knew her well enough to keep quiet at that point, and he had pulled her to him on the bed and held her in his arms until the first departing guests demanded their carriages.

Uncle Thomas was on duty in the Guardhouse that night. When Phebe and I arose in the morning, he was at the table, his head sunk in his hands, his eyes closed. I could see immediately that he was praying. He lifted his eyes to the two of us and there was such sadness in them. We sat down on either side of him, and he told us what had happened.

The Dowager Queen Juliane Marie and her coterie of conspiratorial friends had left the ball and, led by Ove Guldberg, the King's former preceptor, a group of them gained access to the King's bedroom. With difficulty they persuaded the befuddled monarch to sign an order for the arrest of the Queen, Dr. Struensee and Enevold Brandt, who had once physically chastised the King in one of his psychotic rages. No one will ever know what threats might have been made to get the King to sign the order. Or perhaps he just was numbed by drink. For Struensee had truly been the best friend of his life.

Uncle Thomas was then shown the King's order and told to arrest the Queen. He went together with a small band of the conspirators to the Queen's chamber and placed her under arrest, in the name of the King, separating her from her son but letting her keep her nursing infant daughter with her. Her ladies-in-waiting dressed her to be taken to prison. Two other groups of soldiers arrested Struensee and Brandt, and a number of others.

As he tells me this, I can feel my chest rise and fall with each breath, as if I were outside myself watching. Pins and needles pass up and down my body and I start to shake, and then to sob.

"Johanne will be devastated," Phebe whispers.

"Yes," says Thomas, "I fear for Johanne. She was very close to the Queen."

"And to some others too…who will probably protect her if you can't." Phebe's eyes are brimming with tears and sympathy. Thomas looks away and nods.

Chapter Thirty-Eight: Sold

St. Thomas, January 1702

Pierre is in his office, working himself into a lather of fury. Pacing and muttering. Cracking his knuckles violently. "The little bitch!" He spits the words. "She's been carrying on behind my back for years, I bet. And I bet everyone on the island knows." He thinks of whipping her. Of locking her in her room. Of shaving her head. But all those punishments would become public, and shame him as well as her. But there is one thing he could do that the whole island would approve of, and it would be the biggest punishment of all to her. His heart calms as he thinks of it, and a certain glee replaces his fury. He organizes his papers in a neat stack and pushes back his chair. He shuts the door to his office and strides through the courtyard, past the soldiers at the entrance and through the opening in the prickly pear hedge, up the hill to his house.

Maria and Akila are in the back courtyard with the children, having just changed into dry clothing.

Pierre stands on the top step outside the parlor above them and looks down at his wife. Waves of emotion wash over him. Fury, mortification, jealousy. For in truth he loves her, and the thought that he has been sharing her with another man is vile to him. And an Indian. For a moment he thinks of Moriah and her golden skin. Could it be? No not possible. She has his very own blue eyes. But the thought unnerves him.

"Maria," he calls down to her. "Come here. I must speak to you." She looks up at him and smiles.

"I'll be right there."

Staring down at her mass of wild curls, he watches her come up the steps, her sandals slapping. He opens the door so she can pass through.

"Sit down," he says, gesturing to the sofa. "I have something to tell you."

"And what is that?" She does not sit, but stands straight, sensing the need to match his strength. "Something important I guess, from your very formal manner."

"I am selling Akila."

Maria stares at him. She feels as if her blood had stopped moving, had chilled. "You are not," she says, but it comes out in a whisper, not in the shout she wants it to be. And then she finds her voice. "You can't. She is not yours to sell. She's mine. I bought her when I was ten years old. But why ever would you ever want to sell Akila?"

Pierre snorts, a loud snort and then grins at her, a grin so malicious that goosebumps form on Maria's arms.

"You know very well that I can sell her. Everything of yours is really mine. I can perfectly well sell her, and I will. Casper Rysberg has been begging me to sell her to him for years, and what a price he has offered!" Pierre laughs, a cold humorless throaty sound.

"But why? Why would you do this, Pierre? Why would you want to hurt me so?"

He looks at her at for a long moment and then says in a low, ugly voice, "Because you have dishonored me. You and your Indian doctor. And it is very probable that I am the last one on the island to know."

Maria makes a small noise, something between a choke and a laugh. She is galvanized with fear. This is the moment she has so long dreaded.

"No one knows," her voice is squeezed into a thin whisper.

"Well, they do now. Malo saw you and bargained for his foot with the information. You should have seen the pleasure Rufus had in telling me. You little bitch. This is your just reward. I'm taking Akila to the fort right now and locking her up so you can't get to her. And tomorrow Rysberg can come and get her. And I'm spending the night there myself."

Pierre stares fixedly at Maria as he says this, and storms from the room, back down to the courtyard. Maria runs down the stairs after him and tries to seize his arm as he grabs Akila and pulls her from the cookhouse. Akila is so startled by Pierre's rough handling at first she laughs.

"You won't be laughing long, girl."

"The Devil! What's happened to you?" The steady, hard stare of his eyes is like a cold hand on her throat.

"You just come with me." Pierre's face is a frozen mask of anger. Maria has grabbed his arm and is pulling at him. In one swift motion he wrenches his arm away and strikes her across the face with such force she falls to the ground. She tastes the blood in her mouth as she watches Pierre drag Akila to the street. Anger surges over her as she rises. The children are all crying, and Anna and Jean-Baptiste are staring after Pierre.

"Achhh, you are bleeding, Maria. What has come over Master? Let me get you a wet cloth," cries Anna.

Maria stands quietly as Anna ministers to her, thinking of what to do. Then she goes into the house and sits at Pierre's writing desk. She starts to dip a quill into the ink and stops, holding it suspended in the air as she thinks. And then she dips it, and writes on a piece of Company paper: "Pierre knows. He is selling Akila to Rysberg as his revenge. We must get her off the island tonight. She is in the Fort. I will get her out when the moon is high. Where can we hide her?"

She blots the ink and stands staring out the window, down at the street. Then she goes out into the courtyard and beyond, to the pigeon coop. She lifts the latch and the pigeon hops up and coos, waiting for her ministrations. She clips the note to the clasp on its back and whispers "Fly, fly, Princesse, like the wind you must fly."

As she is pulled forcefully along the Kongens Gade, Akila is trying to control her rising panic. She must reason with Pierre. There is only one thing that could make him this angry, she knows. Her arm is hurting where he has hold of it, and her mouth is dry as dust.

"Calm down, Pierre," she says breathlessly. "There's no reason to be so hasty with your vengeance." Her foot slams into a jutting rock and she winces. Blood oozes from her ankle.

"Have you stopped to think what everyone will say? You know Maria loves you…but just not in that way…and I daresay it's the same for you. Why not just accept that you have a different kind of marriage. She's known for a long time what you and Marcus do together. You should not be so surprised that she's found her own solace for that."

At this, Pierre whips her around and slaps her face with his free hand. She puts her palm up to the bruise and stares at him. In a swift moment she sees the whole arc of her life fall to pieces, her husband and her children separated from her. A deep sob erupts from her throat and then she tries to quiet her heart.

"You are not yourself, Master."

"I am very much myself. *Tais-toi!*" he mutters. "You have always thought yourself better than the rest of your kind. Casper Rysberg will knock that out of you."

An uncontrollable sob erupts from the depths of Akila.

At the Fort, Pierre pulls Akila roughly through the great double doors into the courtyard.

The soldier on duty rushes up to them and says loudly, "Halt." Then he stops abruptly, seeing who it is, and mutters an apology.

"Take this bitch to a cell. She'll be staying the night. Casper Rysberg will collect her in the morning. Bring the key to me in my office."

The soldier looks at Akila and his face changes. He blinks, dazed and startled. She is well known to him as a healer of the island, a somewhat feared and much-respected woman. But her eyes are wild. She seems possessed. The expression on Pierre's face silences the question that is rising to his lips.

"Yessir," he mutters, and he takes Akila gently by the arm and leads her away. They go down the stone stairs by the kitchen to the great cavern of cells below.

"Here now, at least you can have the sunset," he says quietly, pulling open the grated door of a cell that looks westward, out across the harbor." He leaves her with a last look of sympathy and a little nod of his head.

In the triangle of the afternoon sun beating through the narrow window, Akila slides slowly into a dark mental void. Even the images of her children have vanished from her mind. She is in the cavernous jaws of the imagined lion that had swallowed her as a child when her mother was killed. She struggles to fix her eyes on a gecko on the wall, trying to hold onto herself, but she is a naked, weeping child wrapped like a small animal in a bloody blanket, unable to speak. The mournful call and response of the slaves echoes in her head. Her skull throbs with the insistent beating of drums. She feels her ten-year-old self cowering in the corner from Mette, and hears the comforting voice of Celine. "Maria will not let this happen," she says aloud, trying to bring herself back.

Pierre goes to his office, pours himself a glass of rum, and paces. He wraps his fingers around the key in his pocket and draws a deep breath. His mind feels like a swamp, buzzing and snapping and slithering. He pours another glass of rum…and then another. The soldier on duty at the gate has meanwhile told every passerby of his prisoner, and the word is traveling around the island like sparks flying off a smoldering log that has been well poked. In the evening a customer arrives at Mette's with the news. It is early, and she and her girls are lounging in the large open room, some in the rocking chairs and some on the couch. Caterina is sweeping up a bit of broken glass in the corner. She stops and stares at the messenger as he utters the news, her mouth agape in soundless incredulity.

"But why?" she asks, her voice breaking in a crack of emotion.

"No one knows the why," the messenger mutters.

Chapter Thirty-Nine: The Parade

Copenhagen, January 19, 1772

I can see the handle of my door turn slowly, and then Phebe is standing over me, her round, steady eyes holding mine, as if willing me back to my life. I know now that she was in her own agony that day, fearing that she was going to lose Antoine. If it hadn't been for the arrests she might have left with him. But she stayed by me.

History records that there is a parade this day, led by the King in a magnificent coach drawn by eight white horses. The King sits looking out at the howling, shrieking people, his face corpse-like, stricken with grief. The populace is wild with emotion, of what precise kind they know not, but they have been led to believe that some kind of tyranny is over. Struensee had been a protector of whores and brothels, so on this day they rip them apart. They do not realize that he had also been their protector.

Phebe and I do not watch the parade, though after much crying we stand on the glass bridge and watch the King's carriage roll through the arch. In a fury I shout down at the roof of the carriage, "You betrayed him, you miserable coward! And you betrayed the Queen."

Chapter Forty: Nightwatch

January 14, 1702

The pigeons have done good work this day, flying back and forth between Isaac and Pundi and Maria. A plan has taken shape. Samuel has been out in the fields, and the hardest thing facing Maria is telling him what has happened. She wants to reach him first, before he hears it from someone else, so she waits as the sun is setting on the path he will take to come home. She sees him walking alone and takes a deep breath, preparing herself. Her lip is bruised and her face is swollen from crying.

"Mistress, what brings you here? What has happened?" Samuel's voice rises with trepidation as he sees the terrible grief in her face. "Where's Keela?"

Hoarse from crying, she whispers, "Samuel, Pierre has locked up Akila in the Fort."

Her voice breaks with a sob. "He has sold her to Casper Rysberg. He found out about Pundi and he has done this to punish me."

Samuel's face moves from astonishment to anguish as he takes in the news. "This cannot be," he says.

"No, it cannot," Maria puts her hands on his shoulders. "We must get her off the island. No good fate awaits her here." Samuel throws his head back and a great wail pierces the air.

At two o'clock in the morning, Maria and Samuel move silently down the path toward the village. The Fort looms in the moonlight with its crenelated walls. The image of Pierre, sodden with drink and passed out on his couch, presses into Maria's mind. She knows him well, but nonetheless her heart is pounding like a blacksmith's hammer. Samuel carries a small trunk on his shoulder. They have discussed at length the next step: getting the guard to open Akila's cell. First they will try a bribe. And if that doesn't work, Samuel will deck the man. Maria knows there is only one guard on duty at this side of the Fort. The others are watching the sea, where the real danger is likely to be. They pass through the prickly pear hedge and approach the entry gate. They are in the shadow of the wall.

"Who goes there?"

"Maria La Salle. Pierre's wife. I must see your prisoner." She is now face-to-face with the soldier and sees he is the young man she has given an aloe cream for his acne. "Hello Ricard." Ricard looks confused.

"Your husband's sleeping."

"Yes, I know. It is not my husband I've come about. It's Akila." A look of panic comes over the boy as he takes in what they are wanting, and the size of the slave with the suitcase. "Don't worry, I'll make it worth your while." She takes a heavy leather pouch and jingles it, smiling at him. Ricard hesitates, then looks again at Samuel. He takes the purse.

"You can say he knocked you out and took the key." Maria smiles at him. "I don't have the key. La Salle has it."

"Oh, what a calamity," Maria mutters. "Well, there's nothing for it but to get it from him. I daresay he's asleep by now." And she pushes past Ricard and goes to the door of Pierre's office. Samuel retreats to the shadows under the eaves of the courtyard. Maria pushes the door open very quietly. She can hear the sound of Pierre's snoring. She opens the door wide to let in the moonlight and she waits while her eyes adjust to this new level of darkness. She is cold, and fear is taking her breath away.

"It will be a miracle if I can get the key without waking him," she thinks, and her mind goes back to the great waterspout on their ocean crossing. "Please Lord," and she says an interior prayer.

Her eyes slowly adjust to the scene. Pierre is lying on the red velvet couch on the left side of the room. His desk is in the center, piled high with documents. Where would he have put the key? Most likely in his pocket, she thinks. But first she checks on the desk, an easier proposition. Just papers, his quill and ink and blotter. She goes to the couch and stands over him, assessing the depth of his slumber. He is snoring like a drunk, she thinks, relaxing a little. She goes behind the couch and leans over, very slowly sliding her hand under Pierre's waistcoat to get to his pocket purse. He stirs. She freezes and waits until his breathing resumes its steady pace. She pulls out the purse and feels the key inside. She takes the purse and quietly backs out the door, closing it behind her. She leans against the wall next to Samuel and heaves a great sigh.

"I got it."

The dungeon is dark but for tiny shafts of moonlight that have escaped through the grates in the cell doors.

"Akila," Maria whispers loudly. "Where are you?" She repeats the quiet cry twice before she hears an answer. They follow the sound of Akila's voice, and struggle to unlock the cell door. It swings open with a wheezing creak and they all freeze. After a moment of silence, the three embrace with quiet sobs.

"Come quickly, Keela, we must get you off the island. Isaac's boat will sail as soon as the two of you are on it."

"Leave the island? Leave you both? My children? How can I do that?"

"Pierre has sold you to Caspar Rysberg and if you do not go, I think you will not live a month."

"She's right, Keela." Samuel can barely utter the words. "Where would you have me go?" Akila's voice is anguished.

"To France. You will make a life there. It makes sense for Isaac too, to take control of that side of their business in France."

Samuel has his arms around Akila, his face buried in her hair. He touches the scars at her temple, her tribal marks.

"But Samuel. I cannot go without him. He must come. And the children too." The plaintive wail cuts Maria to her heart.

"You know they would pursue you all if so many went. And the punishments would be terrible. Oh Keela, it's all my fault. I don't know how you can ever forgive me, but I promise I will devote myself to your children and I will let nothing happen to them. Someday we will bring you back together again. But Pierre has already made this sale, and Rysberg will be here in the morning to collect you. There is no going back from it. I know how your heart is breaking, but you must do this. Pierre will not injure your children. They are his own property, and he wants to see them grown and useful. But he has already made this sale and Rysberg will be here in the morning. There is no going back."

Tears streaking her face, Akila cries in anguish. "I cannot believe it has come to this."

Caterina has left her last customer in her bed, sleeping off his festive evening. She is walking on the road to town in the moonlight to see if she can bribe a guard to let her see Akila. She has a different currency, but it generally works very well. She has tried to think what she might bring to Akila. Her possessions are meagre, but she takes a silk shawl, something from the far east that a customer gave her. She sees a man ahead of her shining white in the moonlight and realizes it is the Indian fellow, Maria and Akila's friend.

"Halloo," she whispers loudly.

He turns and, recognizing her, says, "Where are you going at this time of night?"

"To the Fort. They have arrested Akila. I'm going to try to see her."

Pundi takes this information in silently and starts walking beside her. "You come with me," he says. And they walk into the village. They wait beneath the western walls of the Fort in the shadows of the hedges. Nearby loom the gallows where Mette's husband was hung.

"How are they going to get her out?" Caterina is shivering despite the warm night and her voice quavers.

"They have a plan. Be patient." And as he says this, he sees the three of them in the shadows, rounding the western edge of the Fort. "There they are."

Caterina runs to Akila and throws her arms around her, unable to speak through her tears.

Akila lifts her chin. Caterina sees the ugly bruise on her cheek. "Ooh, he hit you…"

"Don't cry. The bruise is nothing. There's no time for tears. You must come with me." Fresh tears spring to Maria's eyes as she realizes that Caterina will be a kind of child to her.

"Come with you where?"

"To France." Caterina is silent taking this in. Pundi puts his arms around Akila and whispers a plea for forgiveness in her ear. His wet cheeks glisten in the moonlight.

They move quickly to the wharf, where Isaac is waiting in a dory. Sobbing, Akila hugs Maria and then presses herself into Samuel's arms.

"You must go," Maria's eyes close and her face contorts in pain. The two women climb into the dory and Isaac begins to row.

When the sun rises the ship is well away, taking a southern route to avoid pursuers.

Chapter Forty-One: Released

Copenhagen, January 1772

I decipher the last bit of the diary just two days before Struensee's arrest, and I cry as if it had been my own heart that was broken.

"Why didn't she and Pundi go too? Why didn't they all go?" I wonder aloud to Phebe. But she knows full well why.

"Moriah. She wouldn't have left Moriah, and she knew that if she took her Pierre would pursue her." And as an afterthought she says, "And Pundi's business depended on the plants of the island."

But still, I think how different our lives would have been if she had been braver.

"You must eat something," Phebe says to me, bringing a tray into my room. She sets it down on the table by me and then raises the pot, letting a hot stream of tea cascade into a blue and white Chinese teacup. Dark bread and smoked fish have been arrayed in colorful alternation on a plate, in an effort to tempt me to eat. I am sitting by the window next to the sheaf of papers tied in a ribbon that is Maria's diary. Bluish bubbles of rain spatter against the glass and break into little rivulets on the window.

"I am trying to imagine her in Elsinore Castle," Phebe says softly. "The one in Shakespeare's play, Hamlet. What it must be like in this awful weather…so cold and gloomy… with the sea pounding outside. Oh, poor woman, with her little baby. At least she has the baby…" Her voice trails off. But my mind races on, conjuring the rasping claws of rats crawling in the dark. I take a deep breath and stand up, suddenly restless, looking out the window at the dismal day.

"Yes. But don't you think King George will rescue her? He is her brother after all… I can't believe they would let anything truly bad happen to her. But I fear for Dr. Struensee…and I can't believe the things they are saying about him, the very people he served so nobly. People can be so blind, so led by the nose…they will believe anything if it gives them the satisfaction of hating."

"Hate is a powerful thing in the world." Phebe sinks onto the bed.

I look down at the Missy Box on the table. "Yes, but so is love…It must have pained Maria so to put Akila on that ship." I can hear the quaver in my voice as I say this. "And can you imagine what Akila felt, leaving her children and Samuel?"

"Slave women were separated all the time from their families. Not that that makes it any easier. And I think there are many cases of women being closer to their slaves than their husbands. And putting themselves in quite a lot of danger to protect them." Phebe is twisting the end of the duvet in her fingers. We are silent for a few moments, and then I see Phebe's hands go to her cheeks and she squeezes her eyes tight. I can see she is trying to stop the threatening flow of tears. Seeing Phebe's face I say, "Why Phebe, it is very sad, but it was all so long ago." I put my hand out and touch Phebe lightly on her shoulder, puzzled.

Phebe looks at the rain bubbling and rolling on the window.

"I know. It's not that. It's that Antoine is going back to France."

I sink onto the bed beside her, studying her face. I am praying silently. *Lord, speak to me. Tell me what to do to comfort Phebe. Give me strength to rise out of my own sadness and be strong for her.* And as if He is speaking through me I say the words, "Do you want to go with him?"

"He has asked me to marry him," Phebe says simply.

I confess that at this moment I feel I am the stupidest person on earth. For this idea has never occurred to me. That a White man could ask a Black slave woman to be his wife has simply been too far beyond my experience to be believed. I am absolutely still for a long minute, trying to understand.

"Do you want to marry him?"

Phebe looks up at me with an agonized expression, her face glistening with her tears.

"Oh, more than anything. But it cannot be, I know."

"If you want to marry him, I won't stand in your way. I'm going to leave this awful country as soon as I can and go to school in Pennsylvania, so why don't you just go to France with Antoine. It's where your great-great grandmother Akila went, where my great grandmother was from. It seems very right somehow. I will give you your freedom to do it." A great calm settles over me as I make this first real adult decision of my life. At that moment I can see a window into the future for each of us. It all makes sense.

Phebe is silent for a long minute, her eyes closed. She takes my hand and holds it tight. "Are you sure? You know your parents will be very angry. And no doubt Uncle Thomas will do all he can to stop it… Oh Summy, you are so good and dear to me. It will be hard to leave you."

"Well, you must in any case, so you should go where you can find happiness. And freedom. Though I do hope we will always write to each other. You are like a sister to me, and especially after all we have been through in these last two years. You will have to tell me all about France. And who knows? Maybe one day I will go there and see where my great grandmother came from, and where Isaac and Akila had their pharmacy, and visit you." She is crying now and her voice is shaking and the two of us are hugging. There is a knock at the door.

Uncle Thomas calls out, "Do you know where Johanne is?" We both leap up wiping our eyes. "I think she has left," Uncle Thomas says through the closed door.

I pull the door open and look at him open-mouthed. "What did you say?"

Chapter Forty-Two: The Waking

St. Thomas, January 8, 1702

Casper Rysberg is up before dawn anticipating the day ahead with the satisfaction of a man whose long-laid plans have at last reached fruition. Leaving his wife asleep on the bed, he pulls on his pantaloons and yesterday's malodorous shirt and goes to the water basin in the yard to refresh his face and tidy his whiskers. His eyes are bloodshot from an evening of celebration that included fucking his slave woman Jenny. Akila's tea had once had the intended effect on him, but he had figured that out in no time and now knows its source as well. This day will put an end to all that, he thinks, and he moistens his lips.

The Rysberg plantation is well east of the village of Charlotte Amalie, forty-five minutes or so on a walking horse. The house is a mean affair, different from Pierre and Maria's in that it is not raised, but sits directly on the ground, with two large rooms and facilities out back for washing and cooking and slaves. When hurricanes sweep it away it is not difficult to rebuild, being basic wattle and daub. There is no pretense to decor. It is not much different inside from the animal shelters outside, but for a few pieces of rough-made furniture. Behind the house are several shacks for the house slaves and a three-sided stone shelter for cooking. And the latrine and rain barrel.

Rysberg goes to the corral set back from the house and saddles his horse. The first rays of the sun are coming up in the east and he talks cheerfully to the mare. "Going to have a new girl today, we are. Been waiting a long time for this day," and he hurls his short body into the saddle.

By the time he gets to the Fort, the sun is well up and a small group of soldiers are eating from a communal pot in the courtyard. Rysberg strides past the guard and goes to Pierre's office, letting a stream of morning light into the room as he pushes the door open.

"Rise and shine. Big business to do today," he calls out in a guttural whisky voice.

Pierre rolls over and almost falls off the couch. "Achhh. You're very early." He sits up on the couch and rubs his face and eyes. His mouth feels like a sand pit, and acid rises in his throat. He takes a moment to focus his mind on the situation. Rysberg. Akila. Maria. He tries to summon his anger of the day before, but the drink has deflated him. He stands up and runs his fingers through his hair.

"I can hardly wait to get rid of her. But you'll get good service from her," Pierre adds as an afterthought, mindful of the price he has demanded. "Let's get the business done now, and then I'll take you to her. She'll be a handful, I guess."

"I came prepared with ready money," Rysberg says.

And they stand together over the desk in the stream of sunlight while Pierre makes his bill of sale for Akila, Guinea slave, one hundred and fifty rix-dollars. He is getting half again the going rate. Rysberg hands over the bills and they walk together through the door into the bright light of the courtyard. Pierre puts his hand to his forehead to shut out the pain of the sun, and they turn left and head down the stairs to the cells.

The Fort is built high above the water, so even the cells are streaked with beams of sunlight coming through the narrow windows. As they descend the stairs, Pierre pulls the pouch from his pocket and immediately feels that it is empty. The fog in his brain clears in an instant and a short rasping sound escapes him. He quickly composes himself, but his guts are recoiling with panic. And then rage. They walk the entire circuit of the empty cells, until they come to the last, whose grate is open. On the floor is a tray of food swarming with ants. A gecko looks down from the wall.

"Maybe one of the guards has her out for exercise," Pierre mutters, stalling.

As they come up into the courtyard, Governor Lorentz is going into his office. He looks over the two men. Pierre is almost as unkempt as Rysberg. "Pierre, you look awful. What has happened?"

"Escaped slave," Pierre mutters, wishing desperately that the Governor would just go into his office. "One of mine. The best."

"My condolences. Get a search going."

All the guards are assembled and questioned. Ricard stands at attention with the rest. "You were on duty at the gate. Did you let anyone in?"

"Only your wife, who went to confer with you."

"Aach," and Pierre puts his hand to his forehead. "Well, we will find her. Put together a search party."

Rysberg clamps his jaw and snarls, "Give me my money back, you sodden-witted fool."

As the search party is being assembled, Pierre walks back to his house on the hill. He imagines that Maria will have fled to avoid his rage, but he finds her there, sleeping in bed. He stands over her and raises his fist in a convulsive gesture.

"Where is Akila?" he bellows. "You filthy little whore, what have you done with her?" He is truly apoplectic now and has to sit down to avoid falling.

Maria, waking with a jolt of adrenaline, jumps from the bed and goes to him. "Oh Pierre, don't make yourself sick, or any sicker than the drink has done. Akila is gone. She is off the island. You will never see her again, nor will I, and I hope that is sufficient punishment. It is a very dark day for me to lose my most beloved friend."

Pierre looks up at her, utterly exhausted and feeling about to puke. She sees the look and runs to get a bucket from behind the curtain.

"Tell Marcus to go to the Fort and tell them to call off the search." He curls up on the bed, the waiting bucket beside him. The last thing he utters is, "Don't think you're going to get away with this."

That is enough for Maria. She puts together a bag with her modest things, jumps up on Cibonie and rides west to Pundi.

"If I'm going to be punished so, I will take my own happiness, come what may."

Chapter Forty-Three: Fates Decided

Copenhagen, January 23, 1772

The apartment is not large and it takes no time at all to realize that Johanne has truly gone. One lonely brown chemise hangs limply in her cupboard. I sink down on the bed and pull my uncle down beside me, holding tight to his hand. "I am not entirely surprised, Uncle."

"What do you mean, you are not surprised?" His back is rigid, his hand cold.

"I have seen her walking alone with Frederik Karl von Warnstedt. I mean quite often. I thought it rather odd…" I squeeze his hand and my voice trembles. "There seems to be something between them, you know…"

He rises from the bed and starts pacing, clasping his hands together until his knuckles are white.

"God…damn…her."

I bow my head and sit silently praying that God will take this situation in hand. He had been with me just moments before with Phebe… Phebe. I cannot go back on my pledge to Phebe, but I dread contributing to Uncle's misery. "Lord, guide us, strengthen us in our hour of need," I whisper, and my uncle reaches out and clasps my hand.

Chapter Forty-Four: Suspended

St. Thomas, January 1702

Pundi is pacing in the courtyard outside his house when Maria arrives, breathless and disheveled, her hair a wild cascade of golden brown curls. He looks up at her silently and takes the reins while she slides off the horse. He sees a face so bereft he realizes that she is in a kind of delirium. He pulls her to him and holds her for a long time. Finally he lifts her chin and looks into her eyes.

"My darling Maria," he whispers, "you are safe. We are both still here…together. That is what matters." After a minute he says, "Where is Pierre? Does he know?"

"Yes…oh…he has made himself so sick with drink…but I think he will be along shortly." She is trembling as she says this.

"We must be resolute. And calm. And keep him calm. You know his biggest fear is scandal…and being shamed," Pundi says.

Maria begins to pace up and down in front of the ginep tree. "Oh, just look at Isaac's house, with all his wonderful treasures…I can't bear it."

"I will pack them all up and send them to him when his ship returns."

"I am going to miss them both so much… I cannot possibly lose you too."

"I will not let that happen."

Within the hour they hear the sound of hooves drubbing on the road. Pierre trots into the courtyard on his black mare, his own color an unhealthy shade of puce. But his look is rageful, stony.

"You…" The sound is low and guttural, directed at Pundi. Maria steps between them.

"He is not to blame. It was me…it just happened. It is nobody's fault. And you have punished me…" She balls up her fists, her knuckles white, and puts them up to her mouth. "Your punishment has been terrible."

"Not as terrible as I had intended." His voice is a low growl.

"Maybe not, but terrible nonetheless for me." They stare at each other icily.

"You must come home now. Immediately. I insist."

"Only on certain conditions."

"Conditions?" His eyebrows surge. His voice is mocking.

"Yes. My condition is that we shall go on as before. Pundi and I will go on being partners, healers, as we are known to be here on the island. And you will not interfere. We will be discreet. But if people talk, so be it. I will not reveal your secret." She pauses and looks at him meaningfully. His eyes flicker with surprise. "And, if necessary, you will defend my honor." Pierre stares at her for a long moment. His eyes move slowly to Pundi and back to Maria.

"You bitch!" He spits this *sotto voce* and looks at her for a long moment. "So be it. Come home now."

Maria does as he bids, mounting Cibonie in a smooth swinging motion. She nods and smiles faintly at Pundi and then follows Pierre home. In truth, she is worried about Mo Mo and Amalie. She must see them.

She finds them in the courtyard. Amalie, only a year old, is in Kansoleh's lap. It is Mo Mo Maria is worried about. Kneeling, she puts her arms around him.

"Papa has told us." Mo Mo says, stone-faced.

"Oh, Mo Mo," she whispers, and can think of no words of comfort.

At the peak of the afternoon heat she goes into Akila's hut in the courtyard. She lies down on Akila's mat and closes her eyes. She takes between her toes the string of the fan that Akila has rigged over the bed and moves her foot back and forth, tugging on the frond above her so that it stirs the air. Tears slide down the sides of her face. She can hear the banging of pots in the cookhouse nearby. Restlessly she sits up and starts to examine the tiny space. Akila's own space. She sometimes slept with Samuel out in his hut in the fields, but this was always hers.

The light is dim, slivers of sunlight coming through the thatch. There is almost nothing left in the hut. A small reed box lies deep in the shadows. Maria opens it and looks down on a sheaf of folded papers. She lifts them out. The little inkblot eyes of Akila's gris-gris, the gift of Bamadille, stare up at her. And rattling around next to it are the pearl buttons that Akila would twist off her chemise each day in that first year. Maria unfolds the papers and starts to examine them.

It is Rufus MacAllister's trial record. His trial for murder.

When she realizes what she is holding, Maria sits utterly still, staring at the pages. She is salivating. "Where on earth did she get this? And why did she keep it from me?" In this game she is playing with Pierre, she has just come upon a little pile of chips.

She rocks back and forth thinking about this puzzle, and then about what she will do with the papers. It slowly comes to her why Akila never did anything: she was waiting 'til the moment was right, and Maria thinks, "And I will wait too. The time will present itself."

Chapter Forty-Five: Sewing Diamonds

Copenhagen, January 25, 1772

I fidget in the sitting room while Uncle Thomas writes a letter. I walk back and forth biting at my nails. His face is a somber mask and his eyebrows periodically rise in exclamation points as if to punctuate his letter. I am immersed in thoughts of Pierre. Was he really my great grandfather? What had he done to Maria? What had happened to Pundi? I am trying to think of a way to nonchalantly ask my uncle a question that will reveal the answer without revealing what I know. I look over at him and realize he is very intent on what he is doing.

"What are you writing, Uncle?"

"To Mr. Boudinot in New York. I am arranging for you to be collected and transferred to your school in Pennsylvania. We shall get passage for you so that you get there by April.

"Will you stay here alone then?"

"I have requested to be returned to St. Thomas. I am waiting to know if they will give me an appointment."

"Oh, I do hope so. Mama will be so happy to have you home again. And Phebe will be so happy to see her family." I am mildly surprised at my newfound ability to lie nonchalantly. Uncle Thomas gives me a wan smile and an affirming grunt, and I suddenly feel my breakfast stirring. I have never in my life done anything as brave and deceitful as I am doing now.

Phebe and I had stayed up late into the night, carefully taking the diamonds from my necklace off the string and sewing them into the hems of various garments. I imagined as I was doing it that it was just what Celine had done before she and Maria had fled France with these very diamonds. By tomorrow Uncle Thomas will know full well what I have done. Phebe and Antoine will be gone. I will pretend to be surprised myself, but I am not very confident that he will believe me. He will probably know. Or maybe I will have to tell him so that he will not send pursuers after them. All this runs through my mind as I watch him finish the letter, and then I sit down close to him.

"When do you suppose they will start the trial of Dr. Struensee? And what do you suppose will happen to him?" I murmur.

"He will be executed. Beheaded. And I don't expect the trial will be a long one. He has offended every member of the nobility of this country, and they will have their revenge."

I am silent, but the skin on the back of my neck is alive and crawling.

Chapter Forty-Six: Change of Governors

St. Thomas, January 1702

Maria carries on. The weather is clear, the temperature perfect. She rides each morning to Pundi and, finding him lying half-naked in a tangle of sunlit sheets, she cannot resist the animal pull of him. She buries her face in the thick black hair of his chest and inhales deeply. Their lovemaking puts her world right for a time, and they set out together to make their rounds of the plantations, doing what they can for the endless ailments of the slaves.

"They cannot live on so little food. Why do you not supplement their diet?" She repeats this question again and again, to masters and overseers, but they just shake their heads: the system has been worked out. The slaves raise their own food on Sundays, their day off, and they must live on what they raise. It is the custom that has been established, and no one is willing to change it. But it is never enough. Malnourished and overworked, the slaves sicken and die at alarming rates. The whole system is repugnant to Maria. Pundi, a Brahmin from India, is inured. The caste system has similar unbreakable traditions. It is simply man's nature to subjugate others, he tells her. When their day's work is over Maria goes back to her house in the village.

She is tormented at leaving the children, and especially Mo Mo, who at six has gone back to sucking his thumb and won't play with the others. He sits rocking himself. When she is with him she takes him in her lap and they rock together.

"Your mama loves you, Mo Mo. She had to go; she had no choice. But Isaac will take care of her and one day you will see her again."

Pierre goes about the house as if she did not exist. He no longer shares her bed. She imagines that he is sleeping at the Fort, or perhaps with Marcus in his hut. Without Akila to tend to her toilette, Maria's hair is a wild mass of curls, wrapped awkwardly in a bandana, with tendrils sprouting in all directions. She no longer cares.

She visits Mrs. von Bergen one day and finds her laid up with her rheumatism. Maria settles on a stool beside her and massages her aching hands, taking each joint, holding it in the heat of her own hand and rubbing it gently.

"Do you know what is ailing the Governor?" Mrs. Von Bergen asks.

"I did not know he was ailing."

"Surely Pierre has told you something."

"We are not speaking. You know he tried to sell Akila to Caspar von Rysberg. But I got her away at night with Isaac. She's in France by now."

"Tried to sell Akila? Why? What on earth for?"

"To punish me. But do not ask me more."

Mrs. von Bergen is silent and then says, "You did not know then that Governor Lorentz is very ill."

"I did not know. Who is attending him?"

"Oh, some ship's doctor I suppose."

Maria ponders this news as she goes about her business that day. Lorentz has been Pierre's close friend and protector for many years.

In the weeks that follow Maria goes often to the bakery to see Bamadille and Lucien. The bakery is just five minutes from the house and the two men are like fathers to her.

Sometimes when the lines are long, she lends a hand selling the bread and chats for a moment with each buyer, learning the news of the island. And who has fallen ill.

"Oh Missy, our Angus is so sick. You must come. He's too sick to get to the Sangoma." The woman takes the loaves and bows to Maria respectfully and goes on up the dusty path. She may have several hours to walk, but the bread is highly prized. In the past Maria has begged Pierre to let Samuel come away during the week for visits to the sick, but he has always denied the request.

"Samuel is the best field slave we have. We cannot let him go off. There is always another one sick." So his healing work happens on Sundays, in secret, in the Sangoma hut, though occasionally he will pay an evening visit if the sick person is nearby.

It is at the bakery that she hears the news of the Governor's death in the early morning of February 19.

Chapter Forty-Seven: Phebe and Antoine

Copenhagen, January 27, 1772

I sit at my dressing table with my pen suspended in the air as I try to think what to write. I have "borrowed" several pieces of paper from my uncle in case I make a mistake. I am trying to think the document out carefully in advance.

"I, Maria de Malleville Suhm of Christianborg, St. Croix, the lawful owner of the slave Phebe…"

Now what is Phebe's real name? I chew my lip 'til it almost bleeds. It is the same as mine, I think.

"…Phebe de Malleville Suhm, also of Christianborg, St. Croix in the Danish Virgin Islands, hereby grant to Phebe, etc, etc, her freedom."

I cannot think what else to write. "Her freedom to marry Antoine Bouvier." No, that is not a condition of her freedom. "Her freedom, on this the 27th day of January 1772."

I revisit the question of what Phebe's real name is. Perhaps there is no De Malleville in it. But then I think I would rather we have the same name, as if we were sisters, so I decide to include it. Besides, it is a nice French name, a good name to have when she lands in France.

I hold the pen above the paper but find I am trembling too much, so I put it down and make myself breathe, in and out, in and out, until my heartbeat has gone to a normal level and I can hold my hand steady. And then I write. I feel a lead weight on my chest.

The letter written, I sit for a long while and then I rise and take it into Phebe's room.

Phebe is packing her small trunk.

I look at her few things and take a deep breath to try to summon a happier face. "Oh Phebe, I wish I could go to Paris with you and buy you dresses for your trousseau. What fun we would have." She looks up at me and smiles, as if this is the most absurd suggestion she has ever heard.

I hand her the letter. "Read it. Tell me if you think it will do. Really I had no idea what to write." She takes it over to the window to catch the bit of light coming through the January drizzle. When she has read it she places it carefully on the bed and comes over and embraces me silently.

"I think it is perfect."

"I wonder if you will ever have to show it to anyone," I finally say. "I hope it will do if you have to." I go then into my uncle's study and heat the wax that sits in a pot on his desk. I fold the letter carefully and close the back flaps with the bright red seal.

The question remains of how to get Phebe's luggage into the hired carriage and out through the palace gates without arousing suspicion. We are both quite well known by now to the guards. There is no advantage to a night departure. The guards are there at night just as they are in the day. But Antoine, being the man of the stable, is expected to drive various conveyances on occasion.

Eventually we come up with a plan to borrow a carriage from one of Antoine's friends. They bring it into the courtyard and park it under the great arch beneath the glass bridge, where the doorway to the De Malleville apartment is located. The two men quickly load the little trunk into the carriage and depart the way they came. Shortly thereafter, Phebe and I go out for our morning stroll, walking into the busy market area where the carriage is waiting. We stand together and embrace one last time. Then Phebe climbs into the carriage and Antoine drives off with his bride-to-be. They will leave the carriage not far from the town and continue by a series of stages on to Paris in a journey of four days. And I shall walk slowly back to Christianborg Castle and wait for my uncle to come home at the end of the day. It will seem like the longest and loneliest day of my life.

Chapter Forty-Eight: Claus Hansen

St. Thomas: March 1702

"Let us pray…" the minister intones, and of all those in attendance, Pierre is undoubtedly praying the hardest. Governor Lorentz' body was hardly cool before the trumpet was blown to call the island to the service in the Fort. The morning air is languid and the light brilliant, the best weather the island has to offer, but still the body must be interred with haste. As the cart wheels away with the coffin, the planters begin arguing about who will be the next governor.

Pierre de Malleville, a head taller than most of them, commands their attention. "We must make this decision amongst ourselves. We all know we cannot abide by Copenhagen's choice." With that, Joachim von Holten, the Company's man, who is known for his despotic manners, is out. The ensuing discussion is long and vigorous, and at the end of the morning Claus Hansen is the new governor. A lieutenant with little expertise on trade and no great talent with a pen, he will, much to the surprise of the planters, prove to be diligent with the account books.

Pierre retreats to his office, next door to the Governor's. This has been his domain for twelve years, and a profitable one it has been. Through all the chaos of the island's leadership, Lorentz has been his friend and protector. Pierre is bereft. But the loss of a friend is nothing compared to the tidal wave of anxiety that is rolling over him.

He sits in his chair and stares at the ledgers in front of him, wishing he had been more attentive to detail in covering some of his most lucrative transactions. There is much that has never been recorded at all, of course. But in twelve years no one else has ever looked closely at these books, and he can hardly imagine now what a close examination might reveal. He paces with growing anxiety. He chews his nails, a habit Maria had tried fruitlessly to break him of early in their marriage. Then, sighing deeply, he puts on his waistcoat and walks resolutely to Hansen's office next door. Peering through the door he sees that the new governor is, surprisingly, alone.

"Congratulations on your new post, Claus," Pierre hazards, having thought about whether this is too intimate or not, and decided to be bold in his approach. In truth he has never even addressed the man directly before.

Hansen, portly and balding, looks over his spectacles at Pierre for a long moment. "Bring me your ledgers, will you sir? I will spend the next days reviewing things. Seeing what's what, don't you know." He has that irritating habit of saying "don't you know…" all the time. No, Pierre thinks. I don't know. He grinds his teeth.

"Just as you wish. Do let me know if I can be helpful. I've been here for twelve years, you know, through thick and thin."

"Looks pretty thick at the moment to me."

Pierre doesn't know quite what to make of this last statement, so he bows slightly and retreats. In his office he looks at the ledgers, and a chill crawls over him for a moment, raising the hairs on the back of his neck.

"Too late to do anything about it," he mutters softly. "And I wouldn't have a clue how to anyway." He picks up the stack of ledgers and takes them into Hansen's office.

"For your leisure," he says, attempting a smile, and deposits the ledgers on Hansen's desk. But Hansen doesn't smile back. Instead he looks at Pierre solemnly for a long moment.

"Thank you," he intones.

The news of Pierre's arrest reaches Maria at Work and Rest, where she is tending to a group of slaves in the fever tent. A soldier from the Fort arrives on horseback and seeks her out.

"Do not come into the tent. I will come out. These are contagious fevers," she says to him quickly, holding up her hand as he stands in the light at the entry. She wipes her hands on her apron and walks out into the daylight. The soldier stands alert, formal, his eyes somewhere over her head.

"Your husband, Pierre La Salle, has been arrested in the name of the King, for stealing from the Company." Here his eyes flicker to her face and then he resumes. "He has been imprisoned on the

King's ship. He will be sent to Copenhagen for trial. The ship will sail in a matter of days, once the cargo is loaded."

Maria looks blankly at the soldier. And then, as the meaning of his words dawns upon her, she flushes crimson.

"Oh Lord, save us."

She rides on Cibonie back to town. She puts the horse in the small enclosure beside the garden and walks through the courtyard. Kansoleh is there with all the children, Mo Mo and Amalie, and her own Moriah. She crouches down and they come to her for hugs. Moriah rubs her cheek.

"Are you crying mama?"

"I am wondering at God, my sweet. At the strange turns he makes in our lives."

She goes into the house and finds the portfolio tucked deep under the cushion of the chaise longue.

"Do you wish to see your husband, madame?" Hansen's demeanor is formal.

"I came for another reason. To give you this." And she hands him the portfolio. "You will see by these documents that Rufus MacAllister, whom my husband hired as overseer at our plantation, is wanted in Copenhagen for the murder of a woman. If you are sending prisoners to Denmark, he should be among them." She looks him in the eye somberly. "And yes, I will see my husband."

Chapter Forty-Nine: Uncle Thomas

Copenhagen, January 27, 1772

Thomas opens the door and pauses on the threshold. "Summy," he calls out.

"I'm here, Uncle." My voice is just a whisper in the gloom. "Just waiting for you."

"Why are you sitting in the darkness, my child?"

"I am thinking." My voice is solemn, composed. Not the voice of the eager girl child who had arrived a year and a half before. "It is just the two of us now, Uncle. Phebe has gone. I have given her her freedom. She has gone to Paris with Antoine to marry."

As his eyes adjust to the darkness, Thomas sees me sitting on the sofa and moves toward me. He is quiet for a long while, taking in what I have just said. He puts his hand on my head, in the manner of a blessing. "You are a very brave young woman, Maria Suhm. In the eyes of God you have done the right thing." I feel a vast weight lift from me.

"Are not those the only eyes that count, Uncle?"

"Yes. Would that more people were as brave… You know your parents will be very angry." He says this in a matter-of-fact way.

"I know. But I shall be in boarding school." It is hard to hide the smile in my voice. "I couldn't have taken Phebe with me in any case. She will have a better life in France, as her great-great grandmother did."

"You know about that?" Thomas' voice is full of surprise.

"Yes. You would be very surprised at what I know."

"Well, let's light a lamp. And then you can tell me."

I light a lantern and make a pot of tea. We settle down next to each other and I tell him about finding the diary and the many days I have spent decoding each entry.

"What do you know about your grandfather?" I ask Thomas.

"Not very much. He worked for the Company and was lost at sea on a voyage in the early part of this century, when he was called to Copenhagen.

"Do you know why he was called to Copenhagen?"

"I suppose there was some business purpose." Thomas looks at me questioningly. "He was sent to be tried. For theft from the company. Over many years. His ship going down was perhaps a blessing. They might have hung him."

"All this was in the diary?" Thomas puts his hand to his forehead and rubs wearily.

"Yes." I look at him, wondering if he had ever suspected something like this.

"Well, I think that the Lord has guided you…in finding the diary you have gone to the heart of a most extraordinary woman. Though I knew her and loved her as a child, I was not privileged to know her deepest secrets. I think the Lord has guided you to them, or perhaps she guided you. The world is full of great mysteries."

I smile at him. I ponder whether to tell him the story of Pundi, to ask him whether he knew Pundi. I cannot resist.

"Uncle, did you know Dr. Pundit?"

"Your great grandmother's partner in her healing work? He died around the time I was born. She spoke of him often, with great reverence.

"And Isaac?"

"Oh, she used to get letters occasionally from Isaac. He and Akila ended up in Paris. I never really understood how that happened."

"What about Mette?"

"Ah, Mette." Thomas raises his eyes to mine inquiringly, and then unconsciously rubs his nose. "Well, she had a thriving business, as it has done through the ages. And my grandmother had Bamadille fashion a metal nose for her when her own was eaten away by syphilis. She did not live long after that, but her business went on…and there is still a brothel in that spot, though Mette's place burned soon after her death.

"Grandmother sold Work and Rest to Pierre de Malleville after Grandfather was gone, thinking she had got well rid of the business. But of course her daughter Moriah went and married Pierre's son, Jean, so the property ended up in the family after all. Grandmother lived in their house in the town and carried on her healing business with Dr. Pundit. After he died, she moved in with her daughter Moriah and Jean de Malleville. She lived to seventy-five, quite extraordinary in that time and place."

"Amalie and Mo Mo never got to France, did they?"

"I think they were too attached to Grandmother. And their father Samuel. They stayed with Grandmother all her life." He takes my chin in his hand and looks into my eyes. "But now Mo Mo's granddaughter will live France. Thanks to you."

Epilogue

Dartmouth College, Hanover, New Hampshire, 1799

That all happened twenty-seven years ago. My voyage from Denmark to America did not begin until the first week of April of that year, 1772. February and March were very sad, dark months. Uncle and I had clung together in the gloom of the apartment by the glass bridge. We had agreed in a conspiratorial moment that freeing Phebe was the right thing, no matter what the consequences with my parents. My parents were angry, of course, but by letter, so it was hardly punishing. But every time I rounded a corner, I imagined I saw a flash of Phebe's grey dress.

Once I felt her hand on mine in such a vivid way I started to cry. I missed her so.

Heinrich was kind, but he knew I was determined to go, and so his attentions grew more and more distant, though he did come to see me off at the wharf in the first week of April. My uncle, the old judge, came too. Uncle Thomas had given me a new trunk, bigger than the old one, since I had acquired so many beautiful things in Denmark. I left the old one behind, along with the Missy Box and the diary, restored to its secret hiding place.

I had my own snug cabin on the voyage out and dined in the Captain's quarters. I could not help thinking of Maria at ten years old doing the same almost a hundred years ago.

Johan Struensee was very present with me on that voyage. I had loved his boundless cheer and sense of possibility, and I tried to keep it with me as I sailed into a new life. I knew what they would do to him. Uncle Thomas had told me. Cut off first his hand, and then his head. In front of dreadful, howling mobs, who surged vivid in my imagination.

I had knelt in my cabin and prayed for many hours on the day appointed for his execution. And when my knees were sore I went up on deck and prayed, looking at the bow waves leaping in their endless motion. My prayers were not just for his soul, but for all the good he had envisioned. For the end of serfdom, of slavery, and the end of the crushing greed that makes some men so cruel to others. I had prayed for the place I was going—America—that it would be a place less cruel.

I was sailing to America with my own hopes, some of which he had instilled in me. I pictured Phebe in Paris, so happy for her that she was beyond the reach of slavery there. She had sent me several letters before I left Copenhagen to tell me of their arrival. They had gone immediately to visit Antoine's family in Fontainbleau and had greatly amazed them. Phebe related how strange it was not to be regarded as a slave, but simply as a slightly different kind of person. They took it on faith that if their son loved her, she must therefore be worthy of that love.

"And how impressed they were by my French!" she wrote. I was so pleased at that.

And not a little jealous that Phebe had returned to my ancestral home. The second letter told of the little place they had in Paris, and of how Phebe had found the pharmacy that had been Isaac and Akila's. It was in a poor part of Paris where immigrants come when they arrive, but it was a very popular, well-known pharmacy, and wealthier people travelled to it from across the city.

Isaac and Akila were still remembered there, and their portraits were on the wall. It gladdened my heart and has since inspired Phebe to take up studying with a Dr. Hahnemann. She has been his student all these years and has now become a homeopathic physician.

It gives me great joy that I had the bravery as a young girl to free Phebe, and that it was so very simple to do, because Antoine was there to care for her. But the story of slavery is far from over, even in our home here in Hanover. John's father, Eleazar, freed his oldest slave, Exeter, in his will, and gave him land to farm, and "the right of the use of his wife Chloe as long as he should have need of her." (Here I bite my tongue.) But they both died soon after and so had no time to enjoy their freedom or the land he gave to them. He also freed Archelaus upon certain conditions and left him fifty acres of land. But Brister and his family he left to us. I feel deep shame that they were not granted the same land and rights, and now they have all died in the recent diphtheria epidemic.

So we have Angelina, Phebe's sister, and her lovely daughter, Phebe Ann, who is just three years older than my Maria, and such a shining example to her in her love of the Lord. Then just last year, with my mother's death we have taken on the care of her three slaves, who are now too ancient to care for themselves. For them we must surely care, but Angelina and Phebe Ann must have their freedom, though it will break my heart if they leave us. I will inform John of my decision tonight.

I can hear Dr. Struensee's voice of encouragement: "A terrible institution slavery."

Afterword

This book is a work of fiction, although the overall framework is based on real historic events. Maria Bourdoux did come alone to St. Thomas with her nanny, and the names of her progeny are real. Her granddaughter did marry Governor Suhm and her great granddaughter did study in Copenhagen, living with her uncle, Thomas de Malleville, whose role in this story is historically accurate. Other names, characters, and events are imagined. Thomas de Malleville is buried in the small cemetery at the Moravian Church on St. Croix. When I visited St. Croix in 2019, I scrubbed his gravestone clean.

Dartmouth College in 2019 began publicly to explore the history of slavery at the College. There is no doubt that Eleazar Wheelock, founder and first president of Dartmouth College, had slaves, and that they did all kinds of labor: building, farming, husbandry, and domestic work. His will is quite specific in freeing some of them and leaving them land. But not all of them. Some were passed to his son John.

John's wife, Maria Suhm Wheelock (1758-1824), did come from a Caribbean slaveholding family. John and Maria were married in 1786 and had a daughter, Maria Malleville Wheelock, in 1788. When she was born, her Grandmother Beverhoudt gave her an enslaved child, Phebe Ann, who was born on a plantation in New Jersey and just three years old at the time she was "given". Phebe Ann's last name is recorded as Jacobs (whether by birth, marriage, or choice we do not know). A short biography of Phebe Ann Jacobs, written by Mrs. Upham of Brunswick, Maine, mentions that Phebe Ann lived with Maria Wheelock Allen, the daughter of John Wheelock and Maria Suhm Wheelock and the wife of William Allen, president of the short-lived Dartmouth University, 1817-1820, and president of Bowdoin College, 1820-1839. Phebe Ann is reputed to have been the model for little Eva in Harriet Beecher Stowe's anti-slavery novel, *Uncle Tom's Cabin, published in 1852*. Maria and Phebe Ann are buried side by side in the Pine Grove Cemetery in Brunswick, Maine.

Acknowledgements

The idea for this book began when I learned of the existence of a document, *Family Records 1685-1868*, known in our family as The White Book. Written in the late nineteenth century by Elizabeth Lee Allen, The White Book gives the barest outlines of Maria Bourdoux's flight from France as a child and a bit of her descendants' history. Two of my distant cousins, Judith Shea and Joan Ramos, brought it to my attention and helped me piece together some of the real history of the Bourdoux family. Henry Louis Gates put me in touch with his chief researcher, Nick Sheedy, who helped me in trying to track the descendants of the African slaves of the von Beverhoudt family. To all of them I am grateful.

A trip to St. Thomas was essential for research and I was warmly aided by many there: Annice Canton of the Caribbean genealogical library; Aimery Carone; and Levi Farrell who helped me tour the then closed Fort. I am grateful to Senator Myron Jackson, Glenn "Kwabena" Davis who led me around the land which had been donated by Thomas de Malleville to the Moravian Church, Mabel Maduro, Philip Sturm, Kim Holdsworth, Robert Schmidt, Anice Caron and Beverly Smith of the Von Scholen Collection, Sean Krigger, and the Livingston Family. Thanks also to the National Park Service of St. John, Simon Larson, and Malcolm Switzer.

No one contributed more to this effort than my beloved writers group led by Sally Ryder Brady who actually owns the Missy Box that inspired the title. Cynthia Linkas, Miriam Weinstein, Patricia Hanlon, Laura Wainwright, Mical Brownell, Margaret Carlton, and Elizabeth Berges all participated in biweekly critiques of this manuscript as it developed over five years.

In Copenhagen I was greatly helped by Poul Olsen of the Danish National Archives and by Damien Collignon and Katrin May who took me to the remains of Hirschholm Castle which had been destroyed soon after the events that are recorded in this book.

Many have helped in the editing of the book including Susanne Dunlap, Beth Nordberg, and Lawrence Breiner, Professor of Caribbean literature at Boston University. Mangalam Srinavasen gave me guidance on Hindu hygiene and customs.

Special thanks to Don Tingle and Martha DuHamel who both copyedited the whole manuscript at different times, and to my early readers, Melody Allen, Andrew Innes, Leslie Rescorla, and Hannah Burr. I am grateful to my dear husband, Peter Altman, who put up with me for seven years while I was writing this story.

❋ ❋ ❋